unforgettable journeys
EUROPE

unforgettable journeys

EUROPE

DISCOVER THE JOYS OF SLOW TRAVEL

Contents

Previous page Il Sentiero degli
Dei (The Path of the Gods),
along Italy's Amalfi Coast

BY BIKE
116

BY WATER
206

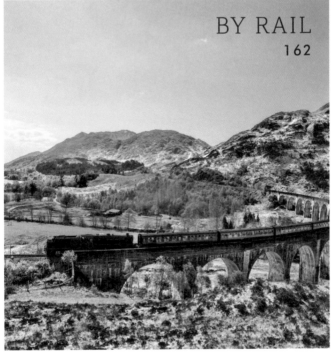

BY RAIL
162

*An empty road
winding toward
Mount Pico in
the Azores*

Introduction

The clue is in the name—the best journeys really are unforgettable. How many times have you traveled somewhere and remembered the journey much more than the destination? Things happen on journeys. Things have time to happen: we travel slower, we take in our surroundings more, we meet new people. Sometimes, we get sidetracked along the way. But that's how it should be—as the Chinese philosopher Lao Tzu said, "A good traveler has no fixed plans, and is not intent on arriving."

Traveling—and the means to travel—has occupied European minds for centuries. One of the oldest walkways in the world lies half-buried in the peat bogs of the Somerset Levels in England. Bikes were invented in Europe, as were motorcars and, before them, trains; a ferry, in one form or another, has been plowing Strangford Lough in Ireland since the 1100s. Europe, in short, has always been ripe for exploring.

In *Unforgettable Journeys Europe*, we've picked out the continent's best adventures, from crossing the Arctic Circle by train to driving through the mountains of Georgia. All the epic trips are here—riding the *Orient Express*, cruising the Rhine, and walking the Camino de Santiago—but we also take you well off the beaten path, cycling in North Macedonia, kayaking through Lithuania, and trekking along the High Coast of Sweden. We've organized the book by modes of transportation, so whether you're an avid hiker or cyclist or like nothing better than hitting the open road, riding the rails, or cruising down a river, you'll find plenty to inspire you. But let flicking through this book be just the starting point. After all, a journey of a thousand miles begins with a single step—or a simple turn of the page.

ON FOOT

Humankind has been traversing the landscape for thousands of years. First, we walked to find food and trade goods; now we scale mountain ridges, tackle long-distance footpaths, and trace entire coastlines. Europe has it all, so put on a pack and go, whether you want to wander through wildflowers in the Alps, trek across northern Spain, or follow the rugged shores of Portugal or Albania.

ICELAND

46

SWEDEN

43

45

NORWAY

44

DENMARK

POLAND

UNITED
KINGDOM

6
4
5

7

IRELAND

8

9

3
1

2

NETHER-
LANDS

21

20

BELGIUM

19

GERMANY

22

CZECH
REPUBLIC

LUX.

18

24

36

SLOVAKIA

FRANCE

23

AUSTRIA

SWITZ.

26

25

HUNGARY

27

28

33

34

SLOVENIA

29

CROATIA

35

BOSNIA-
HERZ.

32

MONTE-
NEGRO

Spanish and
Portuguese Islands

10

AZORES

12

MADEIRA

13

CANARY
ISLANDS

16

30

ITALY

17

31

ALBANIA

38

PORTUGAL

SPAIN

15

11

14

Previous page Hiking through the Bernese
Alps in the shadow of the Eiger, Switzerland

10

AT A GLANCE

ON FOOT

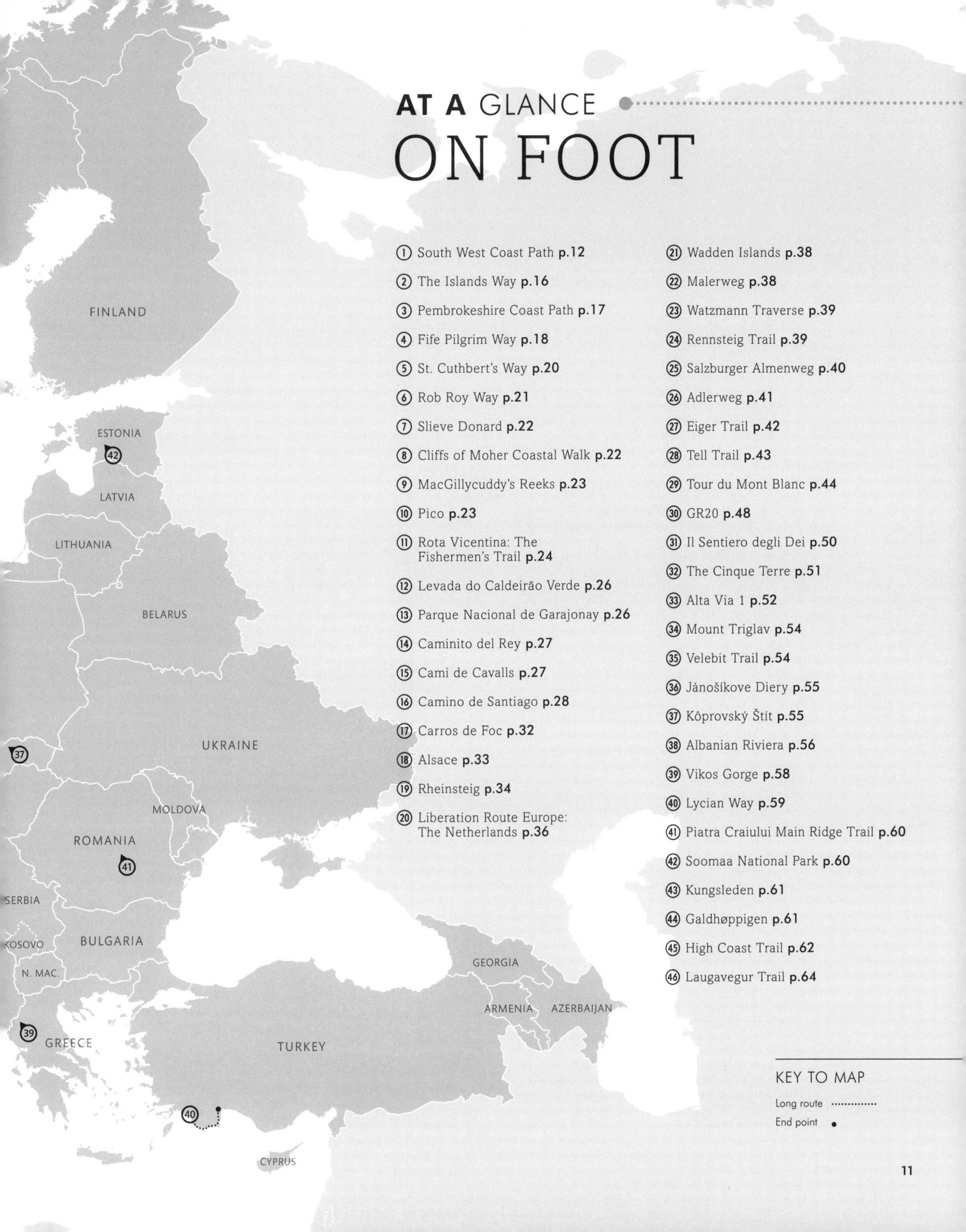
FINLAND
ESTONIA
42
LATVIA
LITHUANIA
BELARUS
UKRAINE
37
MOLDOVA
ROMANIA
41
SERBIA
KOSOVO
BULGARIA
N. MAC.
39
GREECE
TURKEY
40
CYPRUS
GEORGIA
ARMENIA
AZERBAIJAN

KEY TO MAP

Long route ....

End point •

The dramatic coastal scenery at Kynance Cove, on Cornwall's Lizard Peninsula

①

South West Coast Path

LOCATION England **START/FINISH** Minehead/South Haven Point **DISTANCE** 634 miles (1,023 km) **TIME** 6–8 weeks **DIFFICULTY** Moderate, with some challenging sections **INFORMATION** www. southwestcoastpath.org.uk; check tides, ferry timetables, and firing-range restrictions to minimize detours and delays

Follow England's wild southwestern edge for a roller coaster of a trail, which undulates via tiny fishing villages and secretive coves.

There's always someone with you on the South West Coast Path. Not necessarily another human being—for, although this trail traces some of England's most popular shores, it's still easy to lose the crowds. But still, there's always someone—or rather, something—with you here: the ghosts of seamen and smugglers, authors and artists; the cawing choughs, the hovering peregrines, the bobbing seals, and basking sharks. This National Trail, which wraps itself around almost all the sea-facing edges of Somerset, Devon, Cornwall, and Dorset, is wild in nature but has countless stories to tell.

Its roots trace back to the late 18th and early 19th centuries, when import duties were high and bootlegging was rife along these craggy, isolated shores. In response, a coastguard service was founded and a coastal path created, so these new lawmen ▶

> This trail traces some of England's most popular shores

could more easily patrol the multitude of outcrops, inlets, bays, beaches, coves, crannies, and clifftops, looking out for marine miscreants and their ill-gotten gains.

Well, praise be to the smugglers. The path that resulted is one of the best in the world, hugging a varied, spectacular shoreline that's slapped and kissed by a sea shaded emerald, turquoise, and indigo. It's also deceptively tough. Though the South West Coast Path's highest point—North Devon's Great Hangman—is only 1,043 ft (318 m), this trail dips and rears and rolls and plunges so often that by the time you've completed it, you've climbed nearly four times the height of Mount Everest.

It doesn't ease you in, either. From the start in Somerset (most hikers begin in the resort town of Minehead, on the north Somerset coast, and walk counterclockwise), you're soon tackling the outrageously romantic but lung-busting edge of Exmoor National Park, home to the highest sea cliffs in the country. There's respite around Devon's flat Taw-Torridge estuaries, but from the hill-tumbling fishing village of Clovelly, things roller coaster ravishingly into Cornwall, no rest for the thighs.

PASTY POWER

Pasties power many walkers on the path. These classic pastries, stuffed with potato, rutabaga, onion, and beef, were embraced by Cornish miners: they were cheap, portable, and, allegedly, the crimped ridge served as a disposable grip so they didn't poison themselves via their dirty hands. Now, Cornish pasties have protected origin status.

Below The picturesque fishing village of Clovelly *Right* Steps winding down to the rocky arch at Lulworth Cove

STRIDE *through Exmoor's magical, goat-grazed* **Valley of the Rocks**— *aka "Little Switzerland"*

Bristol Channel

▼ Minehead

TACKLE *the stiff climb up* **Golden Cap** *for big views along the Dorset coast*

ENGLAND

South Haven Point ●

SOAK UP *(spurious) Arthurian legends at the dramatic crag-top castle ruins of* **Tintagel**

Celtic Sea

ENJOY *the glorious approach around Bolt Head to enter the well-heeled sailing town of* **Salcombe**

LOOK *for seals from the wild, craggy* **Lizard Peninsula**, *England's southernmost point*

English Channel

The trail around Kernow—as the Cornish call it—is especially smugglery. As well as the county's beautiful (and sometimes busy) golden beaches, there are secretive coves in their multitudes. More contemporary treasures await in the art galleries of St. Ives, the ruined tin mines around St. Agnes, the monastery isle of St. Michael's Mount, and the pasty shops of, well, pretty much everywhere.

In South Devon, the flavor changes again, with a blaze of red cliffs, the busy resorts of the English Riviera, and a splurge of obstructive but idyllic river mouths and estuaries (checking tide times is crucial here). Finally, the trail heads into Dorset and along the Jurassic Coast, where rolling fossil-flecked cliffs lead eventually to South Haven Point. The actual terminus is underwhelming, the trail petering out on the sand beside a monument that seems an insufficient reward. But the South West Coast Path isn't about the finish. It's about every step it took to get there—every valley climb, stream hop, clifftop picnic, and cream tea. And it's about adding your own chapter to this storied trail.

another way

The world's first continuous route around an entire nation's shore, the Wales Coast Path runs for 870 miles (1,400 km) from Queensferry in the northeast of Wales, via Anglesey, the Llŷn Peninsula, Cardigan Bay, Pembrokeshire, and Cardiff, to Chepstow on the Bristol Channel.

②

The Islands Way

La Coupée, the narrow ridge that links Sark with Little Sark

LOCATION The Channel Islands **START/FINISH** Various **DISTANCE** 110 miles (177 km) **TIME** 10 days **DIFFICULTY** Easy to moderate **INFORMATION** www.visitguernsey.com, www.jersey.com

This wonderful multi-island ramble takes in the best of the Channel Islands, from Guernsey's rocky coastline and Jersey's flowery north-coast cliffs to the idiosyncratic isles of Herm, Sark, and Alderney.

A cluster of compact islands scattered in the Bay of St. Malo, just 8 miles (13 km) off France but inherently tied to Great Britain, the Channel Islands provide some of the finest coastal walking in Europe. The Islands Way—five separate circuits of the main isles—takes in every single stride of it.

On Jersey, start your walk in the capital, St. Helier, before moving on to 13th-century castles and pretty harbor villages. The highly scenic North Coast Path is ablaze in spring with yellow gorse; in the fall, clumps of purple heather erupt alongside you. The trail on Guernsey follows a coastline of two halves: pink and slabby along the long west coast and craggy in layers of steely gray in the south, whose bays were captured in a series of landscapes by the French Impressionist Auguste Renoir.

Leave tracks in the sand on tiny Herm— gorgeous Shell Beach is arguably the finest in the entire Channel Islands—before heading on to Sark and hiking the razor-edged isthmus of La Coupée. Alderney, the last stop on your itinerary, rewards with some of the best bird-watching in the region, with the biggest populations of puffins, gannets, and guillemots in the English Channel.

(3)

Pembrokeshire Coast Path

LOCATION Wales **START/FINISH** Amroth/St. Dogmaels
DISTANCE 186 miles (299 km) **TIME** 12–18 days **DIFFICULTY**
Easy to moderate **INFORMATION** www.pembrokeshirecoast.
wales; main walking season Apr–Sept

The extraordinary fringes of the UK's only coast-focused national park combine sandy bays, gnarly cliffs, Norman castles, and the country's smallest city.

The Pembrokeshire Coast Path describes the southwesternmost extremity of Wales. And what an extremity! Along this isolated shore, protected within its eponymous national park, fishing villages tuck into tiny quays, craggy coves alternate with sweeps of golden sand, and towering cliffs are pummeled by Atlantic waves.

Despite its seeming wildness, this is a landscape that's been well lived in: by Neolithic farmers; visiting Vikings; castle-building Normans (you can see the muscular evidence at Pembroke, Tenby, and Manorbier); and streams of Christians—St. Davids, the UK's smallest city, has been a place of pilgrimage since the 12th century. Now, it's largely tourists who come, although this coast—despite its A-list good looks—remains relatively quiet, especially when you leave behind honeypot spots such as the beautiful beaches of Broad Haven and Whitesands Bay and explore on foot. Indeed, tackle the dramatic limestone terrain of the Angle Peninsula or stride out through the bracken toward the lighthouse of Strumble Head and you probably won't see another soul. Just seabirds in the skies above and seals in the bays below.

another way

The Preseli Hills, just inland, make a fascinating detour from the Coast Path—the bluestone used to build Stonehenge was somehow transported to Salisbury Plain from here. An 11-mile (17.5-km) circuit from coastal Newport via the valley of Cwm Gwaun gives a flavor.

Barafundle Bay, just one of many stunning beaches along the rolling coast path

④

Fife Pilgrim Way

LOCATION Scotland **START/FINISH** Culross or North Queensferry/
St. Andrews **DISTANCE** 56 miles (90 km) **TIME** 6 days **DIFFICULTY**
Easy **INFORMATION** https://fifecoastandcountrysidetrust.co.uk/walks/
fife-pilgrim-way

*Riddled with standing stones, solitary abbeys, and
superstitious tales, this meditation in landscape is an
unrivaled way to lose yourself in medieval Scottish history.*

*The ruins of
St. Andrews
Castle, on a
promontory
jutting out to sea*

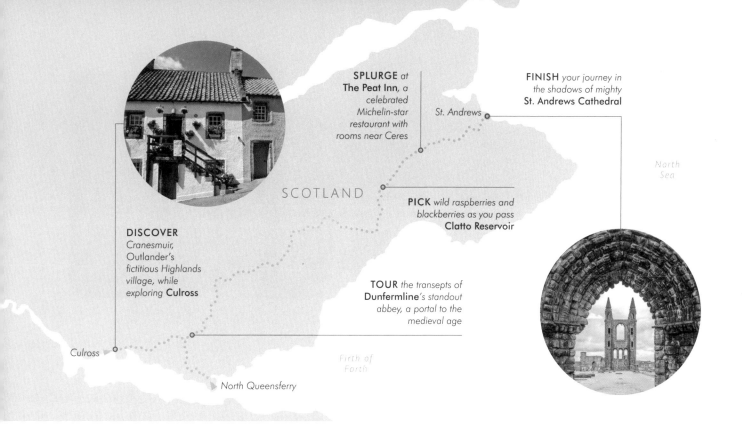

DISCOVER
Cranesmuir,
Outlander's
fictitious Highlands
village, while
exploring **Culross**

SPLURGE at
The Peat Inn, a
celebrated
Michelin-star
restaurant with
rooms near Ceres

FINISH your journey in
the shadows of mighty
St. Andrews Cathedral

St. Andrews

SCOTLAND

PICK wild raspberries and
blackberries as you pass
Clatto Reservoir

North
Sea

TOUR the transepts of
Dunfermline's standout
abbey, a portal to the
medieval age

Culross

Firth of
Forth

North Queensferry

Jerusalem, Rome, Santiago de Compostela, and Lourdes are renowned as holy hot spots, but you can add another to the list: the Kingdom of Fife, a breadbasket of farmland and rolling hills wedged between the cities of Edinburgh and Dundee on Scotland's east coast. Once nicknamed the "Pilgrim Kingdom," the countryside here is a promised land of religious lore, brimming with lopsided abbeys

> The countryside here is a promised land of religious lore, brimming with crooked abbeys

and priories, with the main pilgrimage route to historically rich St. Andrews having captured the hearts and minds of pilgrims for more than 700 years. If it's a tartan Camino you're after, no other long-distance trail offers more spiritual reward.

Pick and choose your starting point from either Culross (production location for TV mega hit *Outlander*) or nearby North Queensferry, beneath the engineering marvel of the Forth Rail Bridge. Then it's a march to Dunfermline, once Scotland's capital, to see the entombed bones of Queen Margaret, the country's only royal saint, and magnificent Dunfermline Abbey; in a city of spirit-lifting architecture, it's the resting place of medieval royalty, including Robert the Bruce. From here, the route trundles through wildflower meadows and whispering barley fields, all while being religiously served by ruined chapels and holy wells. Toward journey's end, the miter-like steeples of St. Andrews parade on the horizon and the trail climaxes at goose-bump-worthy St. Andrews Cathedral.

Dunfermline Abbey, home of the tomb of Robert the Bruce

Left *Early morning mist enshrouding the Eildon Hills*
Above *Melrose Abbey, the start of St. Cuthbert's Way*

(5)

St. Cuthbert's Way

LOCATION England and Scotland **START/FINISH** Melrose/
Lindisfarne **DISTANCE** 62 miles (100 km) **TIME** 4–6 days
DIFFICULTY Moderate **INFORMATION** www.stcuthbertsway.
info; check tide times before walking across to Holy Island
(https://holyislandcrossingtimes.northumberland.gov.uk)

*Follow the story of the Anglo-Saxon saint, from a
magnificent old abbey in the Scottish Borders to the
atmospheric holy isle where he ended his days.*

With fine stretches of moor and woodland, striking ruined
abbeys, and a handsome castle, St. Cuthbert's Way is a winning
mix. It has a fascinating backstory, too, following in the
footsteps of its eponymous saint, from the Scottish Borders
town of Melrose, where St. Cuthbert entered monastic life in
651 CE, to Lindisfarne (Holy Island), where he was abbot of
the monastery and initially buried after his death in 687.

The ornate medieval ruins of Melrose Abbey make an
impressive trailhead; ahead lie the bulbous Eildon Hills and
salmon-stuffed Tweed River, the wild and isolated Cheviot Hills,
and St. Cuthbert's Cave—it's said that after Lindisfarne was
abandoned in 875 due to Viking raids, the saint's body was
hidden here. The grand finale is crossing to Holy Island itself; it's
only possible at low tide, on either the Causeway Road or by
walking barefoot across the sands, as ancient pilgrims once did.

HOLY ISLAND

Lindisfarne, or Holy
Island, was settled by
Irish monks in 635 CE.
The monastery they
established became
one of the most
important centers of
English Christianity,
while their successors
created the superb
Lindisfarne Gospels in
the early 8th century.
The ruins that remain
today date from the
12th century. The
island is also home to
a crag-top castle,
which was built in the
16th century and
renovated in the early
20th, in Arts and Crafts
style, by the architect
Sir Edwin Lutyens.

6

Rob Roy Way

LOCATION Scotland **START/FINISH** Drymen/Pitlochry **DISTANCE** 79 miles (127 km) **TIME** 6–8 days **DIFFICULTY** Moderate **INFORMATION** www.robroyway.com; an optional extension from Ardtalnaig via Glen Almond to Aberfeldy adds 17 miles (27 km)

Hikers on the scenic path that descends from Ben Vorlich to Loch Earn

Track the legendary Rob Roy MacGregor—clan leader and folk hero—across the southern Highlands via sparkling lochs, heather-cloaked moors, sweeping glens, and intriguing villages.

Rob Roy MacGregor is Scotland's most infamous outlaw. Born by Loch Katrine in 1671, this gutsy wee lad became a Jacobite soldier, clan leader, cattle rustler, fugitive, and folk hero; in his eponymous 1817 novel, the romantic writer Sir Walter Scott immortalized Rob Roy, using him to symbolize the disappearing Highlander culture.

Most people walk the trail in his name heading northeast, with the prevailing wind behind them, which means beginning in the village of Drymen, just east of Loch Lomond, and plunging into the Trossachs. This is proper Rob Roy country—Rob drove cattle through Drymen into these oak and Caledonian pine forests, and hid out in caves here. The route continues via the historic Perthshire town of Aberfoyle, beneath the Menteith Hills, to mountain-flanked Loch Earn and Killin's Falls of Dochart. The Way's wildest and highest point (1,854 ft/565 m) lies en route to Ardtalnaig, a stride across exposed moorland. But reward lies ahead, on the last stage from Aberfeldy to the Victorian resort of Pitlochry: not only the joy of those final Highland views but also the pleasures of Dewar's World of Whisky, where you can raise a dram to your almost-completed adventure.

another way

At Drymen, Rob Roy intersects with Scotland's most-tramped trail, the West Highland Way. This busier but bucket-list hike of 96 miles (154 km) runs from Milngavie to Fort William via Loch Lomond and the bleakly beautiful blanket bogs of Rannoch Moor.

A winding mountain footpath leading to Slieve Donard's snowcapped peak

7. Slieve Donard

LOCATION Northern Ireland **START/FINISH** Donard parking lot (loop) **DISTANCE** 5½ miles (9 km) **TIME** 4–5 hours **DIFFICULTY** Moderate **INFORMATION** https://walkni.com; strong winds can make the going tough

At 2,790 ft (850 m), Slieve Donard is the highest mountain in Northern Ireland—and one of the most culturally significant. According to ancient Celtic lore, it's an entrance to the underworld (there are burial cairns dating to 3000 BCE on the summit), while St. Donard used it as a place to preach in the 5th century CE. On top of that, it offers some of the finest views from what is the easiest to climb of all the Mourne Mountains.

That's not to say it's a stroll. After following the Glen River uphill through old oak, birch, and Scots pine, the trail rears more steeply as it meets the Mourne Wall; it then follows this seemingly endless drystone barrier to the summit. But the rewards are worth it: on a clear day, you can see as far as the Isle of Man, Scotland, and Wales.

8. Cliffs of Moher Coastal Walk

LOCATION Ireland **START/FINISH** Moher Sports Field/Doolin Pier parking lot **DISTANCE** 12½ miles (20 km) **TIME** 5 hours **DIFFICULTY** Easy to moderate **INFORMATION** www.cliffsofmoher.ie

Ireland's bedazzling west coast, better known as the Wild Atlantic Way, is—despite its awe-inspiring title—surprisingly short on shoreline-hugging paths, which makes this majestic cliff-top trail the Holy Grail for seaboard-loving hikers. There may be higher cliffs and better spots for solitude-seekers elsewhere, but catching first sight of the Cliffs of Moher, a 9-mile (14-km) limestone rock face dropping vertically into a turbulent ocean, is a memory to cherish. The cliffs rise up to 702 ft (214 m), but it's not just this sweep of wave-pummeled headlands that provides the panoramas: you can spy the Aran Islands and Connemara's mountains in clear weather, and there are three fortifications en route, with O'Brien's Tower, near the UNESCO Global Geopark Visitor Centre, offering the best cliff views. Away from the center, crowds thin and it's just you and the elements.

CORNELIUS O'BRIEN

O'Brien's Tower was built by Sir Cornelius O'Brien, a landowner and Irish politician. A local saying has it that he "built everything around here except the Cliffs": as well as his tower, Sir Cornelius also erected an Arthurian-style Round Table on the clifftops; a wall of Moher flagstones; and O'Brien's Monument, a Doric column (topped by an urn), which he also named after himself.

9 MacGillycuddy's Reeks

LOCATION Ireland **START/FINISH**
Carrauntoohil parking lot, Hydro Road (loop)
DISTANCE 8 miles (13 km) **TIME** 6–8 hours
DIFFICULTY Easy to moderate **INFORMATION**
www.reeksdistrict.com; best time is Jun–Sept;
Nov–Mar the route becomes a winter climb

Known as the backbone of the Kingdom of Kerry, the mighty MacGillycuddy's Reeks were shaped by millennia of glacial erosion and the fierce Atlantic winds that buffet Ireland's west coast.

There are several routes leading to the unassuming iron crucifix that marks the so-called Roof of Ireland. The hardest—and most rewarding—is the Coomloughra Horseshoe, a circular journey incorporating Ireland's three highest mountains: Caher, Beenkeragh, and Carrauntoohil, all over 3,280 ft (1,000 m). The rugged loop showcases the best of the region's scenery, with panoramic vistas at every summit. The climax is the thrilling scramble along Hag's Tooth Ridge, a knife-edge trail running between Beenkeragh and Carrauntoohil. There's no better way to earn a pint of Guinness at day's end.

Tackling the precipitous Hag's Tooth Ridge in MacGillycuddy's Reeks

10 Pico

LOCATION Azores, Portugal **START/FINISH**
Casa da Montanha **DISTANCE** 5 miles (8 km)
TIME 8 hours **DIFFICULTY** Moderate to
challenging **INFORMATION** https://
atipicoazores.com; official guide recommended

Scattered like stepping stones in the mid-Atlantic between Portugal and North America, the Azores feel far, far away. These nine volcanic isles were terra incognita until Portuguese navigators rocked up on their wave-battered shores in 1427—and arriving here today still feels like an off-the-radar adventure.

You'll find an archipelago of fickle weather, surf-sprayed shores, and explosive beauty, whose crater lakes, black-sand beaches, and lichen-draped laurel forests are ripe for Tolkien's Middle Earth. And then there is Pico: a horizon-hugger of a volcano dozing away on its own eponymous island (last eruption 1720). This is Portugal's highest peak at 7,713 ft (2,351 m), and one glance at its perfectly etched cone will have you longing to climb it. The weather can change at the drop of a hat, so go with a guide who knows the shelters and shortcuts. Starting at the crack of dawn, you'll head steeply up and over rippled lava flows and rocky slopes; if you're lucky, above-the-clouds views of the islands will greet you at the top.

another way

To ramp up the challenge a notch, get a 2 a.m. start and join a guided night hike to Pico's summit, with head lamps lighting the way. The volcano has its own magic by moonshine or starlight, and you'll arrive at the crater in time to catch a fiery sunrise.

Rota Vicentina:
The Fishermen's Trail

LOCATION Portugal **START/FINISH** Lagos/São Torpes **DISTANCE**
141 miles (227 km) **TIME** 13 days **DIFFICULTY** Easy, although some
walking on sand **INFORMATION** https://rotavicentina.com

*Head to Portugal's wild and empty Atlantic coast for
world-class walking without the crowds, on a glorious
stretch of the beautiful Rota Vicentina.*

*Picturesque cliffs
along the Rota
Vicentina, near
Carrapateira*

POTTER *around the white-washed fishing village of* **Porto Covo** *and its near-endless beaches*

GORGE *on fresh fish while watching the sun set into the sea at* **Entrada da Barca**

STOP *for a surf lesson on the gentle waves at laid-back* **Odeceixe**

WANDER *the ruined* **Ribat of Arrifana**, *the only Muslim coastal fortress in Portugal*

FEEL *the ocean air on your face at* **Cabo de São Vicente**, *mainland Europe's southwesternmost point*

São Torpes

Atlantic Ocean

PORTUGAL

Lagos

Atlantic Ocean

Most people seeking a Portuguese coastal jaunt flock to the southern Algarve. Which is just fine, because it leaves the country's untamed and underdeveloped Atlantic-slapped seaboard blissfully empty—and the ideal stomping ground for walkers.

Lying largely within the Southwest Alentejo and Vicentine Coast Natural Park, the Rota Vicentina was created by a cohort of independent businesses looking to bring sensitive, sustainable tourism to the region. Its 466-mile (750-km) hiking network comprises various circular routes and two main trails: the Historical Way, which veers into the rural interior, and the Fishermen's Trail, which clings to the sea.

Walking the latter is a window onto the wild western edge of Europe, an unfurling of golden dunes, crumpled cliffs, fizzing waves, and rusting shipwrecks, with the whiff of sea salt, rosemary, and pine. There are unblemished golden beaches—real dazzlers include Praia da Carraca (accessible only by creaky wooden steps), waterfall-tickled Praia da Amália (also tough to reach), 2-mile- (3-km-) long Praia do Malhão, and surfy Praia da Cordoama. There are wildflowers in abundance, especially in spring, when pink thrift, rockrose, and sour fig cloak the clifftops. There are many excellent little tabernas and spit 'n' sawdust bars dotted along the route serving up super-fresh bream, lobster, shrimp, and *percebes* (goose barnacles). And there's brilliant birdlife, from peregrine falcons to the world's only coast-nesting storks. But best of all? You'll find few other people on the trail, leaving all of this for you.

another way

If the coastal path doesn't appeal, tackle the Rota Vicentina's Historical Way instead. This 163-mile (263-km) trail from Cabo de São Vicente to Santiago do Cacém concentrates on the countryside—rolling hills, time-warp villages, and ancient cork trees.

Hiking through cloud forest on La Gomera

(12) Levada do Caldeirão Verde

LOCATION Madeira, Portugal **START/FINISH** Queimadas Forest Park/Caldeirão do Inferno **DISTANCE** 5½ miles (8.5 km) **TIME** 2 hours **DIFFICULTY** Easy **INFORMATION** www.visitmadeira.pt; flashlight required for tunnels

The Portuguese reached Madeira in 1419—and started building *levadas* right away. These narrow channels were carved out of the volcanic rock to direct water from natural springs to lucrative sugar-cane terraces. Now, more than 200 *levadas*, totaling over 1,240 miles (2,000 km), spider the Atlantic isle, still feeding crops but also providing walkers with access to areas that are otherwise impossible to reach.

Built in the 18th century, inland from Santana, the Levada do Caldeirão Verde combines all that's best about Madeira's human-made trails. It's relatively flat but scenically superb: flanked by gnarled laurel trees and rusty beeches, this *levada* delves into the São Jorge valley, mountains rearing on all sides, to finish at a lush lagoon. It's also a real feat of engineering, passing through four hand-dug tunnels and slicing along a sheer hillside. Spectacular—just don't look down.

ROCHEIROS

To farm an island as precipitous as Madeira, early settlers constructed thousands of *poios* (terraces). In order to build the *levadas* to reach these terraces, they relied on *rocheiros*, men who worked in wicker baskets dangling from ropes; these brave laborers hacked platforms out of rock using only axes, hammers, and hoes.

(13) Parque Nacional de Garajonay

LOCATION Canary Islands, Spain **START/FINISH** Laguna Verde/Alto de Garajonay **DISTANCE** 5½ miles (9 km) **TIME** 5 hours **DIFFICULTY** Moderate; some steep sections **INFORMATION** https://lagomera.travel

It's hard to conceive today, but La Gomera's layered rocks bear witness to geological trauma, when magma was funneled to the top of the volcanic island some five million years ago. For centuries, the Gomerans created a network of footpaths and mule trails to adapt to the difficulties of this piton-spiked terrain, and walking their ancient pathways introduces this living museum at close quarters.

A worthy hike is the ascent to the 4,879-ft (1,487-m) bald summit of Garajonay, the highest point on the island. Beginning in the dreamlike woodlands of the national park's interior, a mossy world of tangled ferns and wax myrtle, the trail rises onto a highland plateau of dragon trees and St. John's Wort. By the time the summit is in sight, the full Jurassic-like extent of the erosion-scarred landscape is revealed; in particular, the fist of Roque de Agando, one of five volcanic barbs, which looks like a stone guardian keeping watch over La Gomera's shores.

(14) Caminito del Rey

LOCATION Spain **START/FINISH** El Chorro (loop) **DISTANCE** 4½ miles (7.5 km) **TIME** 2–3 hours **DIFFICULTY** Easy to moderate **INFORMATION** www.caminitodelrey.info

Clinging onto the sheer, honey-hued walls of a narrow Andalusian gorge, the Caminito del Rey (King's Little Path) is one of Spain's most spectacular footpaths. There's a primordial look to the place, with vast faces of bare rock, pockmarked with caverns, descending to a distant turquoise trickle. Closer inspection, though, reveals signs of human life: wooden walkways are fixed to the canyon walls, and hanging footbridges span awesome chasms. Despite its regal name, the path's origins are prosaic—it was built in 1905 to connect two hydroelectric power plants, which sit on either side of the gorge. Over the decades, the path fell into disrepair, and by 2000 it had closed, carrying a dangerous reputation. Extensive renovations were completed in 2015, and it's now safe to explore once again—if you have nerves of steel.

Walkers negotiating a hanging bridge on the Caminito del Rey

(15) Cami de Cavalls

LOCATION Menorca, Spain **START/FINISH** Mahón **DISTANCE** 115 miles (185 km) **TIME** 20 days **DIFFICULTY** Easy **INFORMATION** www.menorca.es

The Cami de Cavalls—Way of the Horses—dates back to the 14th century, when knights would make mounted patrols of the coast to defend Menorca from marauding pirates. What was once for safeguarding is now perfect for strolling.

This gently undulating trail (also known as the GR223) circumnavigates the peaceful Balearic isle, the entirety of which is a UNESCO Biosphere Reserve. It's divided into 20 leisurely sections, each designed so that you could walk a stage out and back in a day. But why skimp on the whole route? The trail passes through the elegant capital Mahón; traces the flatter southern shore's limestone outcrops and brilliant-white sandy beaches; and rounds the rugged, hilly north, via secret coves, holm oak forests, Neolithic burial chambers, Martello watchtowers, and Franco-era bunkers. Short on time? Stage 6, which starts on the beach at Binimel-là, is the toughest but most dramatic, negotiating the island's craggiest cliffs at Binidelfà and the trail's highest point.

another way

Hop over to Mallorca for another historic Balearic trail: the 87-mile (140-km) GR221—or Drystone Route— is significantly tougher but quite magnificent, following ancient cobbled paths and traditional handmade walls to cross the Tramuntana Mountains.

The flat plains of the meseta *rolling out across Castile and León*

(16) # Camino de Santiago

LOCATION Spain **START/FINISH** St-Jean-Pied-de-Port/Santiago de Compostela **DISTANCE** 480 miles (772 km) **TIME** 4–5 weeks **DIFFICULTY** Moderate **INFORMATION** Collect stamps in a *credencial* (pilgrim passport; available at www.csj.org.uk) en route to earn a *compostela* (certificate of completion)

Take on the classic Christian pilgrimage from the south of France across northern Spain to discover a history-rich landscape and to make connections with pilgrims both past and present.

When medieval pilgrims set off for Santiago de Compostela, they were on a religious mission. They walked from all over Europe to pray at the remains of St. James, whose bones had been found in northern Spain in the early 9th century, making it one of the continent's key pilgrimage sites.

And so it is again. Numbers of pilgrims following the Camino de Santiago—the Way of St. James—have boomed over recent decades. In 1988 just over 3,500 *peregrinos* made the journey; in 2019 it was nearly 350,000. Some are still drawn by faith but many come for other reasons: to escape; to connect; to test themselves; to be immersed in nature; to find a new perspective. In an increasingly complicated world, the simplicity of a pilgrimage can offer salvation regardless of belief.

There isn't one definitive route—*caminos* spider across Spain and far beyond. But the Camino Frances (French Way), from the Pyrenean town of St-Jean-Pied-de-Port in France to the Galician city of Santiago de Compostela, is the most commonly walked. Which means unless you walk in the depths of winter—an option for the hardiest and more solitary souls only—you will be far from alone as you hoist your pack, grab your *credencial* (pilgrim passport), and follow the scallop-shell waymarkers (the Christian

ST. JAMES IN SPAIN

What's the Apostle James doing in Spain? Allegedly, after Jesus's resurrection, James traveled from Jerusalem to Iberia to spread Christ's word, before returning home. Following his death and martyrdom, his body was sailed from the Holy Land to Padrón in northern Spain, guided by angels (the stone to which the boat was moored is in Padrón's church), then buried in the countryside. The location was lost until 815 CE, when a hermit had a vision that illuminated the spot.

Along the way are Roman
ruins, medieval towns, quiet
shrines, waving wheat fields,
and welcoming tapas bars

*Top A yellow scallop
shell marking the route
Above Santiago
Cathedral, a memorable
ending Above right
Pilgrims passing through
a sun-baked vineyard
in La Rioja*

symbol of St. James) on this trail. Indeed, averaging around 15 miles
(24 km) a day, you'll meet an array of people of all ages, sizes, and
nationalities; pilgrim camaraderie—sharing hostel dormitories,
bottles of cheap wine, and advice on blisters—is as much a part
of the Camino experience as the walk itself.

It's a good walk, too, which gets off to a challenging start: the
first stage is a stiff crossing of the Pyrenees and over the border
into Spain. But from then on—after you've attended pilgrims' mass
in Roncesvalles, a small border village with a huge abbey—the way
evens out. It plows west through the rural province of Navarra,
passing Pamplona's historic center. It strikes over La Rioja's heady
hills, cloaked in mouthwatering vines. Then it's onto Castile and
León's sun-scorched *meseta* plateau and over the Cordillera

Cantábrica to enter the lush, green valleys of Galicia. Along the way are Roman ruins, walled medieval towns, quiet shrines and chapels, busy cities, waving wheat fields, and welcoming tapas bars. And then, of course, there's the grand finale: UNESCO-listed Santiago de Compostela itself, where, within a maze of cobbled streets, St. James's remains reside.

But while the Camino has a very specific destination, that's not really the point. As awe-inspiring as it is, standing in the Plaza del Obradoiro, staring up at Santiago Cathedral's flamboyant western facade—a masonry riot of filigree, spires, and statuary—it's possible you might feel both elated and a little flat. Because this is a walk about the journey. The challenges faced, the smiles (and sobs) shared, and the serendipitous moments that could never be planned but will never be forgotten.

another way

Many ways lead to Santiago: the 385-mile (620-km) Camino Portugués, which begins in Lisbon, is a popular second choice; the scenic Camino del Norte weaves for 514 miles (827 km) along the Bay of Biscay from San Sebastián; and the Camino Inglés is a compact 68 miles (110 km), starting in A Coruña, on Galicia's west coast.

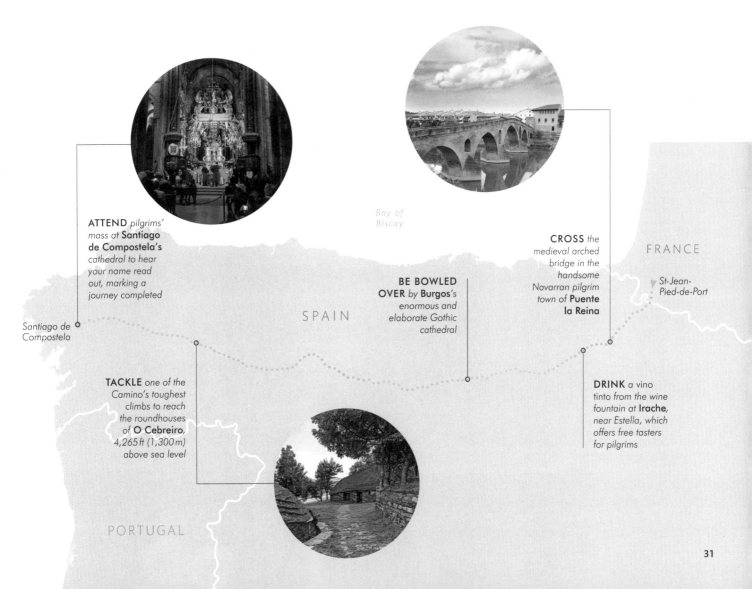

ATTEND *pilgrims' mass at* **Santiago de Compostela's** *cathedral to hear your name read out, marking a journey completed*

Santiago de Compostela

TACKLE *one of the Camino's toughest climbs to reach the roundhouses of* **O Cebreiro***, 4,265 ft (1,300 m) above sea level*

Bay of Biscay

SPAIN

BE BOWLED OVER *by* **Burgos's** *enormous and elaborate Gothic cathedral*

CROSS *the medieval arched bridge in the handsome Navarran pilgrim town of* **Puente la Reina**

FRANCE

St-Jean-Pied-de-Port

DRINK *a vino tinto from the wine fountain at* **Irache***, near Estella, which offers free tasters for pilgrims*

PORTUGAL

31

Carros de Foc

LOCATION Spain **START/FINISH** Espot or Caldes de Boí (loop) **DISTANCE** 34 miles (55 km) **TIME** 5 days **DIFFICULTY** Challenging **INFORMATION** www.carrosdefoc.com; best Jun–Sept; hut reservations (via www.refusonline.com) are essential

Tramp hut-to-hut through the high terrain of the Spanish Pyrenees, with its spectacular mountain lakes and pretty alpine meadows.

In 1987, the rangers of Parque Nacional d'Aigüestortes i Estany de Sant Maurici, in northern Spain, began a 24-hour endurance trek between the park's nine mountain huts. Since then, the Carros de Foc circuit has become one of Europe's hiking greats.

The route starts at either Espot or Caldes de Boí, two mountain villages on the fringes of the park, and meanders through the ethereal wilderness of the Spanish Pyrenees. Here, sharp granite spires fold into pine-fringed lakes and valley floors sequined with wildflowers. Chalking up 30,184 ft (9,200 m) of total ascent across the five days, you'll be thankful for the pit stops at some of the park's rustic mountain huts, where mouthwatering meals and chats with fellow hikers salve the body and the soul.

And the reward for tackling those scree-scattered mountainsides? Cinematic views and the chance to dip tired feet into the crystalline waters of the 200 alpine lakes dotted across the park. The climax of the hike is standing beneath the twin peaks of Els Encantats at the park's namesake lake, when the fog lifts from this "enchanted" mountain and it's reflected in crisp high-definition in the waters beneath.

The peak of Els Encantats towering above crystal-clear Estany de Sant Maurici

*Vineyards lining
the idyllic village
of Riquewihr*

(18)

Alsace

LOCATION France **START/FINISH** Bergheim/Kaysersberg
DISTANCE 14 miles (22 km) **TIME** 2 days **DIFFICULTY** Easy
INFORMATION www.visit.alsace; best Apr–Sept

*Ramble from vineyard to medieval castle, from forest
to fantasy village on this mellow two-day hike through
Alsace, where Germany says bonjour to France.*

Germany fired the imagination of the Brothers Grimm, but it could
just as easily have been Alsace in France. Straddling the German
border, this really is the fairy-tale dream, with ruined castles hovering
above rows of vines, one lovely half-timbered town after the next,
and darkly wooded mountains puckering up on the horizon.

Dipping into the UNESCO-listed Northern Vosges Regional
Nature Park, this gentle beauty of a hike leads from rampart-
wrapped Bergheim to vine-swathed Kaysersberg. Slip into your
own rhythm as you take to footpaths that weave among vines,
fields, and woods, emerging to follow the quiet roads of the Route
des Vins d'Alsace. It's hard to choose the prettiest village, but
Riquewihr and Mittelwihr are way up there, with cobbled lanes,
medieval towers, and gingerbready houses in punchy pastels.

The moments that grab you might be subtler, however: the
whisper of fall in the vines or watching storks clatter in huge nests
atop church steeples. This isn't a region to rush, so allow two days
to take it all in, especially if you want to stop off at family-run
cellars to taste the region's Grand Cru Rieslings and Pinots.

*Colorful houses in the half-timbered
village of Mittelbergheim*

another way

*If you fancy extending your
time in Alsace, you could cycle
or drive the 106-mile (170-km)
Route des Vins d'Alsace (Alsace
Wine Route; www.wineroute.
alsace) in its entirety, which
swings from Marlenheim in the
north to Thann in the south.*

Above The ruins of Drachenfels,
looking down over the Rhine Valley
Left Linz am Rhein, with its
picturesque half-timbered houses

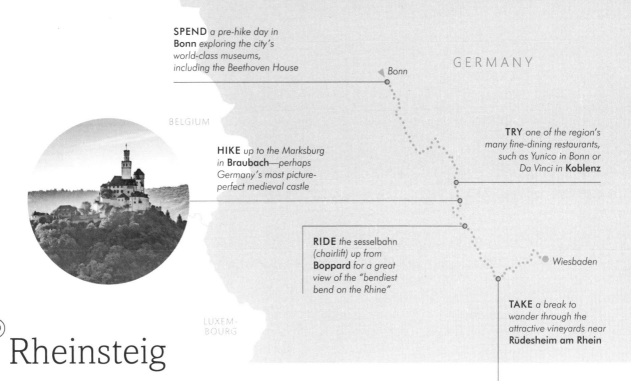

SPEND a pre-hike day in **Bonn** exploring the city's world-class museums, including the Beethoven House

Bonn

GERMANY

BELGIUM

HIKE up to the Marksburg in **Braubach**—perhaps Germany's most picture-perfect medieval castle

TRY one of the region's many fine-dining restaurants, such as Yunico in Bonn or Da Vinci in **Koblenz**

RIDE the sesselbahn (chairlift) up from **Boppard** for a great view of the "bendiest bend on the Rhine"

Wiesbaden

TAKE a break to wander through the attractive vineyards near **Rüdesheim am Rhein**

LUXEM-
BOURG

(19)

Rheinsteig

LOCATION Germany **START/FINISH** Bonn/Wiesbaden **DISTANCE** 199 miles (320 km) **TIME** 21 days **DIFFICULTY** Moderate; some steep sections **INFORMATION** www.rheinsteig.de

Explore some of Germany's most appealing landscapes on this epic hike. The north-to-south trail leads through forest-covered hills, sun-soaked vineyards, and chocolate-box villages.

One of Europe's longest rivers, the Rhine meanders majestically through Germany, from Bodensee to the border with the Netherlands. The Rheinsteig hiking trail may only take in a quarter of the river's length, but its terraced vineyards, volcanic hills, and storybook towns make it one of the more scenic stretches.

Your journey begins in Bonn, the birthplace of Beethoven and erstwhile capital of West Germany. Starting in the city's historic market square, the trail crosses the river before winding southward into the Siebengebirge, a range of undulating hills with sweeping vistas of the river below. For the best vantage point, hop on the Drachenfelsbahn cog railroad up to the old castle ruins.

The path continues through wild woodland and flower-filled meadows to Linz am Rhein, with its colorful, half-timbered houses. From here, it's just a short hop on to Bad Hönningen, famed for both its hot springs and its cool wineries, before the path diverts away from the river and into the foothills of the Westerwald.

You'll soon rejoin the Rhine on the road to Koblenz. Take time to explore this cultural capital's rich Roman history and colossal hilltop forts. Ready to go? Simply follow the Rhine south—through thick forests and lush vineyards, via medieval castles and Gothic churches—until you reach the charming city of Wiesbaden. As one of Europe's oldest spa towns, it's a perfect place to soothe your aching muscles and toast the end of an epic adventure.

another way

Don't have three weeks? There are plenty of shorter walks along the way, whether you prefer a three-day hike from Bonn to Linz or a half-day circular walk around the pretty town of Vallendar.

Liberation Route Europe: The Netherlands

LOCATION Netherlands **START/FINISH** Eindhoven/Arnhem **DISTANCE** 50 miles (80 km) **TIME** 5–7 days **DIFFICULTY** Moderate **INFORMATION** www.liberationroute.com

Step into military history on the former battlefields of Western Europe on a long-distance commemoration route past storied hilltops, landmark bridges, and poignant memorials.

The John Frost Bridge, a key objective in the Battle of Arnhem

READ *eyewitness accounts at the outstanding Airborne Museum Hartenstein in* **Oosterbeek**

HONOR *the fallen soldiers at the John Frost Bridge in* **Arnhem**

North Sea

NETHERLANDS

○ Arnhem

GERMANY

BRAVE *the horrors of* **Camp Vught National Memorial***, a former SS concentration camp for Dutch Jews*

Eindhoven ◄

STOP *in* **Nijmegen** *to discover the Freedom Museum at Groesbeek*

BELGIUM

BEGIN *in* **Eindhoven** *at the Museum Wings of Liberation, where World War II's climax is brought to life*

On the bridge across the Waal River in Nijmegen, there are 48 pairs of street lights. Every night at sunset, each set is ignited at a slow marching pace, lamp by lamp. The somber light show lasts only 12 minutes yet is a nightly tribute by veterans to the Allied soldiers who fought and died for the liberation of the Netherlands from Nazi Germany.

As unlikely as it might sound, war is the reason many come to hike through the Dutch province of Gelderland. This is a critical section of the Liberation Route Europe, the pan-European remembrance trail from London to Berlin that ties together the story lines of the climax of World War II. In September 1944, the Dutch-German border became the main stage for the fighting in Western Europe, and of all the battlefields and memorials to visit along this transnational pathway, the stretch of the Liberation Route between Eindhoven and Arnhem is arguably the richest in historical drama. Here, the past is never far away.

Start with a map of the major sites and events and plot your course through history. At Groesbeek's Freedom Museum, the curators have produced a multi-perspective story of the war, while the Airborne Museum Hartenstein in Oosterbeek re-creates the Battle of Arnhem, in which the Allied Forces at the vanguard of Operation Market Garden were outnumbered by German troops. There are hundreds of other sights along the route, from war memorials to cemeteries, so as well as engaging with the past in new ways, you'll find yourself walking back to a time of siege, sacrifice, and—ultimately—hope.

another way

With enough time on your hands, the entirety of the 1,865-mile (3,000-km) Liberation Route Europe—spinning a web between London and Berlin— awaits discovery. Highlights include the Imperial War Museum in London; the D-Day beaches of Northern France, where more than 150,000 soldiers landed in June 1944; and the story of the Battle of the Bulge at the Bastogne War Museum and Mardasson Memorial in Belgium.

Wadden Islands

LOCATION Netherlands **START/FINISH** Groningen coast/Wadden Islands **DISTANCE** 6–9 miles (10–15 km) **TIME** 3–5 hours one-way **DIFFICULTY** Easy to moderate, dependent on tides and conditions **INFORMATION** www.holland.com; an expert guide is essential

The Dutch have a word for it: Wadlopen—mud walking. That is, hiking out into the sticky mire, the shifting banks, the twisting gullies, and the belly-deep channels of the Wadden Sea, the biggest network of intertidal sand and mudflats in the world.

These UNESCO-listed waters stretch along the coasts of the Netherlands, Denmark, and Germany; the Dutch chunk is protected within the Wadden Sea Conservation Area. It's a landscape in constant flux, so heading out for a stroll here requires an expert guide to monitor the tides and lead you safely across; they will also be able to point out the harbor seals, mussel beds, sea-grass meadows, and myriad birds. The finest muddy hikes are between the mainland of Groningen and the islands of Ameland or Schiermonnikoog—expect to cover up to 9 miles (15 km), whichever route you choose.

Bastei Bridge, built to give visitors easier access to the area's incredible rock formations

EAST ATLANTIC FLYWAY

The Wadden Sea is one of the planet's most important regions for migratory birds—it's used by species making huge journeys along the East Atlantic Flyway between the Arctic and Africa. Up to 12 million birds pass by each year, from barnacle geese to Eurasian spoonbills. In winter, at dusk, watch for massive murmurations of starlings, performing their celestial ballet.

Malerweg

LOCATION Germany **START/FINISH** Liebethal/Pirna **DISTANCE** 72 miles (116 km) **TIME** 8 days **DIFFICULTY** Easy to moderate, largely flat with some stiff climbs **INFORMATION** www.saechsische-schweiz.de

The Malerweg—or Painter's Way—really is pretty as a picture. The route loops through Saxon Switzerland, a region of fantastical rocks, caves, and forests bordering the Czech Republic that has been inspiring artists since at least the 18th century.

The Malerweg has been planned with these creatives in mind. As you follow its eight stages, winding amid the tree-cloaked cliffs and ravines carved by the Elbe River, information panels explain some of the works that have been conjured in these very locations. You can walk where Romantic landscape artist Caspar David Friedrich captured the towering Bastei rocks; where Johann Carl August Richter depicted the monumental Kuhstall Cave rock arch; and where Bernardo Bellotto and Adrian Zingg were moved to draw the hilltop Königstein fortress. Who knows, it might even inspire you to start sketching yourself.

23 Watzmann Traverse

LOCATION Germany **START/FINISH** Wimbachklamm cabin (loop) **DISTANCE** 13½ miles (22 km) **TIME** 2 days **DIFFICULTY** Challenging **INFORMATION** Book huts at www.alpenverein.de; via ferrata kit is required

The UNESCO-designated Berchtesgadener Land in the heart of the Bavarian Alps features nine spectacular mountain ranges, with Germany's most photogenic body of water, the Königssee, as its centerpiece. Towering above its turquoise veneer is the soaring Watzmann massif, with its serrated line of shark-fin peaks.

A must-do mountain hike for many, the Watzmann Traverse takes in the three major peaks of Hocheck, Mittelspitze, and Südspitze, by way of an electrifying 2.8-mile (4.5-km) saw-toothed ridge. This hair-raising section employs a series of via ferrata climbing aids before the trail drops abruptly into the shaded and more sedate Wimbachgries Valley. The journey ends mid-afternoon at Wimbachklamm cabin, where you can share tales of the traverse with fellow "Watzmanners" on the veranda.

Hikers using a system of via ferrata on the Watzmann Traverse's jagged ridge

24 Rennsteig Trail

LOCATION Germany **START/FINISH** Hörschel/ Blankenstein **DISTANCE** 105 miles (169 km) **TIME** 6–7 days **DIFFICULTY** Moderate **INFORMATION** https://germany.travel

Follow the borderland that once marked the start and end of West and East Germany through 700 years of history—and into a fairy-tale landscape straight out of the storybooks.

Two stony peaks edged with wildflowers soar above Thuringian Forest like manicured fists made by giants. A medieval castle, all stone turrets and Rapunzel towers, pokes its head out of the trees in the distance. A timber-frame village appears beneath a great streak of pink, as flushed as the trekkers puffing toward day's end.

Hiking the Rennsteig Trail, the ridgeway track through the Thuringian and Franconian forests in central Germany, changes your perspective on the country. Days can start by a secret dragon gorge near Eisenach or by the peaceful lake of Ebertswiese, breathing in the scent of jasmine, and then end with a bang—on a cedar and spruce ridge, with sweeping views across to Sleeping Beauty–style Wartburg Castle. More than anything, this journey encapsulates the essence of slow travel: there's a sense that this part of Germany is still waiting to be discovered.

another way

Equally beautiful as the Rennsteig Trail, Baden-Baden's four-stage Panoramaweg packs in viewpoints, ridgeline vistas, and waterfalls in only 28 miles (45 km).

(25)

Salzburger Almenweg

LOCATION Austria **START/FINISH** Pfarrwerfen Train Station (loop) **DISTANCE** 219 miles (350 km) **TIME** 1 month **DIFFICULTY** Moderate, some challenging sections **INFORMATION** www.salzburger-almenweg.at; book mountain huts in advance

One for the flower-rich summer months, the Almenweg is a circular hut-to-hut hike through the spectacular slopes of Salzburgerland. It's split into 31 stages, making it easy to sample shorter sections.

Austria is pretty much the dictionary definition of a world-class walking destination, with an extensive chain of superb mountain huts, tens of thousands of miles of well-maintained paths, and—best of all—some of Europe's most giddily beautiful Alpine scenery.

Hiking the entire circuit makes for a highly unforgettable month in *The Sound of Music* mountains, although a big part of the trail's appeal lies in its versatility. The route technically begins and ends at Pfarrwerfen train station, where Stage 1 commences and Stage 31 concludes, but almost

every part of the route can be readily accessed from the towns and villages that speckle the slopes, giving you the freedom to pick and choose your walks as you see fit.

In summer, orchids edge the path and buttercup and eyebright bloom in the Alpine meadows. This is, however, more than just a pretty trail. As well as the myriad riches of the natural landscape—forests, waterfalls, mountain lakes, and all—you'll also be immersed in the deeply enjoyable world of hut-to-hut hospitality, with some 120 Alpine huts dotted on and around the route.

The pretty Alpine town of Radstadt, one of many providing easy access to the daily stages that make up the Salzburger Almenweg

26

Adlerweg

LOCATION Austria **START/FINISH** St. Johann in Tirol/St. Christoph am Arlberg
DISTANCE 257 miles (413 km) **TIME** 2 months **DIFFICULTY** Challenging
INFORMATION www.tyrol.com/things-to-do/sports/hiking/eagle-walk

Incisor-shaped mountaintops, stopped-clock farmsteads, glacial valleys: the Tirol teems with timeless landscapes to explore. This Trans-Tirol adventure will really help you get the most out of the magical terrain.

For hikers who love a challenge, the long-distance Adlerweg—or Eagle Walk—is the one to get in training for. This 33-stage life-definer materializes on the map as the silhouette of an eagle spreading its wings high over the western Austrian state; on the ground it is a zigzagging odyssey that'll have you yodeling in the pastures. There are seven mountain spines to cross—from the granite-faced Wilder Kaiser mountains and Brandenberg Alps in the east to the Lechtal Alps in the west bordering Arlberg—and, as well as having to tackle such knife-edge topography, you'll need to work out the logistics that come with such a monumental trail.

Or trails. This is, in fact, a two-part trail, split into a longer 24-stage North Tirol hike and a shorter 9-stage East Tirol trail between Austria's two highest mountains, the Grossglockner and the Grossvenediger. The overwhelming impression made by the trail, though, is due not only to the magnitude of the Austrian Alps, but also the history that is embedded in these valleys. The pathway charts the story of Alpinism itself, and along with ice caves, waterfalls, and soul-stirring viewing platforms, there are more than 60 classic Alpine huts to eat and sleep in. That alone is reason enough to get back onto the trail the next day.

*Left Among the clouds in Wilder Kaiser **Above** Grossvenediger and idyllic Alpine scenery*

(27)

Eiger Trail

LOCATION Switzerland **START/FINISH** Eigergletscher/Alpiglen
DISTANCE 4 miles (6 km) **TIME** 2–3 hours **DIFFICULTY** Easy
INFORMATION www.jungfrau.ch; open mid-Jun–Sept

*Few European mountains are as iconic as the
mighty Eiger, and this classic half-day hike leads
you directly under its legendary north face.*

The north face of a mountain is generally the coldest, the iciest,
and the most testing to climb. Switzerland's Eiger boasts the
highest and most infamous north face in the entire Alps, which
tells you plenty about the fearsome reputation of this 13,015-ft
(3,967-m) giant. But while countless mountaineers have tested
themselves by attempting to scale its heights, the joy of this
half-day hiking route is that it gets you up close to its for-
midable scenery on an eminently manageable (and largely
downhill) walking path. Even better: the trail's start point is
reached via a scenic cogwheel ride on the Jungfrau Railway.

   Of course, there's far more to the surroundings than the
Eiger itself. The mountain is one of a trio of fabled peaks—
namely the Eiger, Mönch, and Jungfrau (loosely translated as
the Ogre, Monk, and Maiden)—that stand shoulder to shoulder
among the stunning jumble of peaks, valleys, ridges, and cliffs
that comprise the Bernese Oberland. As a way of getting a
quick fix of the celestial landscapes that this corner of
Switzerland calls its own, it's a walk not be missed.

another way

*Rather than hiking the trail, you
can let the Jungfrau Railway take
the strain. After passing through
the Eiger and Mönch, the train
continues up to Europe's highest
train station, the 11,332-ft
(3,454-m) Jungfraujoch.*

*The Jungfrau Railway,
dropping hikers off at the
start of the Eiger Trail*

Tell Trail

LOCATION Switzerland **START/FINISH** Altdorf/Brienzer Rothorn
DISTANCE 97 miles (156 km) **TIME** 8 days **DIFFICULTY**
Challenging **INFORMATION** www.luzern.com/en

Lake Lucerne in all its glory, far below the Fronalpstock ridge

Nowadays William Tell's tale is a mere footnote in history, but it provides the context for this superb hike around a side of the Swiss Alps few people see.

William Tell—apple-shooter, rebel-rouser, national folk hero—is remembered as the liberator of Switzerland, even if most visitors know next to nothing about the man behind the legend. From a certain perspective, though, the collective romantic notions of what it means to be Swiss can be hooked to the Tell myth, and his story— an underdog leading the forest cantons against oppressive Austrian rule—is rooted to the central Swiss Alps and Lake Lucerne, where this long-distance trail begins. It snakes and ladders past six landmark peaks—the Stoos, Rigi, Pilatus, Stanserhorn, Titlis, and Brienzer Rothorn—and tackles valley lows and Alpine highs.

The trail starts overlooking the Rütli meadow before leading hikers around Lake Lucerne, where Tell made his name; the section along the barbed Klingenstock to Fronalpstock ridge soars in the truest sense of the word. You'll also pass Mount Rigi and its historic cogwheel railroad; the world's most advanced cable car on the Stanserhorn; and the historic 13th-century Benedictine abbey of Engelberg. But while the marks of humans and modern life are soul-stirring, it's Mother Nature who leaves the greatest impression. Or, as Friedrich Schiller, German playwright of *William Tell*, wrote: "On the mountains is freedom!"

The Klingenstock to Fronalpstock ridge soars

A hiker pausing to take in awe-inspiring views of the Mont Blanc glacier

(29)

Tour du Mont Blanc

LOCATION France, Switzerland and Italy **START/FINISH** Les Houches (loop) **DISTANCE** 164 km (164 km) **TIME** 9–14 days **DIFFICULTY** Challenging **INFORMATION** www.autourdumontblanc.com; route open summer only, best in mid-Jun or Sept

This classic Alpine route takes you on a loop around the tallest peak in Western Europe, offering the chance to admire the myriad faces of the White Mountain.

Over two and a half centuries ago, Horace-Bénédict de Saussure, a wealthy Swiss geologist studying the Alps, discovered that walking around the Mont Blanc massif—topped by its 15,774-ft (4,808-m) peak, Western Europe's tallest—is, well, actually quite enjoyable. In many ways, little has changed in the birthplace of Alpine tourism since he completed that first lap. True, visitors have proliferated while glaciers have sadly receded, but the experience of gazing at the White Mountain from every angle, and the exhilaration of traversing trails with vistas to rival any on the planet, remain as elemental as ever. Today, the Tour du Mont Blanc is deservedly one of the world's most popular long-distance treks.

Unsurprisingly, given its long heritage, the practicalities are straightforward. Mostly well-made paths, repurposed from ancient shepherds' tracks, link a generous network of mountain huts, *gîtes d'etape* (lodges), and rustic guesthouses and hotels offering more or less comfortable accommodation and hearty food along the trail. Bag transfers are also available if you'd prefer not to lug all your gear between overnights. But despite these comforts, there's no getting away from the fact that the Tour du Mont Blanc is as challenging as it is spectacular: to complete the circuit, you'll have to tackle some 34,000 ft (10,000 m) of ascents and descents.

With the highest point on the official route ▶

The Tour du Mont Blanc is as challenging as it is spectacular

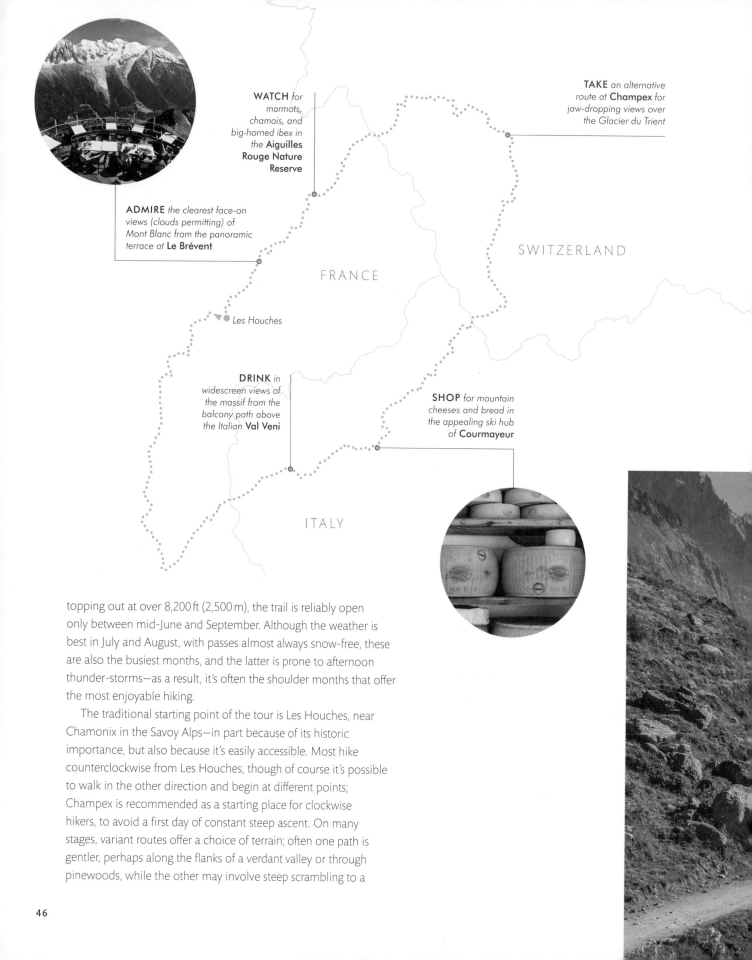

WATCH for marmots, chamois, and big-horned ibex in the **Aiguilles Rouge Nature Reserve**

TAKE an alternative route at **Champex** for jaw-dropping views over the Glacier du Trient

ADMIRE the clearest face-on views (clouds permitting) of Mont Blanc from the panoramic terrace at **Le Brévent**

SWITZERLAND

FRANCE

Les Houches

DRINK in widescreen views of the massif from the balcony path above the Italian **Val Veni**

SHOP for mountain cheeses and bread in the appealing ski hub of **Courmayeur**

ITALY

topping out at over 8,200 ft (2,500 m), the trail is reliably open only between mid-June and September. Although the weather is best in July and August, with passes almost always snow-free, these are also the busiest months, and the latter is prone to afternoon thunder-storms—as a result, it's often the shoulder months that offer the most enjoyable hiking.

The traditional starting point of the tour is Les Houches, near Chamonix in the Savoy Alps—in part because of its historic importance, but also because it's easily accessible. Most hike counterclockwise from Les Houches, though of course it's possible to walk in the other direction and begin at different points; Champex is recommended as a starting place for clockwise hikers, to avoid a first day of constant steep ascent. On many stages, variant routes offer a choice of terrain; often one path is gentler, perhaps along the flanks of a verdant valley or through pinewoods, while the other may involve steep scrambling to a loftier col (pass), rewarded with greater satisfaction and even farther-reaching views of those granite crags and ridges.

Whichever direction, starting point, and variants you choose, days typically follow a similar pattern. After breakfasting in your overnight refuge, you'll follow a path through wildflower meadows and pastures speckled with butterflies, zigzagging up to a col that reveals the glories to come that day. You'll detect subtle differences along the way, of course. Not just between the three countries you traverse—France, Italy, and Switzerland—but also from one valley to the next, in the landscapes and flora, architecture and cuisine.

One thing that remains unchanging, though, is the mountain itself—or, rather, mountains; the massif stretches some 29 miles (46 km) from the southwest to the northeast. It's ever-present on the hike, revealing disparate features as you progress: the stark grandeur of the south face, glaring across at the Italian Val Veni; waterfalls striping forested slopes in the Swiss section above La Fouly; the vast Mer de Glace dripping between crags like icing from a gargantuan birthday cake. It's truly a feast for the eyes, soul, and soles alike.

PIONEER OF THE PEAKS

Horace-Bénédict de Saussure become obsessed with Mont Blanc after visiting the surrounding area to collect plant specimens. In 1767—supported by an entourage of mules, porters, and guides—he pioneered a circuit around the peak, following much the same route as the modern tour. Today, his statue gazes across Chamonix from the bridge by Place Balmat.

Left A couple striding toward snowy peaks *Above* Ibex on a mountain ridge

(30)

GR20

Mountainous Corsica, home to 20 peaks that exceed 6,560 ft (2,000 m)

LOCATION Corsica, France **START/FINISH** Calenzana/Conca **DISTANCE** 109 miles (176 km) **TIME** 15 days **DIFFICULTY** Challenging **INFORMATION** www.le-gr20.fr

Head to the Mediterranean's most mountainous island for a hike across craggy summits, past snow-covered cirques, and through ancient river valleys on one of Europe's most challenging treks.

The Mediterranean island of Corsica feels like a world removed from other parts of France. Rugged mountains cover two-thirds of its territory, and in many of the old stone villages you can still hear the mellifluous tones of Corsican, a language that sounds more Italian than French.

This unique island is home to one of Europe's most demanding hikes, the Grande Randonnée (GR) 20, which courses over the chiseled spine of the interior on grinding ups and downs. Solid preparation, both physical and mental, is the key to success on this alpine roller coaster, which involves some 62,336 ft (19,000 m) of elevation changes.

Despite the arduous terrain, the rewards are immense. You'll experience an astonishing variety of landscapes as you haul up boulder-strewn ridges and descend into deep valleys, traveling past pine forests, boggy marshland, and misty lakes. The weather can be just as mixed, with searing heat, fog, rain, and hail all possible on a single summer's day, thanks to Corsica's unusual microclimates.

Most hikers start in Calenzana and head south, covering the hardest parts of the trail in the beginning. Your first days take you across rushing rivers, above churning waterfalls, and up to dizzying heights where saw-toothed peaks and precipitous

Calenzana

MAKE the side-trip up **Monte Cinto**, *Corsica's highest peak, for mesmerizing views*

BOUNCE *across the iconic* **Spasimata** *suspension bridge, which stretches over the eponymous river*

KEEP *an eye out for wild horses on the green pastures around crystal-clear* **Lac de Nino**

Tyrrhenian Sea

Mediterranean Sea

CORSICA

SOAK *up the vistas of far-away Ajaccio from* **Monte Incudine**, *the highest mountain in Corse-du-Sud*

WIND *past the towering red-rock spires of* **Aiguilles de Bavella** *en route to the mountain hamlet of Bavella*

Conca

another way

If you have just a week to spare, end your hike at the small town of Vizzavona, which marks the halfway point of the GR20. From here, you can catch an onward train or bus to the cities of Ajaccio or Bastia.

valleys stretch in every direction. The later-stage descents are no less dramatic, leading through thick maquis and past glacial lakes, where you might spy wild horses on nearby meadows. Sheep and goats—and shepherds' huts—lend to the scenery, while birds of prey can be seen soaring above.

As you make your final descent into Conca, you'll have no doubts left about how the GR20 got its Corsican name of Fra li Monti—Across the Mountains. From this point, it's a short hop to the glorious sandy beaches of the southeast—a well-earned treat for completing one of Europe's most notorious hikes.

Hikers crossing a stream on the approach to Lac de Nino, on Corsica's Camputile Plateau

(31)

Il Sentiero degli Dei

LOCATION Italy **START/FINISH** Agerola/Nocelle **DISTANCE** 5 miles (8 km)
TIME 3 hours **DIFFICULTY** Moderate **INFORMATION** http://ilsentierodeglidei.net

*This awe-inspiring path hugs the Amalfi Coast, offering spectacular
views of the Mediterranean Sea and the archipelago of Li Galli,
three rocky islets lying between Capri and Positano.*

Hugging the sun-kissed cliffs of the Amalfi Coast, the Sentiero degli Dei conjures mythological landscapes of dramatic cliffs plunging into deep blue waters—a place where heaven meets earth. Translating as "Path of the Gods," this gorgeous trail shimmies its way along a rugged stretch of coastline, with dramatic sea views unfolding at every corner. Cliffs carpeted in vegetation fall away into the sea, where yachts bob up and down in a series of undulating coves. Aromatic herbs scent the air, and in summer it's

> ## This gorgeous trail shimmies its way along a rugged coastline

common to see farmers leading mules laden with sacks of fresh figs. Connecting the villages of Agerola and Nocelle, the walk is shrouded in myth—legend says that Greek gods passed through here to save Ulysses from the sirens of the Li Galli islands. The pathway ends at Nocelle, where you can stop off at the Chiosco degli Dei for a refreshing drink made with locally grown lemons or oranges. You'll need it: from Nocelle, it's a leg-tremblingly long and winding staircase—all 1,700 steps of it—down to Arienzo and then a final walk along the road to Positano.

*View along the
Amalfi Coast
toward Positano*

Left *The colorful houses of Manarola*
Above *A hiker hitting the trail*

32

The Cinque Terre

LOCATION Italy **START/FINISH** Riomaggiore/Monterosso al Mare **DISTANCE** 7½ miles
(12 km) **TIME** 6 hours **DIFFICULTY** Easy to moderate; steep in places **INFORMATION**
www.parconazionale5terre.it/Eindex.php; a Cinque Terre trekking card is required for entry
to some of the trails (buy online at https://card.parconazionale5terre.it)

Explore the impossibly pretty five villages of the Cinque Terre, the jewel in the
crown of the Italian Riviera, traversing old mule tracks and coastal forests as
views of colorful villages and terraced gardens unfold before you.

Lying along the Ligurian coastline like a string of
pearls, the Cinque Terre is archetypal Italian
Riviera: a gorgeous collection of five pastel-hued
villages that cling to the cliffsides in an unlikely
defiance of gravity, tumbling down to picture-
postcard harbors and surrounded by terraced
vineyards. Most of this area is effectively off-limits
to cars, meaning the best way to explore is on
foot; the Blue Path connects all five villages,
through forests and along mountain trails and
coastal mule tracks—all backdropped by
spectacular views over some of Europe's most
photogenic coastline.

The exotic sight of agave bushes, prickly pear cacti,
and jade necklace plants accompanies the first part
of the walk, from Riomaggiore to Manarola. The next
leg sees you traipse up 382 steps to reach Corniglia;
happily, this is an unbeatable spot to gather your
breath over lunch and a limoncino. The seafood is
exquisite in these parts, and a dish of octopus pasta,
followed by honey gelato, is well worth lingering
over. All the senses are in for a feast here—as you
continue on to Vernazza and the home stretch to
Monterosso al Mare, soaking up the fortifying coastal
views, there's the constant aroma of lemon and sea
fennel mingling with the salty ocean breeze.

ⓝ (33)

Alta Via 1

LOCATION Italy **START/FINISH** Lago di Braies/La Pissa **DISTANCE** 75 miles (120 km) **TIME** 8–11 days **DIFFICULTY** Moderate, with some challenging sections **INFORMATION** www.dolomites.org; best mid-Jun to late Sept

Hike into the dramatic Dolomites to get up-close and personal with magnificent mountains, plunging valleys, and wildflower-rife meadows peppered with poignant World War I history.

The Dolomites rise fortresslike across the top of northeast Italy, a gargantuan bastion of spires, turrets, and ramparts hewn from pale-gray limestone and dolomitic rock. During World War, I they became just that: a natural stronghold and a fiercely fought-over frontline, where Italian and Austro-Hungarian forces were locked in battle for four years.

This combination—the region's ravishing good looks and striking history—is what makes the Alta Via 1 such a world-class walk. Crossing north to south, from the forest-flanked shores of Lago di Braies to the trailhead at La Pissa, the route has no shortage of magnificent vistas. You'll get intimate with the monumental monoliths of Tre Cime, the Sennes and Fanes massifs and the pyramidal bulk of Tofana di Rozes. But the trail is also scattered with relics of World War I, from stone-walled trenches to memorials, iron ladders to rock-hewn bunkers. This is most notable around Mount Lagazuoi, a mighty peak—at 9,029 ft (2,752 m), the AV1's highest point—with military bases dug deep inside. Here, you can hike amid the remains of gun emplacements and into long, dark tunnels. Chilling, even on a summer's day.

WATCH the pink late-afternoon light—known as the enrosadira—set the pale pinnacles aglow

Lago di Braies

BRAVE the detour through the long, dark wartime tunnels to Passo Falzarego (pack a flashlight)

SOAK up the views of Alpine pastures rippling in front of the Civetta massif

ITALY

LISTEN for marmots and look for chamois in UNESCO-listed Parco Nazionale delle Dolomiti Bellunesi

● *La Pissa*

VIA FERRATA

During World War I, soldiers stationed in the Dolomites built many via ferrata—"iron roads" comprising fixed lines, ladders, and bridges to help them cross the precipitous terrain. Many remain. You're not required to negotiate any of these more technical obstacles, but you can detour if you're properly equipped—to Passo Giau, for instance, or the challenging Ferrata Marmol.

A line of rowing
boats on stunning
Lago di Braies in
the Pragser Wildsee

Hikers using via ferrata to tackle the final ascent up Mount Triglav

34 Mount Triglav

LOCATION Slovenia **START/FINISH** Krma Valley **DISTANCE** 12 miles (19 km) **TIME** 2 days return **DIFFICULTY** Moderate to challenging **INFORMATION** www.slovenia.info

Mount Triglav is more than a mountain. Soaring 9,396 ft (2,864 m) in the Julian Alps, Slovenia's highest peak features on the country's flag and is a symbol of national identity. Climbing it is a Slovenian rite of passage. And a fine challenge.

There are multiple ways to reach the summit, all of which require hikers to face at least one section of vertiginous via ferrata to get to the very top. The easiest—though longest—option starts in the verdant Krma Valley and climbs relatively gently via forest, alpine pasture, and rocky ridges to the Kredarica Hut (8,251 ft/ 2,515 m). This is a good place to fill up on Slovenian stew and pancakes and get a decent night's sleep before tackling the push up the peak. You'll want to wear a harness (and clip onto the cables) to ascend the final rock face— as far as via ferrata go, it isn't too technical, but a head for heights is definitely required.

35 Velebit Trail

LOCATION Croatia **START/FINISH** Zavižan/ Starigrad **DISTANCE** 65 miles (104 km) **TIME** 5 days **DIFFICULTY** Moderate **INFORMATION** Self-guided treks with www.highlanderadventure. com; shoulder seasons have best weather

Wedged between the Balkans and the Adriatic Sea, the Velebit Mountains are Croatia's largest range and one of Europe's most overlooked alpine landscapes. The Velebit Trail flows through Northern Velebit and Paklenica national parks, known for their rich flora and fauna, including brown bears, wolves, and the Eurasian lynx. Over the course of five days, the trail slides from one landscape to another: weaving in and out of dense pine forest, twisting along rocky ravines, and then breaking out into vast grasslands and over exposed ridges, always with the sparkling Adriatic on the horizon.

The high point of the trek comes on the third day as the trail arrives at Panos, a clearing in the woods just below the summit of 4,347-ft (1,325-m) Panos Peak; the promontory is the perfect spot to watch the sun set over the Adriatic, which lies beyond folding green slopes and more rocky peaks. After reaching the sea at Starigrad-Paklenica, it's impossible to resist diving into its cool waters for a refreshing dip.

another way

The route can be shortened to a 34-mile (55-km) trek that takes three days and ends at Baške Oštarije, a small but civilized campground located alongside a hostel replete with a beer garden. The shorter version enjoys similar scenery but misses out on Panos Peak and a seaside finale.

36 Jánošíkove Diery

LOCATION Slovakia **START/FINISH** Biely Potok (loop) **DISTANCE** 7 miles (11 km) **TIME** 5–6 hours **DIFFICULTY** Moderate to challenging **INFORMATION** Hotel Diery (www.hotel-diery.sk)

Juraj Jánošík is Slovakia's Robin Hood: an outlaw who became the nation's most beloved folk hero. Born and bred in Terchová, he became a notorious brigand, but he now lends his name to the area's magical gorge, the Jánošíkove Diery. Set in Terchová's Malá Fatra National Park, the gorge's moniker translates as "Jánošík's holes," a reference to the myriad hollows and hidey-holes chiseled out by a mountain stream as it churns through a particularly narrow, precipitous ravine, forming delightful waterfalls along the way. The real draw of Jánošíkove Diery, though, is that the entire cascade-spattered canyon is traversed by a hiking trail that threads up the gorge via boardwalks, bridges, and—most thrilling of all—ladders and chains splashed by the raging falls themselves. Dolné diery (lower holes) and Nové diery (new holes) can be explored via short walks, but for the best waterfalls and most heart-in-mouth ascents, head for Horné diery (upper holes), a five-hour round-trip hike from Biely Potok.

37 Kôprovský Štít

LOCATION Slovakia **START/FINISH** Štrbské pleso/Kôprovský štít **DISTANCE** 13½ miles (22 km) return **TIME** 7–9 hours **DIFFICULTY** Challenging **INFORMATION** www.tanap.org

The Tatra Mountains bristle along the Slovakia-Poland border. Formed by receding glaciers more than 50 million years ago, these lofty peaks are the highest section of the Carpathian Mountains. For a classic day hike, tackle Kôprovský štít. Beginning in pretty Štrbské pleso, you'll meander up a gentle incline and emerge at Mengusovka valley. Time your trip to see the valley dotted with spring flowers, or go in September to catch the blushing approach of fall.

As you hike, the scenery gradually transforms from plush valleys and meadows to wind-scoured granite. Pause to admire the shimmering spectacle of Veľké Hincovo pleso, the Slovak Tatras' largest and deepest glacial lake, before trekking steadily up Kôprovský štít itself (7,753 ft/ 2,363 m). From up here, you'll see valleys, meadows and the elegantly tapered peak of Kriváň, a Slovak emblem that is even more majestic viewed from these heights.

The evening sun casting a soft light on a lake near Štrbské pleso, beneath Kôprovský štít

Albanian Riviera

*Hikers tracing
the backbone
of the coastal
Ceraunian
Mountains*

LOCATION Albania **START/FINISH** Llogara National Park/Butrint **DISTANCE**
70 miles (113 km) **TIME** 7–8 days **DIFFICULTY** Moderate **INFORMATION**
www.outdooralbania.com/the-albanian-coast

*On the rocks or with water? When you're hiking along the southern
Albanian coast, you're always within reach of mountain summits and
wild beaches from which to appreciate the deep blue skies and seas.*

When English poet Lord Byron visited Albania in
1809 on his pan-European pilgrimage, he was so
taken by the scenery that he penned a letter to his
mother about it. Albania was "a country of the
most picturesque beauty," he wrote and, despite
the centuries passing, its coastal pathways and
Ottoman-era castles remain untouched—in a
world running short of wild frontiers, this is still
a coast ripe for exploring on grand adventures.

From the capital Tirana, the hiker's path begins
amid the quasi-alpine meadows and ridgeline
forests of Llogara National Park, a swathe of black
pine and ash elevated above the deep blue sea of
the Karaburun Peninsula. The summit of Mount
Çika, the snow-dusted roof of the Ceraunian
Mountains above the Ionian Coast, beckons at
6,706 ft (2,044 m), then it's on to the coast proper,
where the vegetation morphs to become more

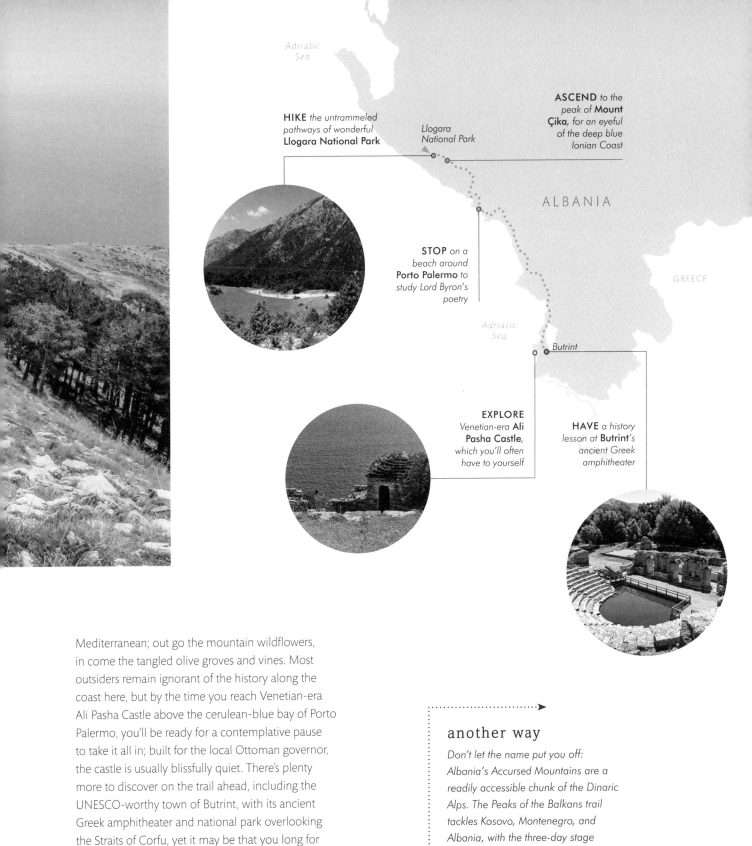

HIKE the untrammeled pathways of wonderful **Llogara National Park**

ASCEND to the peak of **Mount Çika**, for an eyeful of the deep blue Ionian Coast

Llogara National Park

Adriatic Sea

ALBANIA

GREECE

STOP on a beach around **Porto Palermo** to study Lord Byron's poetry

Adriatic Sea

Butrint

EXPLORE Venetian-era **Ali Pasha Castle**, which you'll often have to yourself

HAVE a history lesson at **Butrint's** ancient Greek amphitheater

Mediterranean; out go the mountain wildflowers, in come the tangled olive groves and vines. Most outsiders remain ignorant of the history along the coast here, but by the time you reach Venetian-era Ali Pasha Castle above the cerulean-blue bay of Porto Palermo, you'll be ready for a contemplative pause to take it all in; built for the local Ottoman governor, the castle is usually blissfully quiet. There's plenty more to discover on the trail ahead, including the UNESCO-worthy town of Butrint, with its ancient Greek amphitheater and national park overlooking the Straits of Corfu, yet it may be that you long for beach time and wild swims. Adding an extra few days to your itinerary, surely, is the smart thing to do.

another way

Don't let the name put you off: Albania's Accursed Mountains are a readily accessible chunk of the Dinaric Alps. The Peaks of the Balkans trail tackles Kosovo, Montenegro, and Albania, with the three-day stage from Theth to Doberdol in Albania being an easily digestible highlight.

(39)

Vikos Gorge

LOCATION Greece **START/FINISH** Monodendri/Vikos **DISTANCE** 7½ miles (12 km)
TIME 6 hours **DIFFICULTY** Moderate; steep in places **INFORMATION** If you need to
get back to Monodendri at the end of the trail, tavernas in Vikos can help arrange a taxi

*Descend into the verdant depths of northern Greece's Vikos Gorge,
a much quieter—but no less spectacular—alternative to the famous
Samaria Gorge in Crete.*

Gorgeous doesn't cover it. A great crack in the earth in Greece's Pindus Mountains, the Vikos Gorge is epic both in beauty and in scale. This is the world's deepest gorge relative to its width, and when you're standing at the trailhead, beneath the shadow of the Church of Saint Athanasios in Monodendri village, it feels like it.

Vikos Gorge, snaking through the Pindus Mountains of northern Greece

The fragrance of wild lemon balm, spearmint, and basil accompany the walk, which passes elegantly crumbling stone shrines and shimmering mountain pools. Look amid the undergrowth and you might spot tortoises rummaging through dandelion leaves; cast your eyes skyward and you may meet the watchful gaze of a chamois peering from a distant bluff. Birdsong fills the valley year-round—listen for the song of the nightingale in spring, and the nuthatch in fall.

Gentle though most of the path is, it can still be hot work. Happily, the valley provides: fed by a mountain stream, the crystal-clear Voidomatis springs, toward the end of the hike, make the perfect place to freshen up for the final ascent.

*Right Looking out from Butterfly Valley **Far right** Tombs carved into the rock at Myra*

40

Lycian Way

LOCATION Turkey **START/FINISH** Ölüdeniz/Geyikbayırı **DISTANCE** 335 miles (540 km) **TIME** 29 days **DIFFICULTY** Moderate **INFORMATION** www.cultureroutesinturkey.com/the-lycian-way

Echoes of the ancient world resound at every turn on this Turkish trail, which passes gorgeous coastal landscapes and the rock-cut tombs of the Lycians.

Designed by amateur historians Kate Clow and Terry Richardson in the 1990s, this coastal trail weaves around the Tekke Peninsula in southwest Turkey and is named after the Lycian League, an ancient civilization that ruled this region 2,500 years ago.

Over the course of a month, the trail leads trekkers along a mix of old mule paths and Roman roads, taking in crescent after crescent of brilliant-blue bays, and scaling vertiginous cliffs that fall away into glass-clear waters at scenic spots like Butterfly Valley. All the way, the scent of juniper and pine wafts through the salty air of the Mediterranean Sea, a perennial waymarker in cerulean blue, shimmering away to the south.

The natural views are punctuated by vivid remnants of ancient human life: rock-cut tombs high in cliff walls, and the staggering remains of amphitheaters at Pinara and Myra, are reminders that a great civilization once made its home here. For many, though, the highlight will be the simple things, like sitting with a celebratory raki outside your tent or B&B at the end of another rewarding day on the Way.

SARCOPHAGI

Like their neighbors in Ancient Greece, the Lycian League was a collection of many city-states notable for their highly developed art style. The most vivid illustration of this that you'll see on the Lycian Way are sarcophagi (stone coffins), famed for their huge size and their pointed lids shaped like a bishop's miter. Well-preserved examples along the Lycian Way can be found at the towns of Kaş and Phellus, while there are fantastic rock-cut tombs at Myra.

(41) Piatra Craiului Main Ridge Trail

LOCATION Romania **START/FINISH** Cabana Curmătura (loop) **DISTANCE** 12½ miles (20 km) **TIME** 2 days **DIFFICULTY** Challenging **INFORMATION** www.pcrai.ro

Like the skeletal backbone of some giant prehistoric creature, the Piatra Craiului mountain ridge rises in strikingly white limestone above the hills of Brașov and Argeș County. The ridge itself is so sheer that human influence—even the pastures that are so common in Romanian uplands—has barely impacted the landscape. Brown bears, wolves, and lynx can all be spotted here, but the lure for mountain mavens is the Piatra Craiului's ridge-top hike, among Europe's finest, running from Vârful Turnu in the north up and over Vârful La Om—at 7,342 ft (2,238 m) the trail's high point—to Funduri in the south. At times little thicker than a saw edge, the suddenness with which the ridge falls away on either side defies belief, yet somehow this path threads the length of it. Vertiginous sections where you must cling to chains in the rock face keep you, quite literally, on your toes.

The jagged ridge of central Romania's Piatra Craiului Mountains

Mist draping the marshy landscape of Soomaa National Park

(42) Soomaa National Park

LOCATION Estonia **START/FINISH** Visitor center (loop) **DISTANCE** 3½ miles (6 km) **TIME** 2 hours **DIFFICULTY** Easy **INFORMATION** www.visit estonia.com; all year except spring

Visiting Soomaa National Park feels like stepping into a primeval realm. Located in southwestern Estonia, this wilderness reserve encompasses vast peat bogs veined with meandering rivers, as well as dense forests, rustling grasslands, and rolling sand dunes. Home to creatures such as elk, beavers, and brown bears, Soomaa floods during the spring and is thickly blanketed with snow and ice in winter. Although you can walk along elevated boardwalks, parts of which are wheelchair-accessible, the most memorable way to explore the park is by strapping on a pair of "bog shoes" and striking out on a guided hike across the mire. Although progress can be slow, these walks immerse you in an otherworldly landscape, created during the last Ice Age— and seemingly untouched by humankind.

43 Kungsleden

LOCATION Sweden **START/FINISH** Abisko/Hemavan **DISTANCE** 275 miles (440 km) **TIME** 1 month **DIFFICULTY** Moderate **INFORMATION** https://visitsweden.com/kings-trail-kungsleden

As Sweden's lengthiest and most celebrated hike, the Kungsleden—or King's Trail—has carved a reputation as one of the prime long-distance walks in northern Europe. It justifies the hype. This is, after all, Lapland: thinly populated, sweepingly atmospheric, and fiercely remote. The route lies mostly above the Arctic Circle, meaning glacial valleys, dense birch forests and snow-cloaked mountains, as well as near-constant daylight in high summer. Look out for the tracks of lynx, wolverines, and even bears.

The hike can be tackled as a whole or in separate sections. Many hikers choose to focus on the northernmost (and ostensibly most scenic) stretch between Abisko and Nikkaluokta, but even this takes around ten days. Much of the route passes through the traditional lands of the indigenous Sami people, and you'll see ancient settlements and old herders' huts at various points along the way. This is truly a trail that lives up to its regal name.

◄ ► THE SAMI

Originally hunter-gatherers, the Sami have been herding reindeer since the 17th century, although they no longer lead such a nomadic lifestyle. The Sami have their own language—with more than 300 different ways of saying "snow"—their own flag, and their own parliament, the *Sametinget*. Traditional Sami singing, known as *yoik*, is one of the oldest forms of music in Europe.

44 Galdhøpiggen

LOCATION Norway **START/FINISH** Gjendesheim/Spiterstulen **DISTANCE** 33 miles (53 km) **TIME** 4 days **DIFFICULTY** Challenging **INFORMATION** https://dnt.no

At 8,100 ft (2,469 m), Norway's Galdhøpiggen is the highest mountain in Scandinavia. A journey to its summit showcases a spectacular cross-section of Jotunheimen National Park, the land of the *jötunn*, or giants. Comprising northern Europe's highest concentration of mountains above 6,562 ft (2,000 m), Jotunheimen's titans stand vigil over a magnificent medley of glassy glaciers, plunging waterfalls, and craggy valleys.

The trail begins at the head of Gjende Lake and crosses the ridge into the adjacent valley, skirting Bessvatnet and Russvatnet lakes on its way to the well-maintained Glitterheim and Spiterstulen huts. From the latter, the route is steep and punishing—but sensational.

Wild reindeer roam the verdant lower-level meadows, while the upper slopes harbor gleaming snowfields overlooking the immense Svellnosbreen glacier. Astonishing views of snowcapped peaks are just reward for those who make the final push to the summit.

The mighty snowcapped peaks of Jotunheimen National Park

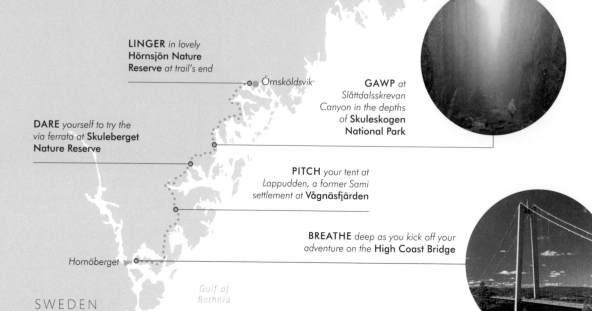

LINGER *in lovely* **Hörnsjön Nature Reserve** *at trail's end* ○ Örnsköldsvik

GAWP *at Slåttdalsskrevan Canyon in the depths of* **Skuleskogen National Park**

DARE *yourself to try the via ferrata at* **Skuleberget Nature Reserve**

PITCH *your tent at Lappudden, a former Sami settlement at* **Vägnäsfjärden**

BREATHE *deep as you kick off your adventure on the* **High Coast Bridge**

Hornöberget ○

SWEDEN

Gulf of Bothnia

FIKA

Not every coffee break is created equal. Sweden is a country ruled by *fika*, an almost mandatory coffee-and-cake break that's a way of life. When hiking in the Swedish countryside, it's never long before flasks appear, followed by sugar-topped cinnamon twists and apple pastries—the ultimate calorie-loader. If you can get your hands on a box of *kanelbullar* (frosted cinnamon rolls) or *semla* buns from one of the bakeries along the route, you'll make hiking buddies for life.

---

(45)

High Coast Trail

LOCATION Sweden **START/FINISH** Hornöberget/Örnsköldsvik **DISTANCE** 80 miles (128 km) **TIME** 5–7 days **DIFFICULTY** Easy to moderate **INFORMATION** www.hogakusten.com/en/highcoasttrail

Evergreen forests, sandy beaches, pretty meadows: all can be found on this life-defining hike that stretches through the entire UNESCO World Heritage site of the same name.

The Swedes do coastal living better than many, so it's little surprise that one of the country's 12 landmark national trails is an out-and-out ode to the sea. This is a route that delivers a succession of forest paths, rocky shores, and nature reserves, and all of it towering over shingle beaches, ancient seabeds and the IKEA-blue sea of the Gulf of Bothnia, the topmost part of the Baltic Sea in northeast Sweden.

Begin in Hornöberget overlooking the High Coast Bridge, then find your rhythm as you stride through a landscape created by post-glacial land-uplift during the Ice Age. Highlights abound, but those likely to top your list are the spectacular swimming beaches at Grönsviksfjärden, the Iron Age fort at UNESCO-worthy Rödklitten, and Skuleberget Nature Reserve. If the hiking is a little too pedestrian, amp-up the drama on the via ferrata—it's one of Europe's longest. Otherwise, the coast is perfection for a contemplative week of vistas and *fika*-fueled coffee breaks, particularly when discovering Skuleskogen National Park, and its standout sight, Slåttdalsskrevan Canyon, a narrow crevice where fog rolls through the landscape like surf. Trail's end brings you to Örnsköldsvik, the Hörnsjön Nature Reserve, and one final swoosh of wonder woods.

*Forested islets dotting the
waters off Skuleskogen
National Park*

Laugavegur Trail

LOCATION Iceland **START/FINISH** Landmannalaugar/Thórsmörk **DISTANCE**
33½ miles (54 km) **TIME** 5 days **DIFFICULTY** Moderate **INFORMATION**
www.fi.is/en/hiking-trails/trails/laugavegur; open mid-Jun–mid-Sept

*Traverse black-sand deserts, hot springs, and forested valleys
hemmed in by glaciers on this magnificent trek, which takes in
the multitude of mind-blowing landscapes Iceland is famous for.*

*Striped rhyolite
mountains contrasting
with black lava fields at
Landmannalaugar*

GET your camera ready for the multicolored mountains of **Landmannalaugar** at the trailhead

Landmannalaugar

REST beside the sputtering geothermal hot spring of **Stórihver**—but don't get too close

TAKE in views over three different glaciers (Tindfjallajökull, Eyjafjallajökull, and Mýrdalsjökull) atop the peak of **Jökultungur** mountain

ICELAND

MARVEL at **Markarfljótsgljúfur**, a dramatic ravine marked by stripes of crimson and green

EARN your adventurer's stripes by fording the glacial river of **Bláfjallakvísl**, fast-moving even in summer

Thórsmörk

ICELAND

Laugavegur Trail

Iceland's longest, finest, and most famous hiking trail takes in the multifaceted beauty of the Land of Fire and Ice, through otherworldly landscapes forged in the country's volcanic furnaces. This manifests not only in black, cracked lava fields, but also in unexpectedly colorful ways: rainbow-striped mountains mark the beginning of the trail at Landmannalaugar; the grass-green cone of a dormant volcano rises from the desert at Mælifellssandur; and the canyon of Markarfljótsgljúfur plunges to an icy river with walls of vivid green and red. Throughout, columns of steam exhale from hot springs, while imperious glaciers stand silent guard, their brittle blue melding with that of the sky.

The Laugavegur Trail promises the kind of adventure that Iceland does so well: mind-bendingly gorgeous, yet only moderately challenging. You'll have to ford a river or two along the way, and it's not uncommon to experience rain, snow, sun, wind, and hail in quick succession. But you'll stay in a series of mountain huts, which, while not exactly The Ritz, are more comfortable than a Scottish bothy—you'll find hot showers, decent beds, and a fully-equipped kitchen waiting for you at the end of each day.

After five days exploring lava fields, hot springs, black deserts, and rhyolite mountains, the trek's final descent feels like a return home. Nestled between three mighty glaciers, Thórsmörk is a gently forested valley, alive with birdsong and wildflowers; its name means the Valley of Thor, and it is truly a divine end to what promises to be a life-changing adventure.

> Rainbow-striped mountains mark the beginning of the trail

BY ROAD

In 1888, when Bertha Benz drove her motorcar south from
Mannheim toward Pforzheim, she was embarking on the world's
first ever road trip. Since then, drivers have been lured by Europe's
open roads: the windswept tarmac of Ireland's Wild Atlantic
Way; the dizzying switchbacks on Romania's Transfăgărășan.
Buckle up and join them—adventure awaits.

ICELAND

SWEDEN

NORWAY

DENMARK

NETHER-
LANDS

GERMANY

POLAND

BELGIUM

LUX.

CZECH
REPUBLIC

SLOVAKIA

IRELAND

UNITED
KINGDOM

FRANCE

SWITZ.

AUSTRIA

HUNGARY

SLOVENIA

CROATIA

BOSNIA-
HERZ.

MONTE-
NEGRO

ALBANIA

PORTUGAL

SPAIN

ITALY

Previous page The gravity-defying
Storseisundet bridge on Norway's
Atlantic Ocean Road

AT A GLANCE
BY ROAD

FINLAND

ESTONIA

LATVIA

LITHUANIA

BELARUS

UKRAINE

MOLDOVA

ROMANIA

㉛

SERBIA

BULGARIA ㉜

KOSOVO

N. MAC.

GREECE

㉝

㉚

TURKEY

GEORGIA ㉞

ARMENIA AZERBAIJAN

CYPRUS

KEY TO MAP

Long route ············

End point ●

Ring Road

LOCATION Iceland **START/FINISH** Reykjavík (loop) **DISTANCE** 828 miles (1,332 km) **TIME** 1–2 weeks **ROAD CONDITIONS** Doable by 2WD; 4WD recommended for trips Oct–May **INFORMATION** www.visiticeland.com; road open year-round, dependent on conditions

Despite Iceland's alien landscapes, huffing volcanoes, and belching geysers, it's quite easy to drive this dramatic road, which runs around the country's fascinating fringes.

Iceland only really has one main road. But what a road it is. The Ring Road—aka Route 1, aka the Hringvegur—loops right around the inhabited edges of the subarctic island, a civilized circle of two-lane tarmac cutting a scenic dash through one of the wildest and most wonderfully weird places on Earth.

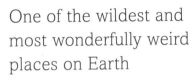

One of the wildest and most wonderfully weird places on Earth

The highway was finally completed in 1974, which also marked 1,100 years since the first settling of the country: it was in 874 CE that the powerful chieftain Ingólfur Arnarson and his wife sailed across from Norway to Iceland and put down roots in what is now Reykjavík. It's a suitably momentous anniversary tie-in for a road that has made it much easier to see more of the country for yourself: to feel the spray from its thunderous waterfalls; to comb its black-sand beaches; to jump into its thermals pools; to walk across its strange burping, steaming, extraterrestrial-looking terrain; and to meet its independent-spirited people. Anyone with a rental car or camper and a spirit of adventure can set off on what feels, at many turns, like driving across another planet.

Technically, it would be possible to make a circuit in two days. But two weeks would be far better, to allow ample time for ▶

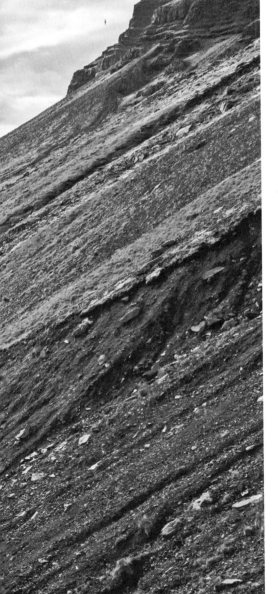

Left The Ring Road following the very edge of Iceland *Below* A sunset view from behind the falls of Seljalandsfoss

Left *A lone car crossing a bridge over ice-blue waters* **Above** *The black-sand beach at Reynisfjara*

HOT SPRINGS

Muscles stiff from sitting in a car? Seek out Iceland's geothermal pools. The famed (and pricey) Blue Lagoon, near Keflavík airport, grabs headlines, but there are many more, from Nauthólsvík Geothermal Beach to Mývatn Nature Baths, and the "People's Pool" at Landmannalaugar. Indeed, there are hot springs dotted all around the country, some out in the wilds, and ranging from tepid to scalding—seek local advice and always have your swimsuit on hand.

stop-offs, photo ops, hikes, and detours, not to mention delays: this is Iceland after all and—especially outside the summer months—snow, ice, storms, and winds could hinder progress.

Lively capital Reykjavík, in Iceland's west, is the obvious starting point. Traveling counterclockwise from here means hitting the busier sights of the southwest first, so that the crowds thin and the sense of wildness intensifies as you go. An excellent way to begin is by detouring off Route 1 entirely, to complete the 190-mile (306-km) Golden Circle loop via the violently spewing Geysir Geothermal Area, colossal Gullfoss waterfall, and Þingvellir National Park, which straddles two tectonic plates. Picking up the Ring Road proper at Hveragerði, the roadside wonders just keep coming: the mighty cascades of Seljalandsfoss and Skógafoss; the pitch-black beach at Vík; and the sparkling glaciers and ice caves of immense Vatnajökull National Park.

Beyond, things get a little quirky. The East Fjords is a place of dramatically serrated coastlines and eccentric villages where the Queen of the Elves lives (just off-route, near Borgarfjörður eystri, in case you're wondering). Returning westward, Mývatn's lava flows, geothermal pools, and glittering lake await, as well as deafening Dettifoss waterfall. It's also worth veering north to the port of Húsavík, where you might spot humpback or even blue whales (best in June and July), or, perhaps, stopping at Akureyri, the bijou "Capital of the North," which sits at the head of Iceland's longest fjord, beneath snow-dusted mountains; it's a fine place to gallery-browse, café-hop, and explore the spectacular surroundings. Then it's back to Reykjavík, to toast your road trip with a shot of potent Brennivín or two.

another way

For another circuit around a dramatic part of Iceland, head northwest into the Westfjords peninsula. Everything that attracts people to Iceland—waterfalls, wild beaches, thermal springs—can be found here, just off the roads (60 and 61) that connect the region's sparse settlements.

ALLOW *a few days for first-rate humpback sightings at* **Húsavík**—*Iceland's whale-watching capital*

Atlantic Ocean

EXPLORE *the forest, rivers and lakes around* **Egilsstaðir***, where the Lagarfljót Worm (the Icelandic Loch Ness Monster) is said to live*

ICELAND

PARK *up in the town of* **Hofn** *to tuck into local langoustine and succulent lobster*

Reykjavík

WALK *right behind the tumbling cascade of* **Seljalandsfoss** *waterfall*

Atlantic Ocean

DIVERT *to the cliffs of the* **Dyrholaey Peninsula** *to look for an improbability of puffins*

Lofoten Archipelago

LOCATION Norway **START/FINISH** Svolvær/Å **DISTANCE** 80 miles (129 km) **TIME** 1 week **ROAD CONDITION**S Well maintained and accessible year-round; the E10 allows for ferry-free access to the islands **INFORMATION** https://lofoten.info

Sense the wonder of Norway at its wildest and most outrageously beautiful, where granite mountains shoot above the sea, fishing villages cling to a ragged coastline, and Viking heritage lives on.

Slinging their hook into the Norwegian Sea, the Lofoten Islands are the Arctic dream—whether you visit in the unending days of the Midnight Sun or the Northern Light raves of winter. Glacial valleys unfurl to great swoops of beach, brightly painted fishing villages still haul in some of the world's tastiest cod, and mountains punch crazily above the sea like the figment of a child's imagination.

In a week, you can drive the archipelago from Svolvær in the north to Å in the south. The joy of road-tripping here is serendipity: keep your itinerary loose and your options open.

Begin on the northernmost island of Austvågøy, dipping into cod-fishing traditions on Svinøya and

visiting pretty Henningsvær. Here you can jump in a kayak to weave around bays and islets, where otters and white-tailed eagles can be sighted. Back behind the wheel, the main E10 road swings south to the island of Vestvågøy. In Borg, the Lofotr Viking Museum shines a light on the archipelago's rich history with its spectacularly reconstructed chieftain's longhouse. Just west of here is Haukland Beach, a perfect crescent of creamy sand melting into turquoise sea and gnarly peaks.

Carrying on south to the island of Moskenesøya ramps up the scenic drama further still in adventure-central Reine and end-of-the-road Å, where land gives way abruptly to roaring ocean.

Left The sun hitting the peaks of the Lofoten Islands *Below* Enjoying a pit stop at Haukland Beach

another way

Lofoten is at the mercy of the sea, making a paddle-camping trip a brilliant way to explore. In a kayak, you can reach bays, islands, and skerries that are otherwise off limits and wild camp under the stars.

TAKE a boat to **Trollfjord**, where sea eagles soar and granite mountains rise up 3,280 ft (1,000 m) above the sea

SPEND a highly atmospheric night in a rorbuer, a quaintly converted fisherman's cottage on stilts, on **Svinøya**

Norwegian Sea

WALK in wonder to the wild, isolated beach of **Kvalvika**, on the north coast of Moskenesøya

N O R W A Y

Svolvær

SCRAMBLE to the top of 1,469-ft (448-m) **Reinebringen** for astonishing views of Reinefjorden and the Lofotveggen

Å

SEE the Northern Lights dance above **Reine**, a prime spot for aurora action from September to April

Múlafossur plunging over cliffs near the tiny village of Gásadalur

③

The Faroe Islands

LOCATION Denmark **START/FINISH** Tórshavn **DISTANCE** 176 miles (284 km) **TIME** 5–7 days **ROAD CONDITIONS** Good **INFORMATION** www.visitfaroeislands.com

Link six otherworldly islands in one unforgettable road odyssey that runs via undersea tunnels and along some of Europe's most savagely spectacular shores.

A broken chain of jagged cliffs soaring above the squally North Atlantic, the Faroe Islands are as close to Asgard, home of the gods in Norse mythology, as mortals ever get. Boats were the go-to mode of transportation until recent years, but with submarine tunnels now connecting the main island of Streymoy with Vágar to the west and Eysturoy, Bordoy, Vidoy, and Kunoy to the northeast, an interisland road trip is now a novel possibility. Your way will wend around lonely fjords and photogenic villages, the elemental coastline seldom leaving your sight. Starting in the capital of Tórshavn, on Streymoy, with its old town of brightly hued turf-roofed houses, you'll dip beneath the sea to Lervík—via the world's first underwater roundabout—drive through pretty Klaksvík and loop around the peak of Malinsfjall. On the homeward leg, stop to hike up Slættaratindur, the Faroes' highest summit, and cross the "Bridge over the Atlantic" to Fossá, the islands' highest waterfall. Then it's out to Vágar for the grand finale: the supernatural beauties of Sørvágsvatn, a huge lake balanced bizarrely on a cliff edge, and Múlafossur, a satin cascade plunging down a cliff face.

SØRVÁGSVATN

Sørvágsvatn, on the island of Vagar, seems like a photographer's fabrication: this snaking lake stretches so close to the cliff edge, with only a wafer-thin wedge of green in between, that the view from certain angles creates an optical illusion whereby the lake appears to hover directly above the North Atlantic.

Atlantic Ocean Road

A bridge linking scraps of land in the North Atlantic, on Norway's Atlanterhavsveien

LOCATION Norway **START/FINISH** Vevang/Kårvåg **DISTANCE** 5 miles (8 km) **TIME** 3 hours
ROAD CONDITIONS Winding; blind bends **INFORMATION** www.nasjonaleturistveger.no

Feel the colossal force of nature in Norway's wild west as you hopscotch over islands, skerries, and the storm-tossed sea on one of the world's shortest, sweetest coastal road trips.

At just 5 miles (8 km) long, Norway's Atlantic Ocean Road (Atlanterhavsveien) seems insignificant on paper. But size isn't everything. These are miles you'll never forget. Snaking and skipping along a fjord-riven, island-speckled coastline that's brutally hammered by the winds and waves of the North Atlantic, this bite-size chunk of County Road 64 is regularly hailed one of the world's most beautiful drives. Believe the hype. You could drive it in 10 minutes if you put your foot down, but you'll probably want to putter along for at least half a day, perhaps more, wholly absorbed by the seascapes.

It really is remarkable the way the road seems to make light of one of Norway's most savage, storm-battered coastlines. Plunging over open water, the road roller-coasters between islands and skerries. Dipping and rising, it builds intensity with every bridge until it reaches Storseisundet, the longest and most gravity-defying of all, before plummeting down to Kårvåg. The road is always extraordinary, but come in fall or winter if you want to see it stormy. It can be lovely on a summer's evening, too, with honeyed light spilling across dark, jagged mountains and a quicksilver sea.

Hebridean Whale Trail

LOCATION Scotland **START/FINISH** Brodick/Tiumpan Head Lighthouse **DISTANCE** 310 miles
(500 km) **TIME** 7 days **ROAD CONDITIONS** Tricky: plenty of single track, with passing places
INFORMATION https://whaletrack.hwdt.org/app

Rocky coastline on the Isle of Harris

Fantastic beasts and where to find them: pack your binoculars and a map and head to Scotland's western coastline, where orca and humpbacks lurk in deep waters alongside minke, basking shark, and the world's largest dolphin.

The morning begins atop a cliff, peering through binoculars and out to sea. It is from this vantage point that you play detective, searching in silence. There's a muted feeling of waiting for the show to begin, and your focus is a chorus line of shearwaters whipping up whitecaps out in the Sound. Hopefully it reveals a clue about the shifting blur below the surface. A minke whale maybe; or in these waters, possibly a basking shark or orca. The prospect alone is thrilling enough.

Scotland's northwest coast is Xanadu for marine life and, with cliffs tumbling down to pogoing seas and imagination-tingling islands to discover, it is the realm of the Hebridean Whale Trail. This self-guided visitor route encourages accessible, low-impact wildlife-spotting from land, with 33 sites earmarked for their extraordinary marine diversity. Dip in for a day—or road trip the route for a week—and you'll get to known a shoreline that's populated by a quarter of the world's largest, most spectacular whale and dolphin species.

All whale-trail adventures start by downloading the Hebridean Whale and Dolphin Trust's app, then plotting a route from the Clyde and Arran all the way up to the Outer Hebrides. If size really does matter, then the lighthouses at Ardnamurchan and Tiumpan Head on the Isle of Lewis are the most successful places to spot the monsters of the deep.

FINISH *beside* **Tiumpan Head Lighthouse** *on the Isle of Lewis*

○ *Tiumpan Head*

The Minch

Atlantic Ocean

TIME *travel at* **Bun Abhainn Eadarra** *on the Isle of Harris, to see ruins of the UK's only remaining whaling station*

SCOTLAND

DRIVE *to the* **Ardnamurchan Lighthouse,** *an orca hot spot on a spit of land jutting into the Sound of Mull*

DROP *into the Hebridean Whale and Dolphin Trust's visitor center in Tobermory on the Isle of Mull*

Sea of the Hebrides

DISCOVER *the legendary whales that once thrived on* **Iona,** *plus porpoise pods*

► *Brodick*

WHALING IN SCOTLAND

The human-cetacean relationship has cast a shadow throughout Scotland's history. The idea of whales as an economic resource was brought into being by whalers in the early 18th century, with the first commercial whalers sailing from ports in Edinburgh and Dundee by the 1750s. There is also evidence of harpooning for blubber as far back as the Bronze Age.

Clifton Suspension Bridge spanning the Avon Gorge in Bristol

Route Yorkshire Coast

LOCATION England **START/FINISH** Staithes/ Spurn Point **DISTANCE** 93 miles (150 km) **TIME** 3–4 days **ROAD CONDITIONS** Good **INFORMATION** https://routeyc.co.uk

England's largest county is regularly dubbed "God's Own Country" by Yorkshire residents, and it's easy to see why when connecting the dots between the coastal towns of Bridlington, Filey, Hornsea, Scarborough, Whitby, and Withernsea. Start east of Middlesborough, then cut through the eastern fringes of the North York Moors National Park from Staithes: the coast and heather moorlands of the national park here are prime territory for hiking and mountain biking. Then it's onward to Whitby—to see the ruined abbey that inspired *Dracula* author Bram Stoker— and to Scarborough, the quintessential seaside resort. A stop-off at Filey Beach—an epic sweep of sand and rock pools—follows, then it's one final leg to Withernsea and its Blue Flag shingle beach, and Spurn Point, Yorkshire's very own Land's End.

another way

The Yorkshire Dales National Park, the heart of the county's famous rolling valleys, tops many road-trip bucket lists. Arguably the most popular route is from Wensleydale to Swaledale, stopping at the cheesemongers of Hawes, before driving the notoriously windy Buttertubs Pass.

Great West Way

LOCATION England **START/FINISH** London/ Bristol **DISTANCE** 125 miles (200 km) **TIME** 4–5 days **ROAD CONDITIONS** Very good **INFORMATION** www.greatwestway.co.uk

There's more to the A4 than meets the eye. Today's asphalt highway was originally one of the six "Great Roads" decreed by King Charles I in the 17th century, and now forms the spine of this modern-day touring route from London to Bristol. The road passes through a number of historical towns, among them UNESCO-listed Bath, but the concept of the Great West Way is very much to meander and detour as the mood takes you—and there are plenty of distractions.

Think of it as a city-to-city journey with side shoots. Aspic-preserved villages, prehistoric stone circles, bluebell woods, and farm shops might all get a look-in. Craft your own itinerary from any number of themed stop-offs, centered on everything from industrial heritage (step forward, Isambard Kingdom Brunel) to TV and film locations (hello, Harry Potter).

⑧ North Coast 500

LOCATION Scotland **START/FINISH** Inverness Castle (loop) **DISTANCE** 516 miles (830 km) **TIME** 5 days **ROAD CONDITIONS** Good **INFORMATION** www.northcoast500.com

It's been described as Scotland's Route 66, but that's all wrong. With its bone-white beaches and heart-quickening clifftop sections, the North Coast 500 is Alba's (equally popular) answer to the Pacific Coast Highway, and while the climate might not be Californian, that's more than made up for by centuries-old castles and floppy-haired Highland cows.

The circular route begins and ends in imperious style at Inverness Castle. Ancient history echoes across the Black Isle, dotted with Pictish stones, while Easter Ross is home to somnolent fishing villages, country pubs, and the Glenmorangie whisky distillery. In Sutherland, crumbling castles dot some of Europe's most dramatic scenery, where mountains collide with the sea, while Wester Ross boasts arcs of sand plucked from a Mediterranean guidebook and lochs cloaked in mist.

A road snaking through the russet hills of the Scottish Highlands

⑨ The Cotswolds

LOCATION England **START/FINISH** Stratford-upon-Avon/Winchcombe **DISTANCE** 64 miles (100 km) **TIME** 1 day **ROAD CONDITIONS** Good **INFORMATION** www.cotswolds.com

This bucolic region is spectacular driving territory, with winding roads lined by aged oak trees, and steep hills affording near-endless views of a patchwork of green fields and quaint chocolate-box villages. Starting from Stratford-upon-Avon, climb into the rolling landscape and get your first glimpse of those golden, oolitic limestone cottages in Chipping Campden—the entire town is painted in honey hues, with a jumble of half-timbered buildings and thatched rooftops. From here, you could detour to Broadway Tower, an 18th-century folly atop a hill that lords over the Worcestershire countryside, or divert to the former home of the English architect Charles Wade at Snowshill Manor. Pass through medieval Stow-on-the-Wold and finish up in historic Winchcombe, where timbered inns and Roman remains offer intrigue enough.

CRAFTY CHIPPING CAMPDEN

The town of Chipping Campden has been a hive of creativity since 1902, when C. R. Ashbee—head of the Guild of Handicraft—moved his artisan colleagues here from the workhouses of east London. Craft and design still thrive today, with world-renowned creatives like Robert Welch and local milliner Louise Pocock setting up shop on the high street. Learn about Ashbee's influence on the area at the tiny but fascinating Court Barn Museum.

Wild Atlantic Way

*Slea Head Drive
hugging the cliffs
along Kerry's
Dingle Peninsula*

LOCATION Republic of Ireland **START/FINISH** Malin Head/Kinsale **DISTANCE** 1,600 miles (2,600 km) **TIME** 3 weeks **ROAD CONDITIONS** Well-maintained paved roads, winding and narrow or single-lane in places **INFORMATION** www.wildatlanticway.com

Running almost the entire length of Ireland's western coast, this camper-friendly route wends its way through charming towns and villages, all the while tracking the jewel-blue Atlantic Ocean.

A wind-buffeted peninsula where Atlantic waves rumble against sheer, craggy rock and grass-carpeted cliffs taper into the ocean, Malin Head is Ireland's northernmost tip and the starting point of your journey. From here, the road picks through the rugged headlands of Donegal, where megalithic monuments loom at every bend and huge swells lash golden-sanded Tullan Strand in Bundoran, Ireland's surf capital. Ireland's west coast is its surf coast, but beach bars around here tend to be the traditional stone-built type: whitewashed cottages

with thatched roofs, real ales, and whisky. As Mayo fades into the rearview mirror and you cross into Galway, you'll notice that English translations on the road signs have all but disappeared. This is the spectacular Gaeltacht region of Connemara, a stronghold for the Irish language, with a name that comes from the Gaelic for "inlets of the sea." Its mellow coastline is laced with pretty coves, sandy bays, and a jumble of offshore islands, plus the region has some incredibly scenic camping and caravan sites.

Malin Head

SEEK out some of Ireland's best surf spots in **Donegal**

TAKE in the sheer crags of **Slieve League**, among the highest sea cliffs in Europe

Irish Sea

SAMPLE the nightlife during **Galway's** International Arts Festival each July

Atlantic Ocean

TRAMP down **Hag's Head** for the best views of the shore

REPUBLIC OF IRELAND

SIP a refreshing pint in one of **Kinsale's** cozy traditional pubs

Kinsale

Celtic Sea

Dawn breaking over Harbour View, a popular overnight spot for campers

As the road ribbons onward into Clare and Kerry, the sprawling karst landscape of the Burren becomes dizzying at the Cliffs of Moher, and on the Dingle Peninsula you'll be at Ireland's most westerly point. Seaside towns turn ever more colorful and picturesque as the often narrow and winding Way meanders gently south along the coast of Cork. You'll thread past historic castles and trace rolling green fields until you reach the gourmet hot spot of Kinsale, a pretty town with a rich history and the perfect place to end your Irish driving adventure.

⑪

Western Seafood Coast

LOCATION Denmark **START/FINISH** Hanstholm/Rømø **DISTANCE** 164 miles
(264 km) **TIME** 4–5 days **ROAD CONDITIONS** Excellent and well maintained
INFORMATION www.visitdenmark.com

*Prepare for plenty of belt-loosening lunches on a road trip along
Denmark's cove-nibbled west coast, plus crowd-free beaches, surf
towns, and historic seafronts.*

It's often reported that Casanova ate 50 raw oysters
for breakfast each day. While this isn't quite true,
it could easily be the case for many residents on
the western seaboard of Denmark. This is a coast
overrun with stocks of the shallow-cupped morsels,
as well as plump shrimp, mussels, and razor
clams—and, most importantly, friendly fishers with
a passion for seafood.

Begin by driving south through North Jutland's
stunning, scalloped-edge coast. Along the way are
Viking burial grounds, working harbors, and
sand-swept beach towns. Klitmøller, with pounding
waves, is known to Danes as Cold Hawaii and is

inviting no matter the weather. From here, the town
of Nykøbing Mors on the Limfjord is the perfect
spot to work up an appetite. At the Danish Shellfish
Center, you can join an oyster hunt for some of
Europe's last remaining wild oysters. Farther south
is Holmsland Dunes, a narrow spit of land
sandwiched between the North Sea and lagoon-
like Ringkøbing Fjord, then the Wadden Sea island
of Rømø, where an astonishing 79,000 tons
(72,000 metric tons) of oysters lie in wait on the
seabed. The local catchphrase is "If you can't beat
them, eat them"—so, at low tide, grab a bucket and
fill it with pearl-shaped shells right from the shore.

*Fishing boats
in a harbor in
North Jutland*

THE WORLD'S THEIR OYSTER

Viking ships once fished along
Denmark's west coast; centuries
later, oysters were shipped across
the Baltic Sea to the palaces
of Catherine the Great in
St. Petersburg. Danish King
Frederik II, meanwhile, loved the
tasty morsels so much that he
introduced the death penalty for
anyone caught thieving his supply.
Absurdly, the law was only
repealed in the mid-1980s.

(12)

Marguerite Route

LOCATION Denmark **START/FINISH** Various **DISTANCE** Varies **TIME** 14–21
days **ROAD CONDITIONS** Excellent and well maintained **INFORMATION**
www.visitdenmark.com

*For Danes, few things in life are better than discovering the
Renaissance-era castles, windswept beaches, and gentle
farmlands of their homeland. Why not join them?*

What could be more ambitious than a tourist driving route that almost
absorbs an entire country? That was the idea behind this all-encompassing
circuit inaugurated in 1991 as a tribute to Queen Margrethe II, the country's
beloved monarch. A collection of some 1,000 attractions that best showcase
Danish landscape and history, from postcard-pretty herring harbors to hilltop
castle ruins, the route is linked through a network of signposts decorated with
the queen's favorite flower—the Marguerite daisy.

In the south, the suggested starting point is half-timbered Bisserup on the
coast of Zealand, with early-stage highlights including Holsteinborg Castle, a
favorite haunt of Hans Christian Andersen, and Borreby, one of Scandinavia's
best-preserved Renaissance castles. Alternatively, begin in northern Denmark
in Jutland, motoring from 12th-century Børglum Abbey to Rubjerg Knude
lighthouse, which tops a gigantic sand dune in Hjørring, then onward to the
east-coast hot spots of Sæby, Voreså, and Præstebro. The choice is yours.

another way

*While the Marguerite Route is
Denmark's longest attraction, it
doesn't, in fact, visit the islands in
the Kattegat. You can hop between
these by small boat, sailing from
one dinky harbor to the next.
Spend a day or two in tranquil
Hjornø before moving on to larger
Endelave and then finally car-free
Tunø, with its chalky beaches.*

85

(13)

Vulkanstrasse

LOCATION Germany **START/FINISH** Bonn/Trier
DISTANCE 174 miles (280 km) **TIME** 3–4 days
ROAD CONDITIONS Well maintained
INFORMATION www.deutsche-vulkanstrasse.com

*Don't be mistaken by Germany's rolling
farmlands and fairy-tale forests—this is
also a land of fire, with crater lakes, cold
geysers, and hollow volcanoes.*

Think of volcanoes and your mind's eye might
picture Iceland and Indonesia, Japan or Hawaii,
home to craters of fire responsible for jaw-dropping
lava displays. But Germany? Perhaps not. And
yet part of the country reveals a secret realm of
spectacular geology. Get to its heart on this driving
route, which follows a chain of almost 350 eruption
sites and nearly 40 sinkholes, crater lakes, quarries,
lava flows, domes, and geysers. Location-wise, it's
a map of 10,000-year-old geological puzzles spun
out from the Rhine River to the Eifel Mountains.

Start by heading south from Bonn to the Laacher
See, a 1.2-mile- (2-km-) wide volcanic caldera. This
lakeside is as pretty as any in Germany, and beyond
the hum of picnicking families there are hikes to
enjoy, Maria Laach Abbey to explore, and boat trips
to take across the placid surface. From here, there's
a quick succession of intriguing volcanic attractions
before the route ends in Trier: Mount Eppelsberg,
whose black bands were the result of several
eruptions; the interactive Meurin Roman Mine,
the ash tuff from which was used to build cities
such as Cologne; and the soothing thermal springs
at Bad Bertrich, a town surrounded by seven
(thankfully) extinct volcanoes.

*Crater lakes and
domes on the
Vulkanstrasse*

Witch-hatted Holsten Gate, an impressive gateway to the town of Lübeck

(14)

Hanseatic League

LOCATION Germany **START/FINISH** Stralsund/Bremen
DISTANCE 300 miles (485 km) **TIME** 7 days **ROAD
CONDITIONS** Very good **INFORMATION** www.hanse.org

*Discover the lesser-visited region of Germany's
Baltic coastline, home to cities that were once part
of a medieval trading union.*

Before the European Union, there was the Hanseatic League.
This medieval alliance of trading guilds and city-states stretched
from the Netherlands to Russia, but it began in the 12th
century with just a handful of north German market towns.
Nine centuries later, this driving tour links the best of them.

This portion of the route begins in Stralsund, in Germany's
far northeast. This pretty, orange-roofed port city is famed for
its UNESCO-listed old town, as well as its status as a gateway to
the chalk cliffs and sandy shores of Rügen island. It's just a short
drive west from here to Rostock, which may lack the classical
charms of its near neighbor but has an appealing harbor and
easy access to the ever-popular Warnemünde beach resort.

Continue west to explore the handsome Hanseatic cities of
Wismar (with its famous wrought-iron fountain) and Lübeck
(home to an iconic red-brick city gate) en route to the
confederation's best-known asset: Hamburg. Spend a few days
here exploring its extraordinary architecture and museums (and
nightlife) before ending your travels in Bremen, where the grand
town hall testifies to the city's rich history as a Hanseatic power.

another way

*Extend your Hanseatic adventure
by continuing down to Cologne,
heading east via Paderborn and
Brunswick, then looping around
Berlin and back up to Stralsund.
The route linking all the major
Hanseatic cities is 1,085 miles
(1,750 km) altogether.*

SIP wine on **Würzburg's** *Alte Mainbrücke (Old Main Bridge)* over the Main River

Würzburg

EXPLORE *the vineyards of the* **Tauber Valley** *by bike*

GERMANY

CZECH REPUBLIC

ENJOY *the Weihnachtsmarkt (Christmas market) in* **Rothenburg ob der Tauber,** *which began in the 15th century*

RELAX *in a convivial beer garden in* **Nördlingen, Harburg,** *or* **Dinkelsbühl**

AUSTRIA

CHANNEL *your inner Sleeping Beauty at* **Schloss Neuschwanstein,** *the castle that inspired Disney*

FRANCE

Füssen

SWITZERLAND

AUSTRIA

(15)

Romantic Road

LOCATION Germany **START/FINISH** Würzburg/Füssen **DISTANCE** 220 miles (354 km) **TIME** 3 days **ROAD CONDITIONS** Well maintained **INFORMATION** www.romanticroadgermany.com

Take it slow on this bucolic route through Germany's southern region, which is peppered with little-known Bavarian villages, walled medieval towns, and historic cities.

This scenic itinerary was dreamed up in the aftermath of World War II to lift the public mood and promote southern Germany's Bavaria and Baden-Württemberg. Most visitors travel north to south, setting their own pace by car. Make sure you drive the German way: in a high-powered coupe or sleek, electric motor—testament to a country that is a powerhouse of the automobile industry.

The romance of this road is undeniable. As the route unfolds from the Main River to "Mad" King Ludwig II's grand Schloss Neuschwanstein, nestled in the northern Alps, it takes in medieval cobbled streets, lively squares, and quiet alleys, lines of vineyards on gently undulating hills, and half-timbered houses with window boxes sprouting brightly colored flowers.

Würzburg is one of two cities along the route (handsome Augsburg is the other) and is famous for its Franconian wine—the Bocksbeutel is king. There's plenty of accommodation here and in the walled towns of Rothenburg ob der Tauber and Nördlingen, which both seem to let out a sigh of relief when the day-trippers depart each evening. Seek out quiet corners and remember that it's the small moments that matter most—sipping Riesling on the Alte Mainbrücke in Würzburg, strolling the gardens of Harburg Castle, or taking in a view of tightly packed gingerbread houses in Dinkelsbühl.

Schloss Neuschwanstein: purportedly the inspiration for Disney's iconic logo

E-Grand Tour
of Switzerland

LOCATION Switzerland **START/FINISH** Various **DISTANCE** 1,000 miles
(1,600 km) **TIME** 2–3 weeks **ROAD CONDITIONS** Well-maintained highways
and paved roads **INFORMATION** www.myswitzerland.com

*Take a ride over high mountain passes and through Alpine
meadows along the world's first road trip designed for clean,
green electric vehicles and guilt-free pleasures.*

In the last few years, Switzerland has leaped forward from the modern way
of life into the world of tomorrow. Tucked-away mountain villages are now
home to eco-friendly hotels, and even the most remote hamlets have
e-chargers for electric vehicles. Between them all, that tallies to almost
1,000 miles (1,600 km) of guilt-free driving through a landscape united
by five soaring Alpine passes, some 22 lakes and a dozen UNESCO World
Heritage sites. There are tilted mountains and powder-blue lakes to see,

Left A zigzagging mountain pass in southern
Switzerland **Above** Chalet-style houses in Gstaad

ELECTRONIC CARS IN SWITZERLAND

The Swiss have been early adopters of e-cars, and the Tesla Model 3 is now the most popular car to buy in the country. Thanks in part to a government keen to bring down its carbon emissions— Switzerland wants to become carbon neutral by 2050—there are now over 7,000 charging points across the country.

of course, but also monstrous glaciers and grand-dame hotels. And the clincher? No range anxiety.

Drive the whole scenic circuit or cherry-pick a few days' worth of highlights to visit—when you're behind the wheel of a next-generation electric car, any trip here will be a memorable experience. For the recommended loop, leave Zurich's watch ateliers behind in the rearview mirror and head northeast to the rolling hills around Appenzell, where you can ride the cable car up from Schwägalp to the Säntis, for views over six countries.

Descend into Italian-speaking Ticino, with your electric car accelerating with all the grace of a Roger Federer serve. Then climb up again to Andermatt. Geography has preserved the traditional Swiss way of life in the mountains for centuries here, and the village is as it once was: woodwork chalets come trimmed with floral balconies, and farmsteads are home to goat herders and jingle-jangle cows. On the slow road out of town, a favorite stop is the Furka Pass, where Sean Connery chased Auric Goldfinger and Oddjob in *Goldfinger*, the 1964 James Bond classic. An electric car isn't as flashy as 007's Aston Martin DB5, but think of the cleaner air. And, if you need a break while the battery is charging, there's a world of lung-filling hiking out your side door—plus e-biking, too, of ▶

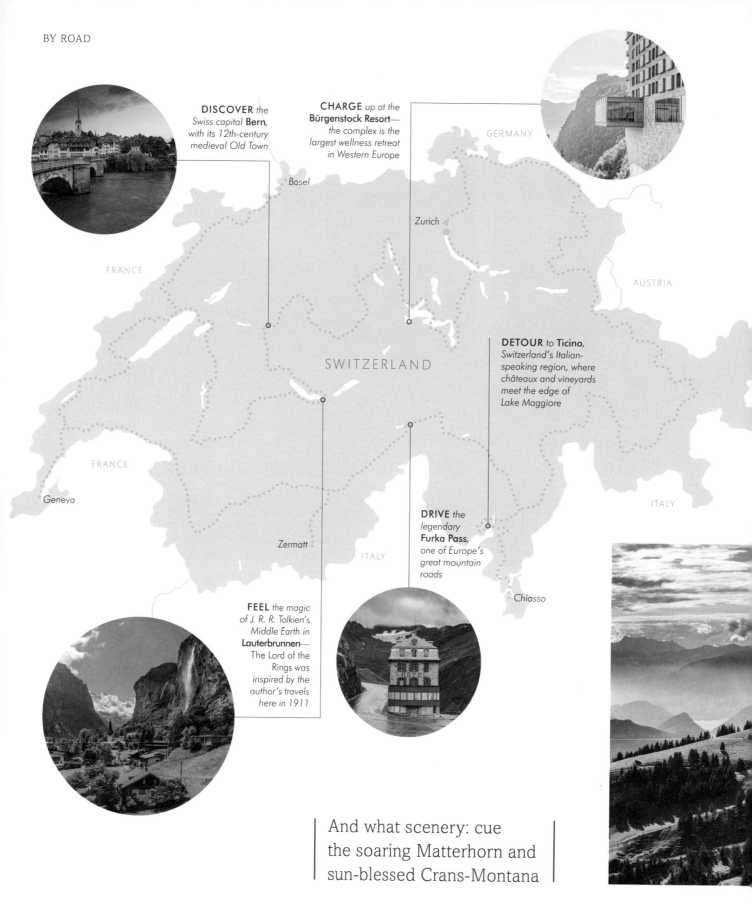

DISCOVER the Swiss capital **Bern**, with its 12th-century medieval Old Town

CHARGE up at the **Bürgenstock Resort**— the complex is the largest wellness retreat in Western Europe

GERMANY

Basel

Zurich

FRANCE

AUSTRIA

SWITZERLAND

DETOUR to **Ticino**, Switzerland's Italian-speaking region, where châteaux and vineyards meet the edge of Lake Maggiore

FRANCE

Geneva

ITALY

Zermatt

ITALY

DRIVE the legendary **Furka Pass**, one of Europe's great mountain roads

Chiasso

FEEL the magic of J. R. R. Tolkien's Middle Earth in **Lauterbrunnen**— The Lord of the Rings was inspired by the author's travels here in 1911

And what scenery: cue the soaring Matterhorn and sun-blessed Crans-Montana course. Onward into the Bernese Oberland, down into the Rhone Valley, and along the border with Italy, playing peekaboo with Swiss Army knife–cut peaks. And what scenery: cue the soaring Matterhorn and sun-blessed Crans-Montana.

The route arcs around Lake Geneva and runs along the north shore of Lake Neuchâtel before delivering you in Lauterbrunnen, an impossibly perfect village scattered along a valley floor; giant cliff faces, squeezing the houses on both sides, and the roaring cascade of the Staubbach Falls complete the picture. Next, your journey speeds north to the unassuming capital of Bern, with its cobbled streets and quaint Old Town. And then it's on to Lake Lucerne, to catch the historic cogwheel railroad of Mount Rigi or to ride in Europe's highest outdoor elevator (the white-knuckle Hammetschwand) to see skyrocketing peaks and nose-diving waterfalls. Your E-Grand Tour ends back in Zurich, where you can charge your batteries—in more ways than one. Of course the Swiss want to keep their country clean, green, and emission-free. Spoiled by such unfiltered beauty, who wouldn't?

another way

Make your trip even greener and tackle the circuit on two wheels instead. Switzerland can be a challenging country to tour by bike, with all those high-Alpine passes and mountain climbs, but the scenery will feel even more dramatic with the wind whistling through your hair.

Below Green pastures providing a lush foreground for the Pilatus and Rigi mountains Right The Hammetschwand Elevator towering over Lake Lucerne

Route des Grandes Alpes

(17)

Snowy peaks providing a dramatic backdrop, the Col de l'Iseran

LOCATION France **START/FINISH** Thonon-les-Bains/Menton **DISTANCE** 435 miles (700 km) **TIME** 5–7 days **ROAD CONDITIONS** Some narrow sections with blind bends; some parts are a white-knuckle ride **INFORMATION** https://provence-alpes-cotedazur.com; Jun–Oct is best, avoiding peak season (Jul and Aug) if possible

France is a mosaic of mountains, lakes, and sultry coast, and this multi-day route connects it all, navigating mountain passes and Alpine meadows and finishing up in the sunny French Riviera. Magnifique!

The Route des Grandes Alpes connects 20 mountain passes, four national parks, and far too many cheesemongers to count. Along this epic drive, you'll encounter incredibly diverse landscapes, ranging from snow-lashed mountains to the eerie Casse Déserte.

Beginning in Thonon-les-Bains, the route crosses the Haute-Savoie region, a realm of high-Alpine pastures and charming wooden

chalets, as well as winter sports hubs like Morzine-Avoriaz and La Clusaz. You needn't step out of the car for dramatic views: fearsome granite mountains rise on one side of the road, rolling green pastures the other. Beyond the Aravis mountain pass is Savoie, an area of high mountains, lakes, and spa towns. Stop to admire the sweeping Vallée du Beaufortain, where soft meadows are framed by snow-dusted peaks,

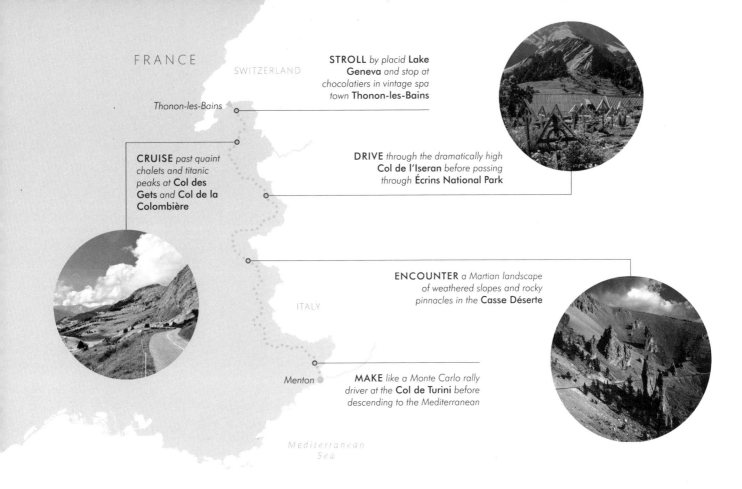

FRANCE

SWITZERLAND

STROLL *by placid* **Lake Geneva** *and stop at chocolatiers in vintage spa town* **Thonon-les-Bains**

Thonon-les-Bains

CRUISE *past quaint chalets and titanic peaks at* **Col des Gets** *and* **Col de la Colombière**

DRIVE *through the dramatically high* **Col de l'Iseran** *before passing through* **Écrins National Park**

ENCOUNTER *a Martian landscape of weathered slopes and rocky pinnacles in the* **Casse Déserte**

ITALY

Menton

MAKE *like a Monte Carlo rally driver at the* **Col de Turini** *before descending to the Mediterranean*

Mediterranean Sea

then continue to meander past elite mountain resorts like Courchevel and Méribel, which draw cyclists to their sunny slopes each spring.

The route delivers some of Europe's highest roads and most nerve-racking hairpin bends. But while the roads can be challenging, the reward is a gallery of gigantic peaks, none more dramatic than during the journey through Vanoise National Park. Just when you thought you couldn't drive any further into the clouds, you'll reach the vertiginous Col de l'Iseran—the loftiest on the entire route—before continuing into the idyllic green Maurienne valley, and onward to Provence. As you steer between hilltop villages, the sparkling Mediterranean rolls ever closer. Park in Menton to toast your journey's end with an Aperol Spritz.

Autumnal mountain scenery near Thonon-les-Bains

another way

Have time on your side and thighs of steel? Then tackle the route by bike. Ideal cycling conditions are between mid-June and mid-July, or September and mid-October. Plan your trip on https://en.routedesgrandesalpes.com.

*Above Vichy's ornate train station **Right** The Sancy mountains surrounding Le Mont-Dore*

(18) Route des Villes d'Eaux

LOCATION France **START/FINISH** Chaudes-Aigues/Vichy **DISTANCE** 234 miles (377 km) **TIME** 3 days **ROAD CONDITIONS** Good **INFORMATION** www.villesdeaux.com/en/home. php; spa at Le Mont-Dore open Apr–Nov

Hot springs bubble up through a fantastical landscape of dormant volcanoes in the quiet Auvergne region. This scenic road trip takes you to hillside caves and glamorous belle-époque towns home to grand old bathhouses.

In Auvergne, the wild heart of France, extinct volcanoes ridge the landscape like the spines of a dragon's back. Below ground, that volcanism still simmers, but its power today is restorative, not destructive. The thermal waters of Auvergne's spa towns are celebrated for their health-giving properties, and this road trip through the region's medieval towns and verdant countryside is a wholesome way to experience them.

Europe's hottest hot springs mark the beginning of the route, at the mouth of the Par River in Chaudes-Aigues. Winding into the volcanic countryside, you'll tour caves where ancient Romans bathed in natural pools before ascending to the mighty mountains of Le Mont-Dore, where the grand bathhouse promises relief from rheumatism and respiratory problems. There are more Roman ruins at Royat, a gorgeous spa town nestled in forested volcanic foothills—although today's spa, Royatonic, is a thoroughly modern affair, all bubbling steam jets and scented bathing pools. Ancient history abides at Néris-les-Bains, home to a Merovingian necropolis and lovely 11th-century church, while the most spectacular stop is saved for last: Vichy is known as the Queen of Spas, and its bathhouses are supremely tempting after time spent behind the wheel. Time to stretch your legs and soothe your muscles.

(19)

Normandy Coast

LOCATION France **START/FINISH** Sword Beach/Utah Beach **DISTANCE** 60 miles (95 km) **TIME** 1 day **ROAD CONDITIONS** Good **INFORMATION** https://en. normandie-tourisme.fr/discover/history

Experience Normandy's key World War II sites on this poignant and moving journey along the region's D-Day beaches.

Utah. Omaha. Gold. Juno. Sword. On June 6, 1944, these five assault beaches strung along Normandy's coast witnessed the largest amphibious invasion in the history of warfare. More than 150,000 infantrymen stormed the sands, to be met by some 50,000 German troops. Thousands of lives were lost on both sides, yet the landings led not only to the liberation of France but also to the ultimate victory of the Allies on the Western Front. A powerful thought as you watch waves wash the shore.

Journeying along the coast today makes for a salutary experience. As well as the beaches themselves—some of which still bear remnants of artificial harbors—the route is peppered with war cemeteries, military museums, and remembrance sites. Among them, the Bayeux War Cemetery holds more Commonwealth World War II graves than any other in France, the remains of the artificial harbor at Arromanches are strewn along Gold Beach at low tide, while the American Cemetery at Colleville-sur-Mer commemorates almost 9,500 lives lost.

◄ ►

WHAT'S IN A NAME?

As D-Day approached, the names attached to the beaches were selected almost at random. The sectors at the center of US operations—Utah and Omaha—are said to have been chosen by a general who asked two of his NCOs where they were from. For British and Canadian troops, the code names originally referred to different fish types—Gold, Jelly, and Sword—but Jelly was altered to Juno in tribute to an officer's wife.

The remains of the artificial harbor at Arromanches

Waves lapping the beach at Malpica de Bergantiños, a fishing village in Galicia

Costa da Morte

LOCATION Spain **START/FINISH** Malpica de Bergantiños/Fisterra **DISTANCE** 93 miles (150 km) **TIME** 4 hours **ROAD CONDITIONS** Good; some blind bends and narrow sections **INFORMATION** www.turismo.gal

Prehistoric tombs, medieval monuments, and clifftop memorials are testament to thousands of years of life (and death) along this ruggedly beautiful Galician coastline.

Epic in both their beauty and their tragic history, the wind-whipped cliffs of the Costa da Morte—the Coast of Death—have lured countless sailors to shipwreck. Happily, driving along the coastal road, the Galician sunshine beating down on the whitewashed lighthouses and Romanesque churches, is a much less perilous affair, with the only clue to the coast's grisly past being the choppy waves lapping the golden sand below.

Beginning in the fishing village of Malpica de Bergantiños, the road passes lonely monuments like the Shrine of St. Adrian of the Sea; gorgeous arcs of honeyed sand such as Playa de Balarés; and Roncudo Point, where stone crosses stand on the cliff in memory of the many sailors who perished on its jagged rocks. This is a poignant place to pause and reflect, but also a fantastic spot for lunch. The barnacles that cling to the rocks here are said to be the finest in Galicia, and are put to delicious use in the restaurants of Corme—a reminder that the Costa da Morte brings forth not just death, but life, too. Indeed, people have been thriving here for thousands of years; the mighty medieval structures that line the route, including the 14th-century castle at Mens, are dwarfed in age by Neolithic tombs like those at Dombate.

As the land draws in on both sides as you enter the route's final narrow peninsula, and the sun melts into the Atlantic, it's easy to see why they called this place Fisterra—the edge of the world.

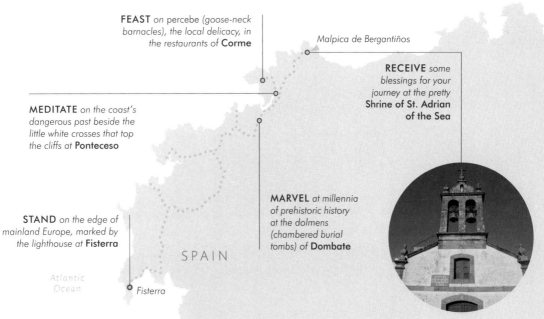

FEAST on percebe (goose-neck barnacles), the local delicacy, in the restaurants of **Corme**

Malpica de Bergantiños

RECEIVE some blessings for your journey at the pretty **Shrine of St. Adrian of the Sea**

MEDITATE on the coast's dangerous past beside the little white crosses that top the cliffs at **Ponteceso**

STAND on the edge of mainland Europe, marked by the lighthouse at **Fisterra**

MARVEL at millennia of prehistoric history at the dolmens (chambered burial tombs) of **Dombate**

SPAIN

Atlantic Ocean

Fisterra

(21) Sicily by Fiat 500

LOCATION Sicily, Italy **START/FINISH** Ragusa/
Messina **DISTANCE** 160 miles (255 km)
TIME 5 days **ROAD CONDITIONS** Good
INFORMATION www.visitsicily.info/en

Buckle up: the eastern coast of this seductive
Mediterranean honeypot runs for around
155 miles (250 km), yet squeezes in so much
history, culture, and wild landscape that it
could take a lifetime to explore. The most
memorable way to see it is in a vintage Fiat 500,
or Cinquecento as the Italians call it, and by
starting in Ragusa, a hilltop cluster of higgledy-
piggledy cathedrals and houses reached by a
drive along a rocky ravine. From here, it's a
rewarding detour through the Baroque hilltop
towns of Noto and Modica—where the Fiat's
dinky dimensions come into their own in the
winding backstreets—to historical Syracuse and
Catania and the smoking crest of Mount Etna,
Europe's highest active volcano. Finally, the trip
north to Messina is not complete without a few
days in Taormina, where houses cling to the
cliffside as if by their fingertips and gorgeous
soft-sand beaches wait to be discovered.

*Ragusa Ibla, Ragusa's
beautiful hilltop old town*

*Blind bends and tunnels on Lake
Garda's Strada della Forra*

(22) Strada della Forra

LOCATION Italy **START/FINISH** Lake Garda/
Pieve **DISTANCE** 3½ miles (6 km) **TIME**
20 minutes **ROAD CONDITIONS** Blind bends
INFORMATION www.stradadellaforra.com

It's no surprise that Winston Churchill described
the Strada della Forra as the Eighth Wonder
of the World. Not for the faint of heart, this
spectacular stretch of road snakes its way from
the shoreline of Lake Garda up to Pieve, winding
through a wild gorge scythed by the Brasa River.
Helter-skelter turns corkscrew up sharp inclines
and steep cliffs plunge down to the lake. You'll
need to keep your eyes firmly on the road;
passengers will be the only ones enjoying the
staggering panorama: lush, verdant vegetation
carpets the rock face, while the deep blue waters
of the lake glisten below. You're likely familiar
with this hairy switchback already; Daniel Craig's
James Bond rallied his way through the road's
tunnels and hairpin bends in an Aston Martin
in the high-speed chase at the beginning of
Quantum of Solace. Drive it if you dare.

23 Ruta Molinos de Viento de la Mancha

LOCATION Spain **START/FINISH** Orgaz/
Madridejos **DISTANCE** 50 miles (80 km)
TIME 2–3 days **ROAD CONDITIONS** Good
INFORMATION www.spain.info/en

Enter the world of Don Quixote, literature's greatest dreamer, on this journey through the windmills of La Mancha. Author Miguel de Cervantes' errant knight looked on these whirring mills and saw fearsome giants. Today, they plot the path of a pleasant road trip through Toledo.

Medieval Orgaz makes an atmospheric starting point, where you can admire the magnificent Church of St. Thomas. Later comes the little town of Tembleque, looked over by a hill crested with three ancient windmills, and Consuegra, which offers the chance to poke around the inner workings of mills that were still grinding flour as recently as the 1980s. The parched plain stretches east from here to Madridejos, where your quixotic quest ends in style at the 400-year-old Tío Genaro windmill, as impressive as it was in the time of Cervantes.

The historic molinos
(windmills) of La Mancha

24 C710

LOCATION Mallorca, Spain **START/FINISH** Port
d'Andratx/Cap de Formentor **DISTANCE** 87 miles
(140 km) **TIME** 1–2 days **ROAD CONDITIONS**
Good **INFORMATION** www.viamichelin.co.uk

Things start at one of the prettiest harbors in the Mediterranean, and they only get lovelier from there on this coastal road through northern Mallorca. Climbing through the forest as you leave Port d'Andratx behind, the scent of Aleppo pine in the air, the trees part to reveal sheer mountains plunging into the shimmering Balearic Sea. The Mirador de Ricardo Roca, a scenic rest point, is just the place to linger—give thanks for the bounty of the Mediterranean over a plate of *pica pica*, a spicy squid stew.

Take time, too, to stop and dip your feet at spots like Cala Deià, a rocky cove harboring still, warm water. A more adventurous diversion can be found at Sa Calobra, where a sheer, rugged canyon opens directly onto the sea. Roman bridges, medieval churches, and prehistoric watchtowers pass by on the final approach to Cap de Formentor, where the Serra de Tramuntana mountains meet the Mediterranean Sea.

another way

You can see more of the area inland from Port d'Andratx on hikes into the pine-forest-clad hills around the village of Galilea. There are several trails to explore, and you're likely to have only the occasional goat herd for company.

Grossglockner High Alpine Road

LOCATION Austria **START/FINISH** Fusch/Heiligenblut
DISTANCE 30 miles (48 km) **TIME** 2 hours
ROAD CONDITIONS Paved road **INFORMATION**
www.grossglockner.at; open early May–early Nov

Find beauty on every Alpine bend on this spirit-lifting ride into Hohe Tauern National Park, which hairpins past jewel-colored lakes and Austria's highest peak.

Just when you think the Austrian Alps couldn't get any more darned spectacular, the Grossglockner High Alpine Road blows that theory out of the water. Hands-down one of Europe's most incredible road trips, this ride from Fusch in Salzburgerland to Heiligenblut in Carinthia is a real treat for motorcyclists, taking you sky high into the Hohe Tauern National Park, corkscrewing past sapphire-blue lakes and wildflower-flecked meadows, and snow-frosted mountains that whoosh above 9,842 ft (3,000 m). Every so often, the shadow of a lammergeier soaring overhead darkens the road.

Hold on tight, it's a steep one: the road lunges around 36 hairpin bends, forcing you to keep a firm grip on the handlebars. On a quiet day, when you switch off the engine, all you'll hear is the rustle of wind, the rush of water, and the shrill whistle of marmots. But don't get too distracted: you'll need to keep your wits about you on the road's 9 percent gradients. And if you think riding the road on a motorcycle is dizzying, spare a thought for the cyclists trying to nail the challenge.

But any efforts are richly rewarded as you crest Edelweissspitze, the road's highest point. From here, it's onward to Heiligenblut, whose 15th-century pilgrimage church is visible from afar. If you want to break the journey, you can camp the night here in seriously scenic surrounds. From Heiligenblut, the road swings on to flag-bedecked Kaiser-Franz-Josefs-Höhe in the shadow of the bell-shaped peak of Grossglockner itself, towering above you at journey's end.

Snowcapped peaks on the Grossglockner High Alpine Road

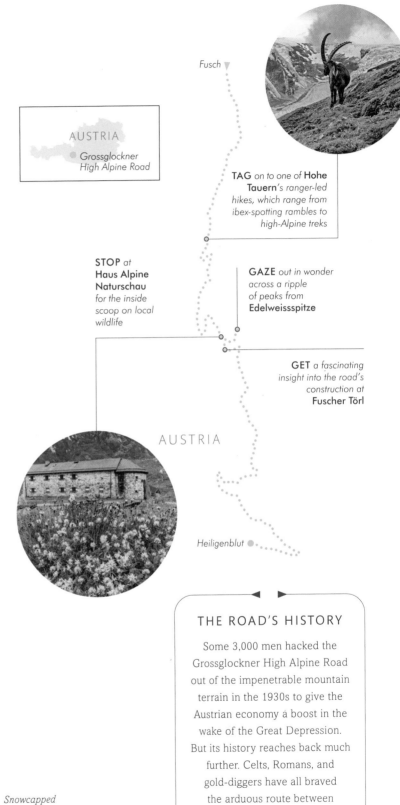

Fusch ▼

AUSTRIA

Grossglockner
High Alpine Road

TAG on to one of **Hohe Tauern**'s ranger-led hikes, which range from ibex-spotting rambles to high-Alpine treks

STOP at **Haus Alpine Naturschau** for the inside scoop on local wildlife

GAZE out in wonder across a ripple of peaks from **Edelweissspitze**

GET a fascinating insight into the road's construction at **Fuscher Törl**

AUSTRIA

Heiligenblut ●

THE ROAD'S HISTORY

Some 3,000 men hacked the Grossglockner High Alpine Road out of the impenetrable mountain terrain in the 1930s to give the Austrian economy a boost in the wake of the Great Depression. But its history reaches back much further. Celts, Romans, and gold-diggers have all braved the arduous route between Villach and Salzburg.

Looking out over Stołowe Mountains National Park

26 Zagorje

LOCATION Croatia **START/FINISH** Zagreb/ Krapina **DISTANCE** 40 miles (65 km) **TIME** 2–3 days **ROAD CONDITIONS** Well-maintained paved roads **INFORMATION** https://visitzagorje.hr

Once a lawless place of bandits and battles, the nexus of a contested trading route between the Ottoman and Hapsburg empires, Zagorje is a region on few traveler itineraries. The landscape of huddled Red Riding Hood cottages and wolf-filled forests north of Croatia's capital Zagreb is the Brothers Grimm fairy tales sprung to life. And it's not just a feast for the senses: a road trip through the undulating valleys around Krapina serves up zero-kilometer-philosophy restaurants and tangled vineyards. Here, every half-timbered house has a plot of dense vines bookended by a *"klet,"* a small house for secret drinking with friends, and the steep-sided furrows of Graševina and glossy Chardonnay grapes unfold as far as the eye can see. Tastings await at the end of a day's drive: at Vuglec Breg, one of Zagorje's leading wineries; at Grešna Gorica, where the wine is accompanied by plates of smoked prosciutto; and at Bodren winery in Hum na Sutli, known for its refreshing ice wines.

another way

A walking tour of Zagreb offers an alternative insight into another Croatian tipple. Rakija, a distilled fruit-based spirit, is ubiquitous in the capital's bars, and a wander along Tkalčićeva Street will turn up flavors that vary from the tried-and-tested— cherry, dried plum, strawberry, and apple—to the out-of-the-blue. Mistletoe, anyone?

27 Droga Stu Zakrętów

LOCATION Poland **START/FINISH** Radkow/ Kudowa-Zdrój **DISTANCE** 15½ miles (25 km) **TIME** 2 hours **ROAD CONDITIONS** Mostly smooth tarmac with some potholes **INFORMATION** www.pngs.com.pl

Known in English as the Hundred Curves Road, the Droga Stu Zakrętów is a favorite among motorcyclists, who come for its sweeping turns and tight hairpins that leave them itching to go knee to the ground. This serpentine strip of tarmac races through the sun-dappled forests of Stołowe Mountains National Park, hemmed in by ruler-straight pine, spruce, and beech that are most spectacular in early fall.

The adrenaline surges as you hit the Stroczy Zakręt; known as the Mother-in-Law's Tongue, this bend folds almost 360 degrees back on itself in an electrifying sweep of tarmac. Mysterious forests whiz by, and you'll find great slabs of flat-topped sandstone seemingly dumped by giant hands on the sides of the road. Clamber to their tops for bird's-eye views of the woodlands and the undulating farmlands beyond.

28 Bosnia Ski Circuit

LOCATION Bosnia and Herzegovina **START/FINISH** Sarajevo/Jahorina **DISTANCE** 30 miles (50 km) **TIME** 3–4 days **ROAD CONDITIONS** Paved **INFORMATION** www.tourismbih.com

Sarajevo might not be the first destination that springs to mind when you're planning a winter road trip. The Bosnia and Herzegovina capital is inextricably linked to the Balkans War, but it's more than 25 years since peace was brokered and it's become one of the most intriguing destinations in Eastern Europe. Sarajevo played host to the 1984 Winter Olympics, and this trip celebrates its legacy by venturing east of the capital into the pine-skirted peaks of Olimpijski Centar Jahorina, where the Olympic torch still burns bright and the slopes are bafflingly empty of the usual ski crowd. The area was devastated by the war but is now all groomed pistes and shiny new gondolas; plans are afoot to join Jahorina with nearby Ravna Planina ski resort, currently reached via a scenic mountain road. Finally, round off your winter-sports tour with a cable-car trip up Trebević, a landmark peak hugged by the war-ravaged bends of the country's former Olympic bobsled track.

TUNNEL MUSEUM

To understand Bosnia and its recent past, pay a visit to the Tunnel Museum, where the scars of the longest siege in modern European history are laid bare. Located opposite Sarajevo's airport, the tunnel was an ingenious escape route that gave the besieged citizens a link to the outside world during the Balkans War—it was used by more than one million escapees.

29 Vršič Pass

LOCATION Slovenia **START/FINISH** Kranjska Gora/Bovec **DISTANCE** 29 miles (46 km) **TIME** 1 hour **ROAD CONDITIONS** Varied **INFORMATION** www.promet.si/sl

It's about the journey, not the destination: an adage that's never been truer than on the Vršič Pass, a tantalizingly filigreed flash of road that's an unmissable thrill for motorcyclists.

Everything about it enlivens the senses. From the picture-perfect ski resort of Kranjska Gora, the road turns into a wicked combination of cobblestones and stomach-churning bends. There are 50 hairpins to negotiate; you'll get a few brief seconds to appreciate the dense forests surrounding you, and the rare gaps in the trees that give glimpses of the mountains beyond.

At the pass itself, the karstic limestone peaks of the Julian Alps mark its high point. Pause here to breathe in the crisp mountain air and prepare yourself for the descent: 24 rippling bows of gray tarmac remain. At the pretty mountain town of Bovec, you'll want to turn back around and do it all over again.

Some of the 50 hairpin bends on the Vršič Pass

Above Maniot tower houses
in the village of Vatheia
Left The inviting turquoise
waters of Marmari beach

This is a place whose
beauty is matched by
its barrenness

TAKE a boat tour into the eerie underwater caves of **Diros**, one of Greece's great wonders

Messenian Gulf

GREECE

Areopoli

LEARN about the Christian history of the Mani at the Byzantine Museum Manis in **Areopoli**

Laconian Gulf

ENJOY ocean-fresh seafood in a taverna overlooking **Chalikia Beach**—grilled octopus is a local specialty

Paralia Marathos

VISIT the site of Greek mythology's gateway to the underworld, where Hercules captured Cerberus

STAND on Europe's southern frontier at the **Cape Matapan lighthouse**, gazing toward Libya

(30)

Mani Peninsula

LOCATION Greece **START/FINISH** Areopoli/Paralia Marathos **DISTANCE** 44 miles (71 km) **TIME** 1–2 days **ROAD CONDITIONS** Mostly good **INFORMATION** Tower houses can be booked at www.manitowerhouses.com

Myth and legend shroud every corner of this gorgeously rugged peninsula in Greece's Peloponnese region, where a road trip takes in mountain villages home to mysterious tower houses.

"Every rock and stream is a myth." So wrote travel writer Patrick Leigh Fermor of the Mani, a mountainous peninsula drenched in sunlight and legend which extrudes from southern Greece into the Mediterranean Sea. This is a place whose beauty is matched by its barrenness—life is hard here, and it's easy to believe the Maniots' claim they are the modern descendants of the Spartans.

The myth of the Mani is evident from the route's starting point, Areopoli, named for Ares, god of war. Down the coast at the Diros caves, cross the threshold into the underworld as you leave terra firma behind and take a punt into a network of caverns ceilinged with stalactites. Heading south, the Mani's unique character reveals itself in the Maniot tower houses, which rise from the barren earth—the fortified homes of the warring clans that long lived here.

Just occasionally, the sharp cliffs and rocky bluffs that characterize the Maniot coastline are broken up by sandy coves. One such is Marmari, a lovely spot for a cooling dip before the approach to Cape Matapan: the second-most southerly point of Continental Europe, marked by a modest lighthouse. This is where Greek legend placed the gates of Hades, though as you make the wild drive up the east coast to finish on the beach at Paralia Marathos, it's hard to think of the Mani as anything less than heavenly.

THE DEATH ORACLE

Just to the east of Cape Matapan, a brown sign beside a low-slung, ruined building signals the site of the Death Oracle of Poseidon Tainarios. Greek mythology holds this place to be the gate of hell, guarded by the many-headed dog, Cerberus; tradition has it that there was an oracle here who consulted the souls of the dead.

(31)

Transfăgărășan

LOCATION Romania **START/FINISH** Intersection of Hwy DN1 and Hwy DN7C/Bascov
DISTANCE 91 miles (146 km) **TIME** 6 hours **ROAD CONDITIONS** Multiple hairpin
bends and sharp ascents/descents; ice and snow at high elevations **INFORMATION**
https://romaniatourism.com/scenic-drives-romania.html; usually open Jun–Oct

*The Transfăgărășan's topography-defying tarmac is reminiscent of a ball
of string unraveled by a giant for some fantastical purpose, for logic surely
never made a road so loopy or mountainous.*

The nicknames bestowed upon the Transfăgărășan,
a route traversing the Carpathian range's Făgăraș
mountains in sheer dissent of gradient and common
sense, offer clues to its character. It has been dubbed
the "road to the sky," as it climbs to 6,700 ft (2,042 m),
and "Ceaușescu's folly," after the Romanian dictator
who built the thing at huge cost to defend against
a potential (and imagined) invasion by the Soviet
Union. This is the road trip every Romania-bound
traveler wants to try for its ridiculous twists, turns,
rises, and falls, many on hairpins so acute they
almost defy the laws of physics. Although it is the
68 miles (110 km) between Cârțișoara and Curtea
de Argeș, open only for a few snow-free months
each year, which really quicken the pulse. From
Cârțișoara, the Transfăgărășan launches on a loopy
ascent of over 5,000 ft (1,525 m) to reach Balea Lac
above the tree line. Then come the helter-skelter
sections that you see in the tourist brochures,
unfurling before you down the mountainside. You'll
pass the trailhead to Romania's highest peak, Vârful
Moldoveanu; the long, lovely lake of Lacul Vidraru;
and, lower down, Poenari Castle, former residence
of Vlad the Impaler—and thus the closest you can
get to Dracula's lair outside fiction. Fitting really, for
a road that you simply couldn't make up.

*The road's
dizzying
switchbacks,
looping through
thick forest*

The startling Buzludzha Monument

(32)

Central Mountains

LOCATION Bulgaria **START/FINISH** Veliko Tarnovo/Plovdiv
DISTANCE 124 miles (200 km) **TIME** 1 day **ROAD CONDITIONS**
Paved but quality varies: get ready for potholes, bumps, and
multiple blind bends **INFORMATION** https://bulgariatravel.org

*Navigate the sinuous mountain roads of central
Bulgaria to encounter battlegrounds and ancient
tombs—and a structure reminiscent of a UFO.*

Driving between Veliko Tarnovo and Plovdiv is about much more
than epic scenery. Yes, you'll clutch the steering wheel along
serpentine mountain passes, and see yawning valleys and
impenetrable forests. But this route across the Stara Planina
mountains also plunges you deep into the heart of Bulgarian
history, with centuries of storied sights along the way.

After driving south into the Shipka region, you'll climb the flanks
of 4,360-ft (1,329-m) Mount Stoletov, cresting the summit to
admire a peerless panorama of sheer cliffs and green valleys. Up
here, you'll find the Shipka Monument, a stern gray tower that
memorializes a series of key battles during the late 19th century. A
bumpy, eastbound road leads you to an even more intriguing spot:
the UFO-shaped Buzludzha Monument. Tickle the accelerator to
make your way steadily up to this abandoned Socialist assembly
hall, complete with mosaics and a giant red star.

After driving back downhill, you'll reach the Kazanlak Valley, the
so-called Valley of Thracian Kings; watch for low, grassy hills, the
burial places of warriors from millennia past. It's a regal finale to a
trip that ends shortly after in equally historic Plovdiv.

◀ ▶

SHIPKA'S LEGENDARY BATTLES

Battles at Shipka Pass
helped secure
Bulgaria's freedom
after more than 500
years of Ottoman
control. In 1877 and
1878, more than 7,000
Bulgarian and Russian
soldiers succeeded
in securing the
strategic pass, despite
the Ottoman army
outnumbering them
many times over. The
battles at Shipka
remain legendary;
today they're
synonymous with
Bulgarian resilience
and courage in the
face of desperate odds.
Step inside the Shipka
Monument's museum
to learn more.

(33)

Black Sea: Istanbul to Doğubayazit

LOCATION Turkey **START/FINISH** Istanbul/Doğubayazit **DISTANCE** 1,553 miles (2,500 km) **TIME** 10 to 12 days **ROAD CONDITIONS** Variable **INFORMATION** Ensure all your paperwork is at hand, as Anatolia is marked by a heavy military presence; weather best Jun–Sept

Following the shores of the Black Sea from Istanbul to Doğubayazit, this remarkable route takes you through land blessed with centuries of history and shaped by the Silk Road.

From the collision of modernity and ancient cultures in Istanbul, prepare to embark on a road trip deep into a crossroads of empires and along time-worn trading routes, where ancient civilizations have left churches, palaces, castles, and mosques in their wake. Traces of the Ottoman Empire abound here, with preserved towns of skyline-piercing minarets and stone mansions that speak of their once great prosperity as stopping points along the caravan routes of the Silk Road.

> Embark on a road trip deep into a crossroads of empires

Your destination is Doğubayazit in the far east of Turkey, on the border with Iran. How you get there is entirely up to you. For those on a schedule, highways let you make swift work of some sections. But the true magic of this journey is in the slow-going minor roads, where every bend gives onto breathtakingly beautiful beaches, lush fields of tea and tobacco, and the dramatic landscapes of the inland mountain plains. As you drive, you'll trace a route along the Black Sea's wriggling coastline before crossing inland into the sparsely inhabited high mountains and arid plateau of eastern Anatolia. If you've time to dedicate to this trip, you'll be paid judiciously. In fact, take the lead from those across the centuries: there are ▶

Left Sumela Monastery, defying belief with its cliff-side location **Below** A road winding down Kaçkar mountain

plenty of places to pause—for days if you wish—in the plethora of sleepy towns and postcard-perfect beaches along the sea's shores.

At Trabzon, head inland to gasp at Sumela Monastery, a 4th-century Greek Orthodox monastery that appears to have sprouted directly out of the cliffs, clinging miraculously above the evergreen forests of the Altindere Valley. From here, head back to the coast to take a scenic detour along the D925. This mountain road clambers up to trace the contours of the 13,120-ft (4,000-m) Kaçkar range, where snow clings year-round to its barren, scree-filled slopes, and the road careers south through arid steppe. Dropping 3,280 ft (1,000 m), it reaches the city of Erzurum, whose magnificent mosques from Seljuk, Saltuk, Mongol, and Ottoman eras make it a worthy destination in its own right.

At each and every stage, the route offers more magic, more history, and more enchantment. As you enter the final few hundred miles, the shores of Lake Van are a tranquil place to while away a day or two. Drive up to the crescent-moon crater lakes of the

MOUNT ARARAT

According to the Bible, Noah's Ark landed on the mountains of Ararat—which many Christians have taken literally to mean Mount Ararat, Turkey's highest mountain. Discoveries of wooden remains buried on the mountain's upper reaches have been met with skepticism by archaeologists and historians alike.

Far left The Armenian Apostolic cathedral on Akdamar Island *Left* Traditional Ottoman houses in Safranbolu *Below left* A stream running through Kaçkar's foothills

dormant Nemrut volcano on its eastern shores and spend an afternoon mesmerized by the medieval Armenian Apostolic cathedral on Akdamar Island, with its biblical relief carvings and backdrop of snow-dappled mountains.

Doğubayazit marks the end of the road. Positioned on a high mountain plateau, the town sits in the shadows of Mount Ararat, a mountain many Christians believe to be the landing place for the fabled Noah's Ark. Bring your trip to a close by heading up to the Ishak Pasa Palace, a grand 17th-century Ottoman complex of Persian-inspired domes and arches built to manage traffic along the Silk Road. From its commanding vantage point, you can look back across the route you've traveled and pause to take it all in.

another way

Cyclists will find the narrow roads of the sleepy Black Sea coastline a hilly but worthy challenge, where idyllic and mostly untouched beaches, plus stunning coastal views, are the reward. Allow at least three weeks.

ADMIRE epic Byzantine architecture in the 6th-century Hagia Sophia mosque in **Istanbul**, which has been both a church and a museum.

WANDER the charming streets of the well-preserved Ottoman town of **Safranbolu**, a UNESCO World Heritage site

EMBARK on a quest to find Noah's Ark with a trek to the peak of **Mount Ararat**

CHOW DOWN on traditional Turkish Abant kebabs in gastronomic capital, **Bolu**

TAKE IN dazzling views of the Altindere Valley from **Sumela Monastery**'s remarkable vantage point

BULGARIA

GREECE

Istanbul

Black Sea

GEORGIA

ARMENIA

Doğubayazit

IRAN

TURKEY

SYRIA

Mediterranean Sea

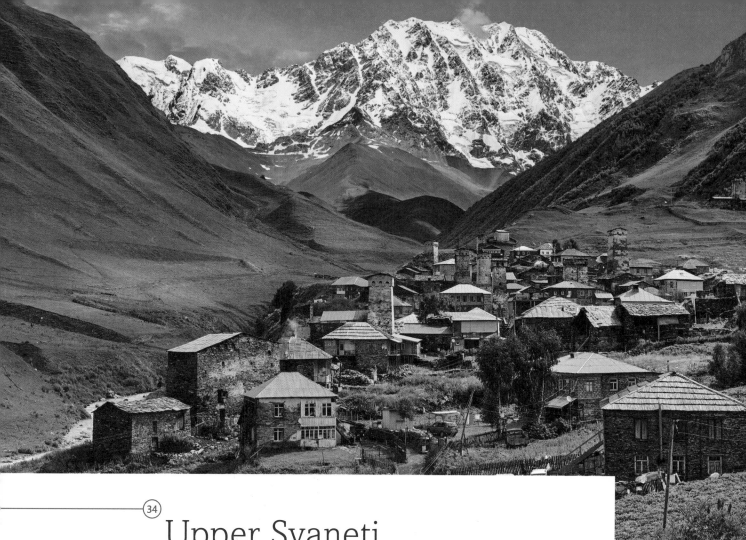

Upper Svaneti

Ushguli and its distinctive Svan tower houses

LOCATION Georgia **START/FINISH** Kutaisi/Ushguli **DISTANCE** 100 miles (163 km) **TIME** 4–5 days **ROAD CONDITIONS** Challenging—consider a 4WD **INFORMATION** https://georgia.travel

A visit to Ushguli, the most remote medieval village in Europe, is just one aspect of a road trip across the Upper Svaneti, a hidden corner of Georgia that was forgotten by the world for centuries.

Few places capture the beautiful, if forlorn, isolation of medieval Europe better than the Upper Svaneti. It has an age-old feel. Like Middle Earth meets Narnia, or Czarist Russia crossed with Westeros. The Svans, the ethnic subgroup of Georgians who live in Svaneti, call their homeland the "heaven of the mountains," an impression you can't shake when road tripping here.

Begin in Georgia's second city of Kutaisi, before driving north toward the border with Russia, stopping between Mazeri and Tvebishi at the foot of Mount Ushba, a spectacular raw knuckle of rock. Here, you'll find fortified 9th- to 13th-century tower houses that punctuate the skyline. Known as *kors*, these are the skyscrapers of the Caucasus and look like they've been built to break into the heavens, with hundreds looming on the road east toward Mestia; a handful have reopened as museums and guesthouses.

HIKE to **Shdugra waterfall**, the tallest in Georgia and an unstoppable force of nature, on the border with Russia

LEARN about Svan culture in **Mestia**'s Svaneti Museum of History and Ethnography

GO skiing at **Mount Tetnuldi**, the newest hiking and skiing destination in Georgia

USE the **Grand Hotel Ushba** as a base camp for hiking and horse riding to remote villages in the surrounding valleys

RUSSIA

Ushguli

RUSSIA

Kutaisi

Black Sea

GEORGIA

STEP back in time in **Ushguli**, with its collection of lopsided, crooked chess-piece towers

TURKEY

ARMENIA

AZERBAIJAN

From Mestia, the journey deeper into the mountains, up and over hills that concertina spectacularly to Ushguli, is about more than just scenery. The highest mountain village in Europe, located at the end of a twisty-turny road beneath jaw-dropping summits, Ushguli is a place where identity has been sharpened by isolation. The village is the natural home of Svan culture, and there's a sense upon arriving that you are walking through a living ethnographic museum. Heaven of the mountains indeed.

another way

Georgia lays claim to being the oldest wine-producing region on Earth. A spectacular road trip for oenophiles leads from the capital, Tbilisi, to Signagi, the most important winelands of the Kakheti region. The area is known for its semisweet reds, which you can try in tastings at the Cradle of Wine Marani, Okro's Wine, and Pheasant's Tears wineries.

BY BIKE

Europe's cycling pedigree is unrivaled. A German invented the bike, while the world's most prestigious cycle race spans the perimeter of France. Europe's bicycle routes cross borders and follow rivers from source to sea, but it's the little details that will leave a lasting impression: the creak of windmills by a Dutch canal; the smell of wildflowers in the Austrian Tyrol. Now that's pedal power.

AT A GLANCE
BY BIKE

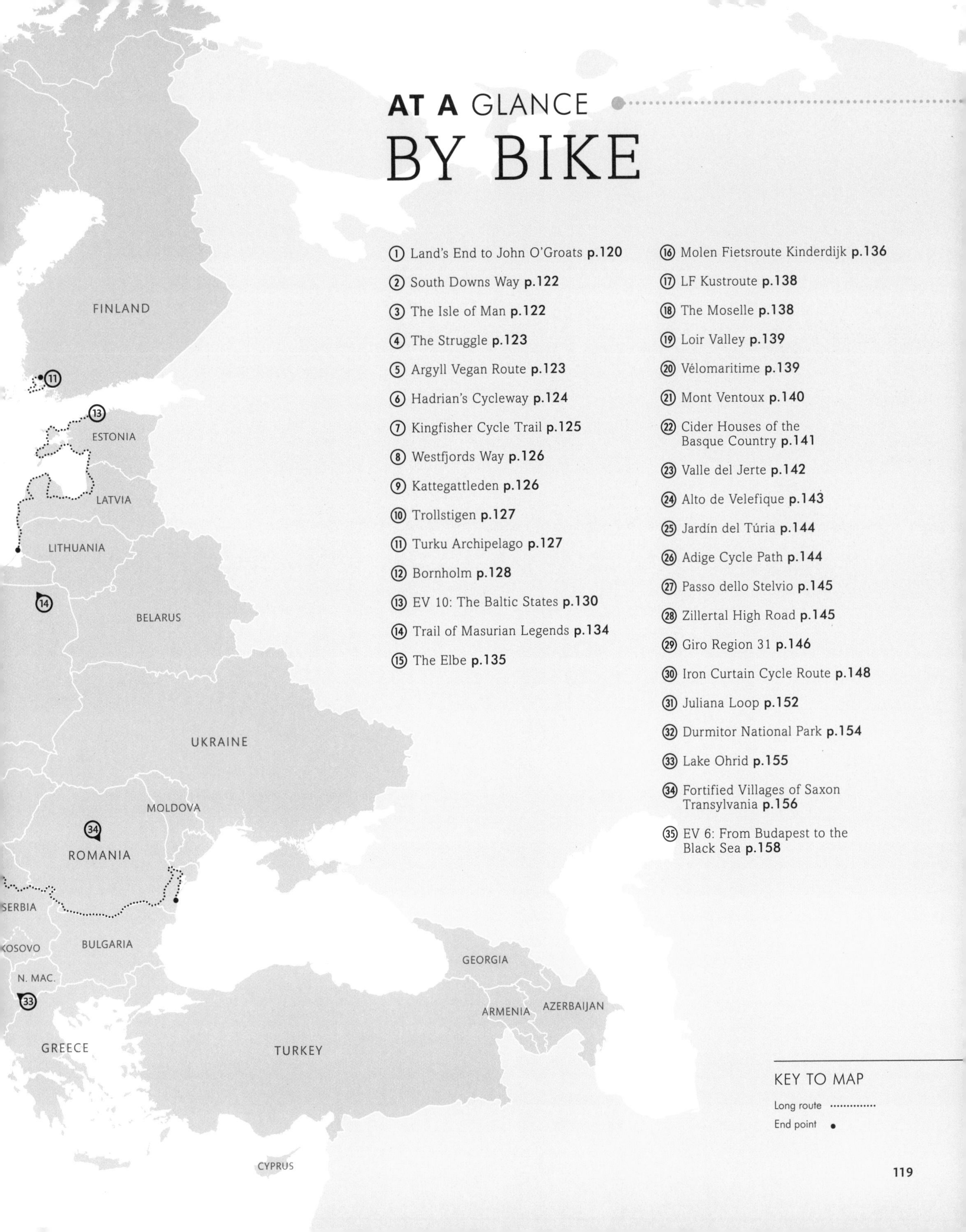

FINLAND
11
13
ESTONIA
LATVIA
LITHUANIA
14
BELARUS
UKRAINE
MOLDOVA
34
ROMANIA
SERBIA
KOSOVO
BULGARIA
N. MAC.
33
GREECE
TURKEY
GEORGIA
ARMENIA
AZERBAIJAN
CYPRUS
KEY TO MAP
Long route
End point

○1

Land's End to John O'Groats

*Bluebells
carpeting the
Quantock Hills
in Somerset*

LOCATION England to Scotland **START/FINISH** Land's End/John O'Groats
DISTANCE 1,100 miles (1,770 km) **TIME** 16 days **DIFFICULTY** Challenging
INFORMATION www.cyclelejog.com

*Want to see the UK? Hop in the saddle and cycle the length of the British
mainland on this timeless route, on a cross-border ride as rewarding as
it is far-reaching.*

Call it the End to End. Call it LEJOG (or JOGLE, if
you're pedaling north to south). Call it the ultimate
British cycling experience. Whatever name you
hang on this iconic ride, which wriggles its way
from the southwesterly extremity of England to
the northernmost tip (or as close as it gets) of the
Scottish mainland, it's a challenge for any self-
respecting cyclist to relish.

There are various routes to weigh up, none of
which are official. If you're keen to blast from A to B

as swiftly as possible, you'll see plenty of main
roads, while if you stick to National Cycle
Network Routes, you'll add around 310 miles
(500 km)—and probably considerably more
enjoyment—to the ride. What attracts a thighs-of-
steel club rider might not appeal to a more casual
bike tourist, so plan accordingly.

Ultimately, though, it all adds up to the same
thing: Britain spooling underneath your wheels.
Expect billowing coastal scenery and village greens;

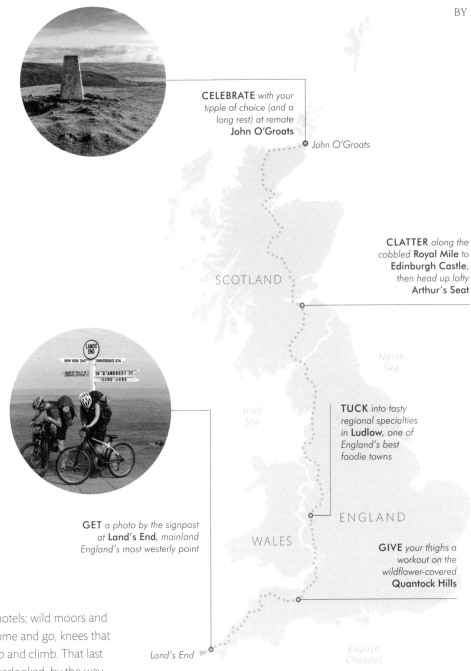

CELEBRATE with your tipple of choice (and a long rest) at remote **John O'Groats**

John O'Groats

CLATTER along the cobbled **Royal Mile** to **Edinburgh Castle**, then head up lofty **Arthur's Seat**

SCOTLAND

North Sea

Irish Sea

TUCK into tasty regional specialties in **Ludlow**, one of England's best foodie towns

ENGLAND

WALES

GIVE your thighs a workout on the wildflower-covered **Quantock Hills**

GET a photo by the signpost at **Land's End**, mainland England's most westerly point

English Channel

Land's End

traditional pubs and remote hotels; wild moors and winding valleys; towns that come and go, knees that ache and stiffen, lanes that dip and climb. That last word—climb—shouldn't be overlooked, by the way. Whichever direction you're traveling, Cornwall and Devon will give you a sharp lesson in how hilly the UK can be.

Book your accommodation ahead of time, particularly in high season—you'll find everything from hotels and B&Bs to hostels and campsites—and do the same with your transportation to and from the start and end, especially if traveling with a bike by train. After all, unless you're superhuman, the last thing you'll want to do is cycle home.

another way

Thinking of doing LEJOG on foot? Well, why not? Plenty of people walk the full length, a hike that typically takes between two and three months to complete—but as ever, plan well.

The rippling chalk cliffs of the Seven Sisters, one of the finest sights on the East Sussex coast

② South Downs Way

LOCATION England **START/FINISH** Winchester/ Eastbourne **DISTANCE** 100 miles (160 km) **TIME** 2–4 days **DIFFICULTY** Moderate to challenging **INFORMATION** https://south downsway.org

Running along a range of chalk hills that stretches from the heart of Hampshire to the East Sussex coast, the South Downs Way is among the most rewarding, and challenging, national trails in the UK. Although you can hike and horse ride along its tracks and bridleways, the route is best explored on two wheels. Despite its proximity to London, the trail whisks you through a sparsely populated and surprisingly varied landscape of ancient woodlands and rolling grasslands, winding ridges and breezy clifftops, much of it protected by the South Downs National Park. Avid cyclists can complete the route in as little as two days. But it pays to take a more leisurely approach, with regular detours to picture-postcard pubs, nature reserves, and historic sites such as Bignor Roman villa and the eye-catching Long Man of Wilmington, the largest chalk figure in Europe.

③ The Isle of Man

LOCATION British Isles **START/FINISH** Douglas (loop) **DISTANCE** 37½ miles (60.5 km) **TIME** 3 hours **DIFFICULTY** Challenging **INFORMATION** www.isleofmancc.com

Midway between England, Ireland, Scotland, and Wales, this small emerald island—independent from the UK and the EU—is just 30 miles (48 km) long by 10 miles (16 km) wide. The countryside of this island nation is famous for hosting the annual Isle of Man Tourist Trophy (TT) motorcycle race, but its patchwork of fields and sweeping glens, undulating hills and sharp bends is also classic cycling terrain. Pedaling the route of the famous race to and from Douglas takes in 2,132 ft (650 m) of ascent—plus some remarkable views of the Irish Sea. The course record is under 1 hour 24 minutes, but as you have to tackle the central mountainous ridge that includes looming Snaefell (which means "snow mountain" in Norse), it will probably take the average rider a little (a lot) longer.

MANX CYCLISTS

Mark Cavendish is one of the greatest road sprinters of all time: he rode for the Isle of Man and Great Britain at the Commonwealth Games and Olympics respectively, and won 34 Tour de France stages. The winner of the first-ever female Tour de France (1955) was Millie Robinson, another Manx cyclist, who only took up competitive cycling when she was 25.

④

The Struggle

LOCATION England **START/FINISH** Ambleside/
Kirkstone Pass **DISTANCE** 3 miles (4.5 km) **TIME**
1 hour **DIFFICULTY** Short but challenging
INFORMATION https://climbfinder.com

Ah, the Lake District. A region of romping fells,
Michelin-starred restaurants, and lung-busting
cycle routes. "The Struggle" is the apt name given
to the punishing ride from Ambleside up to
Kirkstone Pass, a beast of a climb that clocks up
almost 1,312 ft (400 m) of vertical ascent and,
at its steepest, reaches a gradient of almost 20
percent. If you're looking for a leisurely pedal
to take in the Lakeland scenery, you'd be best
steering yourself elsewhere.

Which isn't to say it's not beautiful. Ambleside
itself sits on the northern shore of peak-ringed
Windermere, the largest lake in the national park,
while lofty Kirkstone Pass gives a show-stopping
view across surrounding hills—you'll just need
to get your breath back to enjoy it. And there's
more good news. The Kirkstone Pass Inn stands
close to the summit of the climb, providing just
the place for a restorative post-ride drink.

*A cyclist testing his leg muscles on the winding
but scenic ascent of The Struggle*

⑤

Argyll Vegan Route

LOCATION Scotland **START/FINISH**
Lochgilphead/Appin **DISTANCE** 52 miles
(84 km) **TIME** 2–3 days **DIFFICULTY**
Good roads but hilly and winding
INFORMATION www.wildaboutargyll.co.uk

What's the beef with the UK's first vegan route?
Well, for starters, it's one of five self-guided Taste
Trails, from seafood to farm produce to spirits,
that have been developed by local producers
and food advocates who know Argyll and its
west-coast Scottish isles intimately. The vegan
route is underpinned by animal- and planet-
friendly B&Bs, vegan cafés, and plant-based
menus, but also takes in scenery that's more than
just a side garnish. Consider Kilmartin Glen's
standing stones; Dunadd Fort, from where the
ancient kings of Argyll ruled; and Knapdale forest,
where the UK's most famous vegans—the
flat-tailed and herbivorous Eurasian beaver—
have been successfully rewilded. It's a case of
choose your own pace and direction, but the
exquisite Loch Melfort Hotel and The Pierhouse
in Appin help bookend a bike route where piling
on calories is as important as burning them.

another way

*For pescatarians, Argyll's Atlantic
waters and sea lochs deliver some of
the most stunning and sustainable fish
and shellfish in Europe. The region's
Seafood Trail, which spins out from
crustacean capital Oban, tells a story
of unassuming beach cafés, salty-dog
fishermen, and sensational restaurants.*

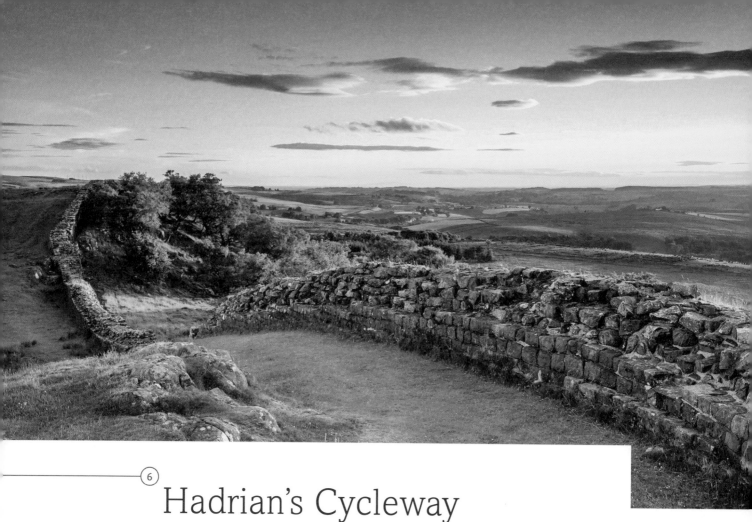

Hadrian's Cycleway

(6)

Hadrian's Wall snaking across Northumberland

LOCATION England **START/FINISH** Ravenglass/South Shields **DISTANCE** 170 miles (274 km) **TIME** 4 days **DIFFICULTY** Moderate **INFORMATION** www.sustrans.org.uk/hadrians-cycleway

Loosely following the 1,900-year-old frontier of the same name, this coast-to-coast ride follows quiet roads from the Irish Sea to the North Sea, combining a stirring sense of history with sensational rural views.

When, in 122 CE the emperor Hadrian ordered the construction of a military barrier across the entirety of the British mainland, he might have been shocked to learn that a couple of millennia later, people would be traveling its length on two-wheeled machines. But hey, it's a heck of a ride.

The nearby presence of the Hadrian's Wall Path National Trail means that the journey is more commonly completed on foot than in the saddle, although the cycleway more than deserves its reputation as a top-notch bike route. Largely following National Cycle Route 72, it leads from

Ravenglass in the west to South Shields in the east, passing numerous Roman sites in the process, including big-name attractions such as the Roman Army Museum, Vindolanda, and Housesteads Fort.

Other than a few well-surfaced off-road sections, most of the route is on minor roads, and while the central section has several hills to negotiate, both the start and end of the ride are largely flat. Speedy cyclists can power through in three days or less, but far better to take your time and enjoy the shifting panoramas as the wall wends its way from one sea to another.

(7)

Kingfisher Cycle Trail

LOCATION Ireland **START/FINISH** Enniskillen Visitor Centre (loop)
DISTANCE 300 miles (480 km) **TIME** 8 days **DIFFICULTY**
Moderate **INFORMATION** https://kingfishercycletrail.com

Follow quiet country roads on this scenic figure-eight route through Ireland's border counties—keeping your eyes peeled for the eponymous bird.

The Kingfisher Trail traces a large double-loop through the border counties of Fermanagh, Leitrim, Cavan, Donegal, and Monaghan, beginning—officially, at least—in the Northern Irish town of Enniskillen. One of the beauties of the route, however, is that it can be picked up at any point. If you want to power around the whole thing in a few days, go for it. If you'd rather choose a stretch and take your time, overnighting where the mood takes you, more power to your elbow. It's a dip-in-and-out, do-as-you-please cycle ride. Some might call that the best kind.

So what to expect? Canal-side paths, tree-shaded lanes, minimal traffic, colorful birdlife—the kingfisher has long been associated with the watery environs in these parts—and an immersion in the unrushed day-to-day of rural Ireland. In addition to the scenery and hospitality, you'll also find some impressive set-piece attractions, including Neo-Classical Castle Coole, the natural limestone grottoes of the Marble Arch Caves, and the prehistoric dolmen tomb on the banks of freshwater Lough Scur. And if you're lucky, you might just spy the flash of a kingfisher en route.

another way

The 242-mile (387-km) route between Belfast and Ballyshannon is Ireland's first fully signed coast-to-coast cycle trail, leading from the Northern Ireland capital to the shores of County Donegal, via the Sperrin Mountains and Fermanagh Lakelands.

Taking a break by a lake in Donegal

*Deserted beaches and wild Atlantic waves
on Iceland's Westfjords Way*

⑧ Westfjords Way

LOCATION Iceland **START/FINISH** Various
DISTANCE 575 miles (925 km) **TIME** 6–8 days
DIFFICULTY Moderate **INFORMATION** https://
vestfjardaleidin.is

The latest and greatest place to visit in Iceland isn't the Golden Circle or Vatnajökull National Park. For loveliness on a more visceral scale, your road should lead west into the Westfjords, a place where there's rarely any road traffic to worry about—here, sheep outnumber people 20 to 1. Essentially, the trail is a loop around the country's least-inhabited fjord lands, zigzagging back and forth along the coast of one of Europe's last great wildernesses, while proposing stops at hot springs, remote villages, and windswept beaches. Scale the pass between Hrafnseyri and Þingeyr, cycle along the Látrabjarg Cliff, or stop off at the Sea Monster Museum. Pit stops aside, what you'll love most are the bountiful moments to appreciate having the road in front of you to yourself. But this is also an area notorious for headwinds and unpredictable weather. Pack smartly and have a plan for accommodation and drying out your gear should the skies of Valhalla open above you.

⑨ Kattegattleden

LOCATION Sweden **START/FINISH**
Helsingborg/Gothenburg **DISTANCE** 240 miles
(390 km) **TIME** 8 days **DIFFICULTY** Easy
INFORMATION www.kattegattleden.se;
best May–Sept

Civilized, modern, organized, comfortable—what typifies Sweden also typifies its first national cycle-touring route. Car-free paths and quiet lanes trace the west coast, from Helsingborg to Gothenburg, past a smörgåsbord of historic towns, cozy fishing villages, nature reserves, and sandy beaches. The going is as smooth and as flat as a Swedish pancake, and daily distances are small because there's plenty to explore here—for culture lovers and foodies, sea-swimmers and hikers. At the ice-cream stalls and farm shops en route, you'll meet everyone from e-biking couples hopping between spa hotels to wild campers enjoying the natural landscapes on a budget. Despite your fellow cyclists, it's quiet here, too: the only sounds at your bayside bistro come summer's 10 p.m. sunset will be the birds and the breeze—and maybe the clink of glasses.

another way

The similar Sydostleden route, on the opposite coast, runs 168 miles (270 km) from inland Växjö, the self-proclaimed Greenest City in Europe, south past lakes, mountains, and forests to the coastline of Simrishamn. A link to the Kattegattleden is planned.

(10)

Trollstigen

LOCATION Norway **START/FINISH** Åndalsnes/
Trollstigen Plateau **DISTANCE** 11 miles (17 km)
TIME 1 day **DIFFICULTY** Challenging
INFORMATION www.fjordnorway.com; open
May–mid-Oct

Wiggling up the mountain in a series of 11
hairpin bends, Trollstigen (Troll's Ladder) is an
incredible feat of 1930s engineering. Your nerves
will start tingling as soon as you clap eyes on this
corkscrewing, heart-stoppingly steep section of
Norway's Route 63, with the Romsdal Alps
thrusting high above. There's no denying it's a
backbreaking, thigh-burning beast of a climb, but
it's also an unforgettable ride.

Pedaling away from the fjord-facing town
of Åndalsnes, you'll soon swing past great
boulders—petrified trolls, according to legend.
Just make sure you save energy for the climb
up to 2,815-ft (858-m) Stigrøra and the bridge
spanning Stigfossen waterfall, which dives over a
sheer cliff face. Enjoy the view—and the sense of
achievement—from the steel-and-glass platform
that juts out into the mouth of the abyss before
rolling gleefully back down to Åndalsnes.

(11)

Turku Archipelago

LOCATION Finland **START/FINISH** Turku (loop)
DISTANCE 124 miles (200 km) **TIME** 4 or 5 days
DIFFICULTY Easy **INFORMATION** www.
visitfinland.com; some ferries are seasonal

Time loses meaning on the Turku Archipelago, a
cluster of laid-back islets hanging off the southwest coast of Finland. The landscape here is
imbued with a natural sense of calm and, unless
you're racing to catch the next ferry, there's little
reason to hurry. It would take a lot of languid
days to pedal round all 20,000 islands that make
up the chain, so opt for the Archipelago Trail for
a watery week-long meander.

Setting off from the lively city of Turku, the
route winds alongside rocky bays and through
rustling forest. Pedal along the pretty harbors of
Korpo and Naantali and pause to admire the
ship models that are a feature of many churches
here. Take time, too, for exploratory detours
down quiet side roads or forest paths, or simply
perch on sun-warmed granite and look out over
the inky-blue, island-speckled sea.

*The squiggling,
serpentine road
of the Trollstigen*

⑫

Bornholm

LOCATION Denmark **START/FINISH** Rønne (loop) **DISTANCE** 65 miles (105 km)
TIME 2 days **DIFFICULTY** Easy **INFORMATION** https://visitbornholm.com

*The island of Bornholm is farming-and-fishing-village Denmark, but with
a dash of scenic drama. Encircled and criss-crossed by generous bike-
only paths, it's the ideal destination for a stress-free cycling trip for all.*

Not much happens when you cycle on Bornholm.
But it happens delightfully. Bicycles are the
dominant transportation here, and the island works
at their pace—it's appropriate that the fine sand
from the many beaches is used for hourglasses.

The landscape is about as vertically dramatic as
Denmark gets: rocky cliffs, cool woods, and gently
billowing farmland. The crystal-clear Baltic light
gives an intensity to the island's colors, and you'll
stop often to take it all in: brightly painted cottages

and boats bobbing in the harbor; dark green firs
and light green meadows; the endless blue-gray of
the water. Even the salty tang of sea air and heady
pine aromas are in sharp focus. And it's quiet.
Mostly, the only sound is the rustle of leaves in
the sea breeze and the hum of your tires on
smooth tarmac.

Bornholm has 143 miles (230 km) of well-
surfaced cycle routes, much of them traffic-free
paths and former rail trails. The circular Route 10 is

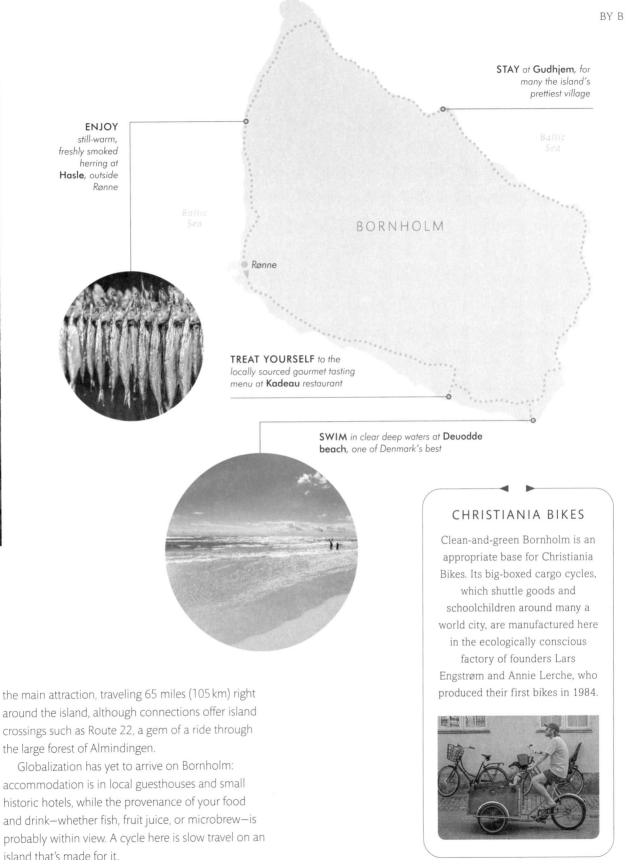

STAY at **Gudhjem**, for many the island's prettiest village

ENJOY *still-warm, freshly smoked herring at* **Hasle**, *outside Rønne*

Baltic Sea

BORNHOLM

Baltic Sea

Rønne

TREAT YOURSELF *to the locally sourced gourmet tasting menu at* **Kadeau** *restaurant*

SWIM *in clear deep waters at* **Deuodde beach**, *one of Denmark's best*

CHRISTIANIA BIKES

Clean-and-green Bornholm is an appropriate base for Christiania Bikes. Its big-boxed cargo cycles, which shuttle goods and schoolchildren around many a world city, are manufactured here in the ecologically conscious factory of founders Lars Engstrøm and Annie Lerche, who produced their first bikes in 1984.

the main attraction, traveling 65 miles (105 km) right around the island, although connections offer island crossings such as Route 22, a gem of a ride through the large forest of Almindingen.

Globalization has yet to arrive on Bornholm: accommodation is in local guesthouses and small historic hotels, while the provenance of your food and drink—whether fish, fruit juice, or microbrew—is probably within view. A cycle here is slow travel on an island that's made for it.

⑬

EV 10: The Baltic States

LOCATION Estonia, Latvia, and Lithuania **START/FINISH** Tallinn/Nida
DISTANCE 955 miles (1,537 km) **TIME** 2 weeks **DIFFICULTY** Moderate
INFORMATION https://en.eurovelo.com/ev10

Pedal along the coastline of the three Baltic countries on this seductive section of the mammoth EuroVelo 10. Expect quiet roads and a real insight into the local way of life.

The three Baltic states—namely, from north to south, Estonia, Latvia, and Lithuania—are often misunderstood or overlooked, seen by some as lands of cheap vacations, or a cartographic blind spot between Western Europe, Scandinavia, and Russia. Naturally, the reality of these proud, history-rich countries is an infinitely layered thing, making this long-distance ride along their interconnected coastlines a deeply rewarding one. If you're looking for a corner of the continent that offers scenery, culture, and a distinct sense of character—with little in the way of crowds and much in the way of wild camping options—you're very much in the right place.

This route actually forms part of the colossal 5,282-mile (8,500-km) EV 10 circuit, which leads right the way around the Baltic Sea coastline via Scandinavia and Poland, so you can think of this shorter, tri-nation section as a more-than-worthy taster of a far longer coastal ride. That said, you'd be wrong to see it as purely a seaside cycle—much of the route veers slightly away from the coast itself, through the sedate ▶

The immense Curonian Spit, a UNESCO World Heritage site

Above Cycling through forest in Klaipėda, Lithuania **Right** Sunset over Rīga's Old Town

THE EUROVELO NETWORK

If EuroVelo 10 piques your interest in long-distance cycle trails across Europe, you're in luck—there's plenty more where that came from. The EuroVelo network comprises 17 different routes, totaling more than 56,250 miles (90,000 km) and collectively covering almost every corner of the continent, from the balmy shores of Malta to the extreme Arctic north of Norway, and from the Black Sea coast of Bulgaria to the mountains of the French Pyrenees.

pinewoods and farms of the Baltic countryside—but the briny tang of the waves is never far away.

This is evident from the very start. After leaving the cobblestoned Estonian capital of Tallinn, you head west toward Haapsalu and the ferry across to the islands of the Moonsund archipelago, a UNESCO Biosphere Reserve. Cycle along the Baltic beaches of Saaremaa before heading back to the mainland and the resort town of Pärnu, known as Estonia's Summer Capital. Wide-open rural views soon return, as the Latvian border approaches to the south.

After the well-oiled outdoor infrastructure of the Estonian section, the Latvian stretch—while rich in sweeping scenery and bucolic atmosphere—is a little less slick, both in terms of signage and facilities. If you're riding in summer, however, those long Baltic evenings will give you ample time to find the perfect wild-camping spot, where your only company is likely to be the call of birdlife and the murmur of the maritime breeze.

A series of small settlements and serene roads leads you into capital city Rīga—all Gothic spires and lively squares—then later through the spa resort of Jūrmala, the river-laced town of Kuldīga, and the prison and former Soviet military base of Karosta. As an arm of the Atlantic Ocean that laps the shores of some nine separate countries, the Baltic Sea is an enormous body of water, and you'll get a fuller sense of its scale as you travel along the Latvian coast.

By the time you reach Lithuania, having racked up countless more revolutions past mellow woods and long beaches, you're not far from journey's end. Indeed, once you've made your way along the narrow causeway of the Curonian Spit—a natural thread of sand surrounded by seawater and held together by pine trees—the little village of Nida represents a memorable finish line, a mere whisper from the Russian territory of Kaliningrad.

another way

Rather be on two feet? The 1,338-mile (2,141-km) Forest Trail opened in 2021, linking the Dutch city of The Hague with the Estonian capital of Tallinn and passing through all three Baltic nations.

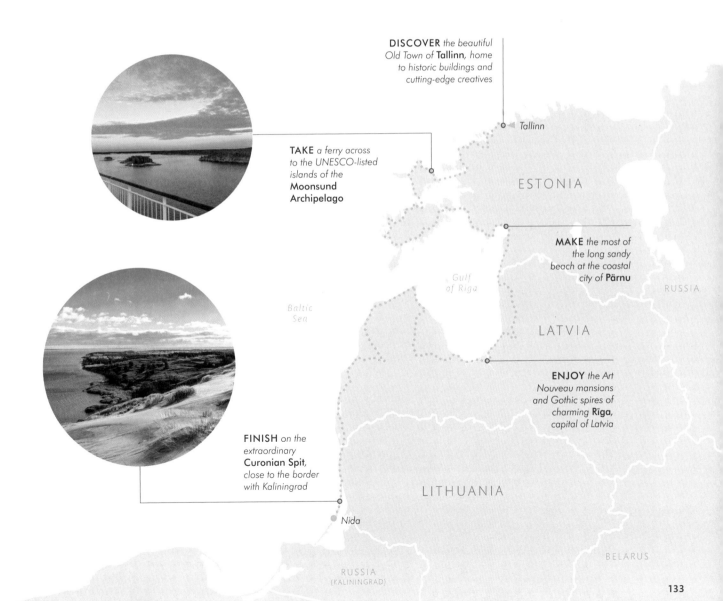

DISCOVER *the beautiful Old Town of* **Tallinn**, *home to historic buildings and cutting-edge creatives*

Tallinn

ESTONIA

TAKE *a ferry across to the UNESCO-listed islands of the* **Moonsund Archipelago**

MAKE *the most of the long sandy beach at the coastal city of* **Pärnu**

RUSSIA

Gulf of Riga

Baltic Sea

LATVIA

ENJOY *the Art Nouveau mansions and Gothic spires of charming* **Rīga**, *capital of Latvia*

FINISH *on the extraordinary* **Curonian Spit**, *close to the border with Kaliningrad*

LITHUANIA

Nida

RUSSIA (KALININGRAD)

BELARUS

⑭ Trail of Masurian Legends

LOCATION Poland **START/FINISH** Pozezdrze (loop) **DISTANCE** 60 miles (100 km)
TIME 2 days **DIFFICULTY** Moderate to challenging; remote unsigned stretches,
GPS recommended **INFORMATION** www.greenvelo.pl; storyboards en route

*An off-piste, sometimes spooky immersion into a land of myths and
legends, this ride offers a glimpse of Eastern Europe's ancient sagas
on remote lanes and forest roads where nature reigns.*

Poland's unspoiled northeastern corner is a remote
area of lakes, marshes, forests, and meadows—and
legends. Here, fantasy and reality merge: stories
abound of visitors to Regułówka being haunted
by a mysterious black dog; of evil spirits lurking in
Gębałka; and the ominous "Flux" that inhabits Lake
Wolisko. This circular trail visits 30 or so places that
feature in the area's folk tales, collected from local
people after World War II. Each one is marked by
a sculpture and storyboard.

The terrain isn't flat, especially in the northern
part of the Borecka Forest, but the rewards for
nature lovers are big. There are plenty of wild
animals to spot, notably European bison (seen more
frequently on the labels of Żubr beer bottles), who
thrive here. Head to the village of Wolisko, deep in
the forest, for the best chance of seeing them.

It's remarkable how far away from it all your
bike can take you in a day or two; picnicking by the
area's largest lake, Gołdapiwo, you'll likely have the
whole place to yourself. The village of Pozezdrze is
about as connected as it gets up here, and makes
a good start or end point for your journey into a
Poland of folklore and fairy tales.

*Mist creeping through
the trees of the
Borecka Forest*

another way

*To enjoy Poland's more modern
side, the Baltic Route north of
Gdańsk runs for 28 off-road (but
paved) miles (45 kilometers) from
Puck to the beach resort of Hel,
along a narrow sand spit that
extends far out to sea.*

(15)

The Elbe

LOCATION Germany **START/FINISH** Dresden/Hamburg **DISTANCE** 375 miles (600 km) **TIME** 10 days **DIFFICULTY** Easy **INFORMATION** www.elbe-cycle-route.com

Embark on a gentle ride through an often-turbulent period of history that generated some of Central Europe's most extraordinary achievements in music, art, and architecture.

Slicing northern Europe in two as it maneuvers from the mountains of the Czech Republic to the North Sea marshes, the Elbe lays claim to Germany's most popular cycle route. This stretch is a living museum. At one end lies Dresden, Germany's great capital of music and arts, its Baroque buildings laboriously reconstructed after World War II. At the other is Hamburg, a business heavyweight that pulses with galleries and modern concert halls. And in between: a parade of storybook medieval towns and villages apparently unchanged since the Protestant church broke away here 500 years ago.

Along the German Elbe, the past opens like a pop-up book. Stop for lunch in a colorful market square and listen to the locals' tales about life in the old East Germany—the Elbe was part of the Iron Curtain, and some evidence remains. But Germany is never serious for long. Keep an eye out for the marquees of village fêtes, park your bike, and join in the fun: hearty local food and drink; live bands; convivial chat. The Elbe can unite as well as divide.

STORK VILLAGE

Rühstädt, in the Brandenburg section of the Elbe cycle path, is officially known as "Stork Village." Every year, breeding pairs of the giant birds return from their wintering grounds to the dozens of room-size nests that sit on chimneys, rooftops, and posts around the village. Watch—from restaurant tables—as the parents shuttle back and forth to feed their young, clacking noisily as they do so.

Windmills lining the watery horizon around Alblasserdam

Molen Fietsroute Kinderdijk

LOCATION Netherlands **START/FINISH** Alblasserdam (loop) **DISTANCE** 26 miles (42 km) **TIME** 3 hours
DIFFICULTY Easy **INFORMATION** www.kinderdijk.com; the World Heritage site is normally open 9:30 a.m.–5:30 p.m.

Enjoy a relaxed ride through a classic Dutch landscape of watery meadows, old farms, and riverside willows, taking in the 19 traditional windmills of the Kinderdijk UNESCO World Heritage site.

Apart from clogs and tulips, nothing says the Netherlands as much as a windmill. And here, amid the drains, dykes, and ditches of UNESCO-listed Kinderdijk, there are windmills galore. This route runs in a clockwise circuit from Alblasserdam, and while there's plenty of enjoyment to be had in the tranquil polder setting that accompanies the ride, the majority of the main sights are clustered together shortly after you cycle out of town.

Turning onto the trail that bisects the waters of Het Nieuwe Waterschap, you're immediately into an avenue of mighty *molens* (windmills), standing proud into the wind. On one side, the stone mills of the Nederwaard; on the other, the wooden mills of the Overwaard, their conical tops covered in thatch.

Both rows work together to pump water from the Lower Basin—this might be a World Heritage site, but it is still very much a living landscape. Take a moment to hop off your saddle and listen to the creaking of the blades, their ground sails almost scraping the ground with every monumental turn.

Pop in to see the millers at work—the family at windmill number 5 are the tenth generation of a Kinderdijk miller dynasty, who can trace their lineage here back to 1746—then pedal on to the *Alles Heeft een Tijd*, a restored barge that screens short films on the water system of the Alblasserwaard and the impacts climate change can have on this exposed region of the Netherlands. Beyond lies the polder countryside, and more magnificent mills.

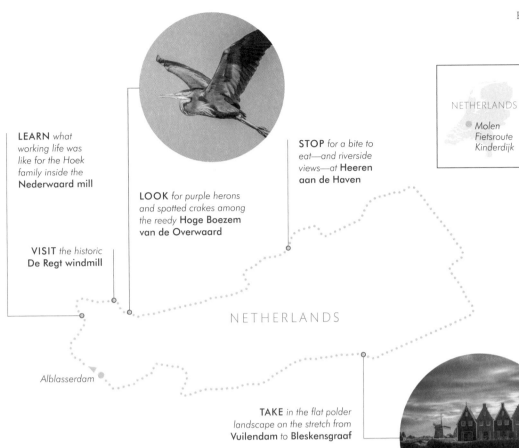

NETHERLANDS

Molen
Fietsroute
Kinderdijk

LEARN *what working life was like for the Hoek family inside the* **Nederwaard mill**

LOOK *for purple herons and spotted crakes among the reedy* **Hoge Boezem van de Overwaard**

STOP *for a bite to eat—and riverside views—at* **Heeren aan de Haven**

VISIT *the historic* **De Regt windmill**

NETHERLANDS

Alblasserdam

TAKE *in the flat polder landscape on the stretch from* **Vuilendam** *to* **Bleskensgraaf**

Passing the stone windmills of the Nederwaard

THE ROOT OF DUTCH DEMOCRACY

In the 13th century, Count Floris V of Holland ordered the founding of District Water Boards, to bring the locals together in an effort to keep the waters at bay. Three water boards were founded here (Alblasserwaard, Overwaard, and Nederwaard), each with a director who was elected by a vote—thus kick-starting a democratic tradition that still determines how the Netherlands is governed today.

The Afsluitdijk disappearing into the distance of the Zuiderzee

⑰ LF Kustroute

LOCATION Netherlands **START/FINISH** Cadzand-Bad/Bad Nieuweschans **DISTANCE** 379 miles (610 km) **TIME** 11 days **DIFFICULTY** Easy **INFORMATION** www.lfkustroute.nl.com

Tracking the North Sea coast from one Dutch border (Belgium) to the next (Germany), the LF Kustroute is 11 stages of wind-in-your-hair, salt-on-your-skin pedaling through one of the least densely populated parts of the Netherlands. Long stretches of dunes punctuate the route, forming a sandy foreground to the islands of South Holland and Zeeland, while seaside resorts, artists' colonies, and traditional "mound" villages—built on hills of earth and manure—provide charming pit stops en route. This being the Netherlands, there are plenty of dykes to cycle along as you work your way up to Bad Nieuweschans, notably the Afsluitdijk, although the most momentous crossings might just be along the series of defensive dams that protect the exposed mainland here from North Sea floods—the imposing Oosterscheldekering, or Eastern Scheldt Storm Surge Barrier, is the largest and best-known link in this remarkable system.

⑱ The Moselle

LOCATION Luxembourg and Germany **START/FINISH** Schengen (loop) **DISTANCE** 70 miles (112 km) **TIME** 2 days **DIFFICULTY** Easy **INFORMATION** www.visitluxembourg.com

Rising in France's Vosges mountains before meandering northeast to Koblenz, the Moselle is one of Europe's prettiest rivers. And its central stretch along the Luxembourg–Germany border is perhaps the most beautiful of all.

This cycling trail begins in Schengen, a little-known border village with a world-famous name. Head north on the Luxembourg side of the Moselle to follow a riverside path that gently winds through charming villages backed by lush vineyards. Before you know it, you'll be across the German border and into Trier, a city with stunning Roman remains, including a blackened city gate and vast amphitheater.

After a good breakfast on day two, jump in the saddle and head back south; this time on the German side of the river. This is a more rural stretch, so stop often to soak up the stunning scenery and sip a small Riesling at a village *winzer*, before crossing borders again back into Schengen.

> ### THE SCHENGEN AGREEMENT
>
> Signed in 1985 in the border village of the same name, the Schengen Agreement allowed free travel between five neighboring Western European countries: Luxembourg, Belgium, France, the Netherlands, and West Germany. Today, the Schengen Area comprises no less than 26 European countries, stretching from Iceland to Greece.

The medieval Arche des Grands Prés spanning the Loir in Vendôme

⑲ Loir Valley

LOCATION France **START/FINISH** St-Éman/ Angers **DISTANCE** 200 miles (320 km) **TIME** 5 days **DIFFICULTY** Easy **INFORMATION** www. loir-valley.com

Good news for cyclists: this ride is (in principle) all downhill. This little-known gem of a route follows the Loir River, from source to mouth, as it meanders west across northern France. Even better, these quiet country roads serve up the classic rural-France experience on a plate, often literally. Lunch might be a waterside picnic with village-bakery baguette and local produce from the morning market; dinner could just as easily be a rustic bistro improvisation as a Michelin-star gourmet experience, washed down with wine from the vineyards you just rode past.

The lazy pace lets you explore: stop off at stone villages, abbeys and châteaux, nature reserves, and even cave-dwellings (the latter found in the steep-sided valleys after the grand island city of Vendôme). A night in the castle at Château de Durtal, or in the safari lodge at La Flèche amid bears and wolves, can add a touch of magic, before the river—and your route—runs out, its waters flowing into the mighty Loire.

⑳ Vélomaritime

LOCATION France **START/FINISH** Roscoff/ Mont-St-Michel **DISTANCE** 265 miles (430 km) **TIME** 9 days **DIFFICULTY** Moderate; brief climbs **INFORMATION** www.lavelomaritime.com

The northwest lands of Brittany have a different feel to the rest of France, perhaps most impressively in the giant natural sculpture park of its rugged pink-granite coast. Cycling the westernmost section of the Vélomaritime leads through attractive port towns and charming inland Celtic villages. You can snack on boat-fresh seafood, crêpes, or slices of butter cake, all good fodder for the rides from one mysterious megalith to the next.

Climbs are short—the altitude never exceeds 328 ft (100 m) or so—and the sea views, particularly at the cliffs of Cap Fréhel and over the Emerald Coast, are consistently superb. The route climaxes at the striking walled town of St-Malo, the oyster village of Cancale, and— entering Normandy—the extraordinary part-time-island commune that is Mont-St-Michel.

The incredible island of Mont-St-Michel, the end point for this coastal section of the Vélomaritime

(21)

Mont Ventoux

LOCATION France **START/FINISH** Bédoin/Mont Ventoux **DISTANCE** 13½ miles (21.5 km)
TIME 1½–2½ hours to the top **DIFFICULTY** Very challenging; steep ascents in weather-exposed terrain **INFORMATION** www.clubcinglesventoux.org; road open mid-Apr–mid-Nov

Follow in the tire tracks of Tour de France heroes at Mont Ventoux. This is the toughest bike ride in Provence, but reaching the top earns you sublime views and serious bragging rights.

Cycling in Provence isn't just about pedaling through lavender fields and seaside towns. The region's steep hills can put even hardened cyclists to the test—and the most brutal ascent is up Mont Ventoux.

Standing 6,266 ft (1,910 m) tall, Ventoux is known as the Géant de Provence (Giant of Provence). There are three ways up, all of which require tackling unrelenting uphills (with an average gradient of 7.5 percent) while being buffeted by the chilly mistral wind. The Bédoin Route, spanning a grueling 13½ miles (21.5 km), is the true test of whether you can sweat it out like a Tour de

France rider. The route begins easily enough, but it isn't long before your thighs start burning. The road snakes upward through forests, with no switchbacks to give your stinging leg muscles a break. Pace yourself: heat exhaustion and dehydration are dangerously common.

Once you're above the tree line, the scenery shifts to bone-white limestone, and you're at the mercy of the wind all the way to the top. Reaching the summit is exhilarating, but take a moment to admire the panoramic views, from the Alps to the Mediterranean, and to get ready for that knuckle-whitening descent.

another way

If you want to achieve membership of the legendary Club des Cinglés ("Crazy Club"), you'll need to cycle all three routes—Bédoin, Sault, and Malaucène—in 24 hours.

Enjoying the descent of the Bédoin Route

(22)

Cider Houses of the Basque Country

LOCATION Spain **START/FINISH** San Sebastian/Astigarraga **DISTANCE** Varies **TIME** 2–3 days **DIFFICULTY** Easy-going **INFORMATION** www. sagardoa.eus

San Sebastian is one of the most celebrated gourmet destinations in Europe, but more tasty treats await in the surrounding fields, a little-known land of deep-rooted cider rituals.

The cider house holds a special place in the Basque Country, not that many visitors would know it. Straw-yellow when held up to the light, the naturally fermented drink is produced in *sagardotegi*, family-run cider houses that are central to community life and identity. On the shout of *"Txotx!,"* a toothpick-size spigot is plucked from a gigantic chestnut barrel and a golden arc of apple cider gushes from the wooden drum, with the amassed revelers rushing haphazardly to fill their glasses. It's a tradition that started in the 15th century, and today 80 *sagardotegi* remain defiantly open—Astigarraga, outside San Sebastian, has become something of a cider Shangri-la.

Handily, the Basque Country Cider House Association has mapped plenty of ways to dip in and out of this unique gastronomic experience. Pick three or four cider houses to try, and take it easy on a slow-paced route along back roads that most of Spain has forgotten. The Basques say *"Gutxi baina sarri"* (A little, but often), so pace yourself, especially if your trip coincides with the annual cider festival, a routine that creates chaos and jubilation in equal measure.

A farmhouse amid lush green fields in the Basque countryside

HISTORY OF BASQUE CIDER-MAKING

Cider-making was first documented in the Basque Country in the 11th century; 400 years later, the Basques decided to replace drinking water onboard whaling ships with cider, and the currency of the *sagardotegi* soared. By the 18th century, there were some 2,000 farms across the Gipuzkoa region alone. Numbers have dwindled since, but the tradition very much lives on.

(23)

Valle del Jerte

LOCATION Spain **START/FINISH** Barco de Ávila/
Plasencia **DISTANCE** 45 miles (70 km) **TIME** 5 hours
DIFFICULTY Moderate **INFORMATION** www.spain.
info/en/discover-spain/jerte-valley-caceres; buses
take bagged bikes

*This Spanish natural wonder delivers a
springtime feast for the eyes—and the
stomach—in a thrilling freewheel.*

For ten days from late March to early April each year,
the Valle del Jerte in lofty, dry, central Spain provides
one of the country's most spectacular natural sights.
The blossoming of two million cherry trees here
turns the long, straight mountainsides snowdrift-
white—a show that's best enjoyed by bike.

The steady climb from the village of Barco
de Ávila takes you to the summit viewpoint at
Tornavacas, after which it's a 3,280-ft (1-km) descent
through those unending cherry orchards. The N-110
runs all the way; side roads offer a more intimate
alternative, but the main road is never that busy, the
surface is good and gradients are even.

Don't freewheel all the way to Plasencia too
quickly, though, as interesting as the walled historic
town is. In season, the dozen or so villages and
towns along the valley buzz with parties—markets,
tastings, open-air fiestas—celebrating those prized
picota cherries. The delightful staples of Spanish
cycle-touring are here all year—*chocolate con churros*
from a café, tapas and drinks from a bar, fixed-price
set meals al fresco in a village square—but from
March to May there's that extra fruity flourish.

*Cherry blossoms turning
the Valle del Jerte—and
its roadsides—white
during spring*

Riding through the rocky Tabernas Desert near Almería

(24) Alto de Velefique

LOCATION Spain **START/FINISH** Tabernas/Alto de Velefique **DISTANCE** 20 miles (30 km) **TIME** 3 hours **DIFFICULTY** Challenging **INFORMATION** www.epicroadrides. com/cycling-spain/almeria/alto-de-velefique-tabernas

An undercelebrated climb that rivals any of France's iconic Alpine passes, this multi-hairpin ascent from southern Spanish deserts up to the Alto de Velefique sees virtually no traffic—not even other cyclists.

The arid wastelands around Tabernas, north of Almería, look like the deserts of Arizona—the 1960s "spaghetti westerns" starring Clint Eastwood were in fact filmed right here—and make a suitably parched backdrop for the ascent of the Alto de Velefique. The long, hot, lonely haul up the 20 perfect hairpins of the AL-3102 is one of Europe's most spectacular and little-known road-cycling challenges. There are no roadside bars once you leave behind the whitewashed houses of the tiny old mining town of Velefique. There's nothing for miles, in fact, but mountain scrub and the occasional prickly pear bush— and, on the blue-gray tarmac, graffitied messages to cycling legends who have dragged themselves up here in races past.

Toward the top, the copses of conifers—and the cool mountain air—come as a welcome surprise. A short section of track leads to the peak proper, from where the view over the distant ginger peaks is vast, gauzy, and austere. Traffic up here is unlikely; you'll probably have this far-flung rooftop to yourself, the lone star of your own movie masterpiece.

another way

Not far from the Alto de Velefique, Spain claims Europe's highest paved road: the Pico de Veleta, at 11,148 ft (3,398 m). This most epic of road-cycling climbs starts at Granada (at 2,461 ft/750 m) and reaches the summit 25 miles (40 km) later.

The Jardín del Túria and Valencia's spectacular City of Arts and Sciences

25 Jardín del Túria

LOCATION Spain **START/FINISH** Parque de Cabecera/Ciudad de las Artes y las Ciencias **DISTANCE** 5½ miles (9 km) **TIME** 1 hour **DIFFICULTY** Easy **INFORMATION** www. visitvalencia.com

Valencianos are rightly proud of the Jardín del Túria, a magnificent ribbon of gardens that follows the former course of the Río Túria, curling around the Old Town and running down toward the sea. After severe flooding in the 1950s, the river was diverted south of the city, and now locals and tourists alike come here to jog and bike along its tree-lined cycle paths.

Leafy Parque de Cabecera, at its western end, gives a good idea of how the Río Túria would have once looked. From here, it's a relaxed pedal past monasteries and glass-domed music venues and under a series of striking bridges—watch for the Puente de las Flores, covered in over 10,000 flowers. If the ride itself is wonderfully low-key, the ending is spectacular: Santiago Calatrava's City of Arts and Sciences, a dazzling ensemble of cutting-edge architecture, is one of the most stunning sights in Spain.

26 Adige Cycle Path

LOCATION Italy **START/FINISH** Resia Pass/ Verona **DISTANCE** 174 miles (280 km) **TIME** 3–4 days **DIFFICULTY** Easy **INFORMATION** www. visittrentino.info

The scenic Adige Cycle Path begins at the Resia Pass, close to the Austrian border, and meanders down the Dolomites toward Lake Garda and on to Verona. It's easy, perfect for a first taste of a multi-day cycling trip. The route passes wonderful mountain landscapes of granite peaks, peppered here and there with Alpine meadows, home to grazing livestock. It follows the course of the Adige River, which roars its way through the Venosta Valley, passing sleepy villages dotted with vineyards and apple and apricot orchards, before reaching Bolzano. From here, cycle south along the lower Adige Valley, stopping off for a refreshing dip in Lake Caldaro before pedaling on to the medieval city of Trento. The route ends, dramatically, in fair Verona.

another way

The Giro del Vino 50 winds its way through the Rotaliana plain between Trento and Bolzano in the verdant Adige Valley, passing delightful vineyards (stop off for a little wine tasting en route) and charming villages.

Peaceful Piazza Duomo, Trento

Streams gushing down into a valley in the Tux and Zillertal Alps

(27) Passo dello Stelvio

LOCATION Italy **START/FINISH** Prato/Passo dello Stelvio **DISTANCE** 15½ miles (25 km) **TIME** 2–4 hours **DIFFICULTY** Challenging **INFORMATION** www.vinschgau.net; open end May–end Oct

Dubbed the "Queen of the Alpine roads," the Passo dello Stelvio is a masterpiece of engineering, built between 1820 and 1825 to connect the Italian region of Lombardy to the rest of the Austrian empire. At 9,049 ft (2,758 m), it's the highest pass road in the Italian Alps, and one of the most challenging—and famous—climbs in the country. Join the avid cyclists who flock here in summer to tackle the 48 hairpin turns that zigzag up the mountainside; as you climb up toward the Swiss border, you'll be rewarded with dramatic mountain scenery and magnificent views of the glacier and rock formations of the Ortles mountain range. It's extremely popular among motorists, too—TV host and car enthusiast Jeremy Clarkson was sufficiently impressed to name it the best road in the world in an episode of *Top Gear*—so your best bet for a care-free ride is to tackle the pass's switchback turns on Stelvio Bike Day, when the road is closed to motorized vehicles.

(28) Zillertal High Road

LOCATION Austria **START/FINISH** Ried im Zillertal/Hippach **DISTANCE** 22 miles (35 km) **TIME** 1 day **DIFFICULTY** Challenging **INFORMATION** www.zillertaler-hoehenstrasse. com; open Jun–early Oct, snow permitting

Throwing you in at the Tyrolean deep end, this long, steep mountain climb opens up sensational views of the Tux and Zillertal Alps. Built in the 1960s to help farmers manage their pastures, the lightly trafficked route is a full-on day of road cycling, taking you from valley to peak as it loops and curves dramatically from Ried im Zillertal, at 1,879 ft (573 m), up to an altitude of 6,627 ft (2,020 m). The peaceful mountain scenery will make you want to yodel out loud, with cows grazing lazily in meadows freckled with flowers, dark-timber chalets clinging to steep hillsides, and pine forests sweeping up to glaciated peaks. Your reward for the grueling climb? A slice of Austrian life and cheese-rich mountain grub in the old-fashioned taverns that help break up the ride.

29

Giro Region 31

LOCATION Austria **START/FINISH** Rattenberg (loop) **DISTANCE** 72 miles (116 km)
TIME 1 day **DIFFICULTY** Very challenging **INFORMATION** www.tyrol.com has a
guide to the route; Jun–Sept make for the most spectacular riding conditions

*The beautiful
village of Alpbach,
deep within the
Tyrol region*

*Starting from Rattenberg, this triple-loop ride through Austria's Tyrol
region takes in lush meadows, traditional farmhouses, towering
mountains, and the country's prettiest village.*

The greatest rewards require the hardest work. At
least that's the mantra you'll find yourself repeating as
you tackle the 8,200 near-vertical feet (2,500 m) of
ascent packed into this thigh-burningly challenging
circuit. From the start and end point at Rattenberg,
a charming medieval town that takes the crown as
Austria's smallest, this route loops into the mountains
of Tyrol, showcasing Alpine landscapes better known
when buried under a foot of snow. Instead, catch

them in their glorious summer attire: think flower-
strewn meadows, glittering lakes, and lush valleys
dotted with cute-as-a-button villages.

The adventure begins at the Notburga-Brunnen
fountain at the center of Rattenberg. Warm your legs
with the first climb: a steady 5 miles (8 km) of ascent
that passes through scatterings of traditional wooden
chalets where pastel-hued geraniums peek out from
window boxes. From here, you'll roll into Alpbach, a

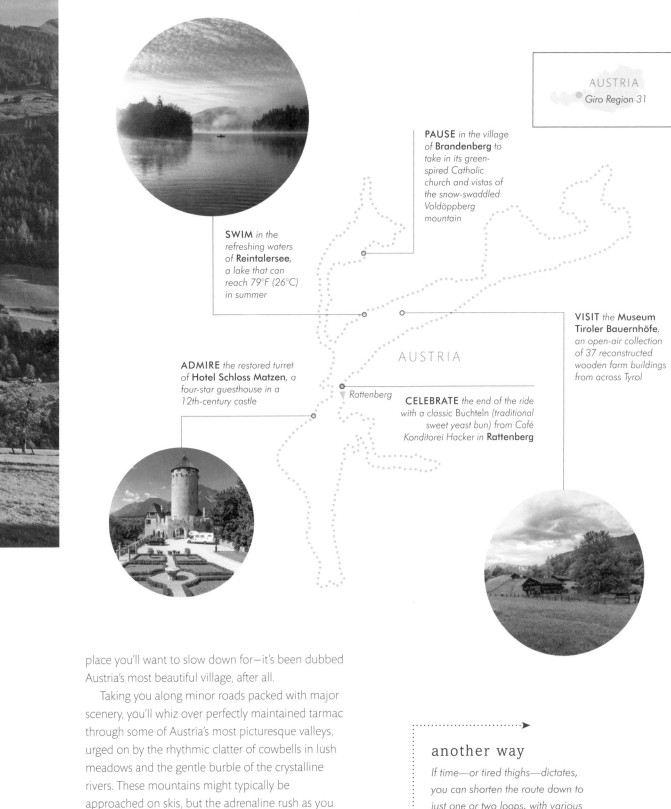

PAUSE in the village of **Brandenberg** to take in its green-spired Catholic church and vistas of the snow-swaddled Voldöppberg mountain

SWIM in the refreshing waters of **Reintalersee**, a lake that can reach 79°F (26°C) in summer

AUSTRIA
Giro Region 31

VISIT the **Museum Tiroler Bauernhöfe**, an open-air collection of 37 reconstructed wooden farm buildings from across Tyrol

AUSTRIA

ADMIRE the restored turret of **Hotel Schloss Matzen**, a four-star guesthouse in a 12th-century castle

Rattenberg

CELEBRATE the end of the ride with a classic Buchteln (traditional sweet yeast bun) from Café Konditorei Hacker in **Rattenberg**

place you'll want to slow down for—it's been dubbed Austria's most beautiful village, after all.

Taking you along minor roads packed with major scenery, you'll whiz over perfectly maintained tarmac through some of Austria's most picturesque valleys, urged on by the rhythmic clatter of cowbells in lush meadows and the gentle burble of the crystalline rivers. These mountains might typically be approached on skis, but the adrenaline rush as you power down each and every descent, just a blurred figure on two wheels, is all the more rewarding knowing you've got there under your own steam.

another way

If time—or tired thighs—dictates, you can shorten the route down to just one or two loops, with various roads giving the opportunity to bow out of the longer circuit by taking you back to Rattenberg.

An old windmill standing alone in the rolling fields of South Moravia

30

Iron Curtain Cycle Route

LOCATION Czech Republic **START/FINISH** Aš/ Břeclav **DISTANCE** 540 miles (860 km) **TIME** 2 weeks **DIFFICULTY** Moderate to easy **INFORMATION** www. cyclistswelcome.cz

This borderlands odyssey of nature reserves and historic towns—plus sobering remains of the Iron Curtain itself—cuts right across Eastern Europe.

The "Iron Curtain" was a rigidly enforced border that separated Western and Eastern Europe following the end of World War II. Its wide stripe down the whole continent was cleared of all settlements, so when the boundary was dismantled after the fall of the Berlin Wall, it fortuitously left a mighty green corridor—which now forms the epic Iron Curtain Cycle Route. As EV13, the route runs for around 6,200 miles (10,000 km) from the Barents Sea, at the far north of the Finnish-Russian border, through 20 countries, to the Black Sea in Turkey.

The EV13's most scenic, varied, and rewarding section lies on the southern Czech border, dipping in and out of Germany and Austria, rarely more than 3 miles (5 km) from the frontier. Nature soon reclaimed the former no-man's-lands here, and wildlife thrives in what is now a 30-mile- (50-km-) wide European Green Belt. Cycling services—cafés and restaurants, ▶

POLAND

EXPLORE superbly preserved historic centers in towns such as **Slavonice**

Aš

CZECH REPUBLIC

COOL *off from the summer heat in Bergwerksee in* **Langau**

SPOT *birds at* **Hohenau's** *wetlands, some of the most pristine in Europe*

GERMANY

VISIT *a winery in* **Znojmo's** *lush vineyards and try the fragrant local whites*

SLOVAKIA

Břeclav

AUSTRIA

EXPERIENCE *what the world might have once looked like on a ride through* **Žofín Primeval Forest**

FREEDOM TRAIL

From the 1960s to the late 1980s, up to 500 people are believed to have died while attempting to flee Eastern Europe over the Czech section of the Iron Curtain. At Mikulov, near the Břeclav end of the route, storyboards along the Freedom Trail chart some of these desperate efforts, including escape attempts by hot-air balloon and tunnel. The 53 people known to have died trying to cross here are each commemorated by an iron post.

picnic areas and rest stops—are discreetly available, and overnights are usually had in characterful old buildings, although many cyclists camp their way along the trail.

The route's mountainous first half clambers through the hilly forests of Bohemia and Bavaria, giving way to the flatter terrain of South Moravia, a land of wine centered around Znojmo, whose historic center is (literally) built on vineyards. The landscape changes by the hour, a shifting backdrop of woods, orchards, scrubland, and wild fields overflowing with poppies.

The pastel-colored facades, whitewashed walls, and red roofs of exquisite little hill towns and villages punctuate the endless green, while thickset monasteries and fortresses, centuries old, stand starkly alone, seemingly in the middle of nowhere. Follow the Švarcenberský Kanál, a navigational channel built to float logs down from the forest; weave your way through Thayatal and Podyjí, two adjoining national parks that claim some of Europe's most stunning natural scenery.

There are plenty of reminders of those divided times en route: the open-air museum in the Nové Hrady Mountains; the bisected train station at Železná Ruda; various monuments to the era and its victims. Perhaps the most striking of all can be found at Čížov, where a section of the old border fence, complete with watchtower, remains intact.

another way

For a three-day self-contained Iron Curtain bike ride, the 100-mile (160-km) Berlin Wall Trail is an easy, varied, circular route in and around the German capital. Memorials remember those who perished, and a few lengths of the original wall and fences remain.

Left *The castle town of Hardegg, Podyjí National Park*
Below *Remnants of the Iron Curtain near Čížov*

Thickset monasteries and fortresses, centuries old, stand starkly alone

(31)

Juliana Loop

LOCATION Slovenia **START/FINISH** Bohinjska Bistrica (loop) **DISTANCE** 180 miles (290 km) **TIME** 1 week **DIFFICULTY** Easy to moderate **INFORMATION** www.slovenia.info

The pretty little island monastery on Lake Bled

Seven stages; a variety of trails, bridges, and tracks; and a colossal ascent through the Julian Alps make this one of the most exciting— and perhaps exhausting—bike trails in Europe.

Strap in for a blockbuster bike ride. This 180-mile (290-km) circular trail in eastern Slovenia has some of the finest scenery in Europe, one of the bluest rivers you'll ever set eyes on, and a few tricky stretches that'll keep you on your toes. Starting and finishing in Bohinjska Bistrica, it glides through valleys and up and over mountain passes that'll take your breath away—as much for their beauty as for their physical challenge—and sees you riding in the

shadow of Mount Triglav, a peak that tops out at nearly 10,000 ft (3,000 m).

Cycle across the Pokljuka Plateau, forested with towering spruce trees, before descending into the Radovna Valley where the handsome town of Radovljica is a welcome respite, with its medieval architecture and brilliant views of the Julian Alps and the Karawanks. Then there's Lake Bled, one of Slovenia's most popular tourist

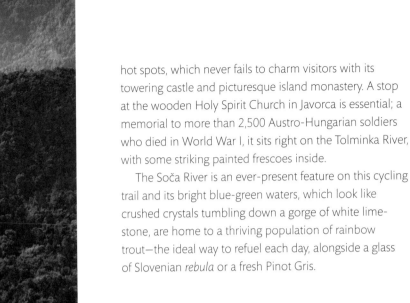

hot spots, which never fails to charm visitors with its towering castle and picturesque island monastery. A stop at the wooden Holy Spirit Church in Javorca is essential; a memorial to more than 2,500 Austro-Hungarian soldiers who died in World War I, it sits right on the Tolminka River, with some striking painted frescoes inside.

The Soča River is an ever-present feature on this cycling trail and its bright blue-green waters, which look like crushed crystals tumbling down a gorge of white limestone, are home to a thriving population of rainbow trout—the ideal way to refuel each day, alongside a glass of Slovenian *rebula* or a fresh Pinot Gris.

THE GOLDHORN

This is the Kingdom of Goldhorn, a fabled golden-horned mountain goat who, according to folklore, could grant access to a trove of treasure atop Mount Triglav. The story goes that after Goldhorn was injured by a hunter, magical flowers sprouted from his spilled blood, and as he tore down the mountainside, the gaping holes left behind filled with water to create what is known today as the Triglav Lakes Valley.

TACKLE *Slovenia's highest mountain pass at 5,285 ft (1,611 m) high*

ITALY

SPEED *down the slopes of* **Kranjska Gora***, the country's top ski resort, overlooked by its highest peak*

AUSTRIA

SAMPLE *Slovenian wine in charming* **Bovec**

LOOK *down over* **Lake Bled***'s glassy waters from a centuries-old castle*

Bohinjska Bistrica

SLOVENIA

SEE *the astonishingly blue-green flow of the mighty* **Soča River**

32

Durmitor National Park

LOCATION Montenegro **START/FINISH** Pluzine/Žabljak **DISTANCE** 30 miles (48 km) **TIME** 1 day **DIFFICULTY** Challenging **INFORMATION** www.visit-montenegro.com/destinations/zabljak/attractions/durmitor

Winding its way through awe-inspiring mountain scenery, this challenging route through Montenegro showcases the dramatic limestone peaks and windswept meadows of this off-the-beaten-track country.

Montenegro's geological wonders are never far away on this ride, which treats adventurous cyclists to some mind-bending scenery. Shortly after leaving the tiny waterside town of Pluzine, you'll get up close and personal with the Piva Gorge, as you take the bridge across its blue lake and ascend through a series of tunnels blasted out of the cliffs.

Eventually, the lofty views of the gorge give way to deciduous woodland and alpine meadows. The foliage becomes sparser as the road winds higher, and the gray karst stone of the Durmitor massif starts to erupt from beneath the greenery. The road tops out at 6,562 ft (nearly 2,000 m), and you'll find yourself wanting to stop regularly, to catch your breath as much as to watch the light dance across Durmitor's rippling limestone peaks. There follows a twisting descent, past shepherds' huts and occasional roaming cattle, to Žabljak. This tiny resort town is the perfect place to take in even more incredible mountain scenery—this time with your feet up.

It's hard to imagine a more scenic place to end than Žabljak's Crno Jezero, where the scene of your adventures—the frosted peaks of Durmitor—are reflected in the lake's glassy surface.

> Watch the light dance across Durmitor's rippling peaks

The bridge crossing Piva Lake, near the Piva Gorge

Left *Monastery of St. Naum* **Above**
Cycling gravel paths along the lakeshore

(33)

Lake Ohrid

LOCATION North Macedonia **START/FINISH** Ohrid/St. Naum **DISTANCE** 19 miles
(30 km) **TIME** 1 day **DIFFICULTY** Easy **INFORMATION** https://ohrid.com.mk

*Byzantine monasteries, sleepy fishing villages, and gorgeous beaches
line the shores of ancient Lake Ohrid, a life-affirming place rich in
beauty, both natural and human-made.*

Ancient history and natural beauty collide on the primordial shores of Lake Ohrid—
one of the oldest lakes in the world, and among the most biodiverse. On this gentle
ride, you'll be immersed in the life that teems around the lake: chamois peer warily
from mountain ridges; red foxes flit through the undergrowth; and the scent of
elder-flowered orchids hangs in the air in spring and summer.

Everywhere, too, is evidence of the human civilization that has thrived here for
thousands of years. The town of Ohrid (like the lake, UNESCO-listed) is known as the
Jerusalem of the Balkans for the religious zeal that permeates its cobbled alleyways—
there are 365 churches here, including several magnificent Byzantine structures. To the
south, the city gives way to somnolent fishing villages clustered around a succession
of sandy bays—pause to dip your feet at Jungle Beach, where the pine forest runs all
the way to the water's edge and restaurants serve trout fresh from the lake.

Beyond here lies the Bay of Bones, where a reconstructed Bronze Age village sits
on stilts on the water—extraordinary architecture, yet surpassed by the Monastery of
St. Naum, which crests the lake's southern shore at the end of the ride.

LAKE OHRID'S BIODIVERSITY

The great age and
depth of Lake Ohrid,
combined with a
relative lack of
pollution, combine to
make it one of the
most biodiverse lakes
in the world, with
some 50 percent of its
fauna found nowhere
else on Earth. These
include the Ohrid
sponge, Ohrid trout,
and various carp.
Amazingly, 85 percent
of the snail species
found here live only in
Lake Ohrid.

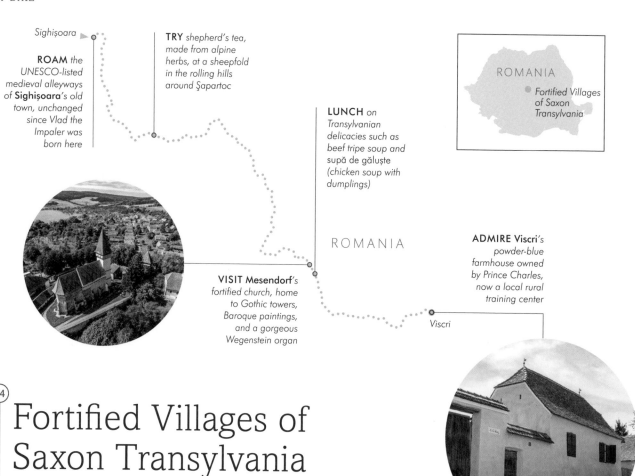

Sighişoara

ROAM the
UNESCO-listed
medieval alleyways
of **Sighişoara**'s old
town, unchanged
since Vlad the
Impaler was
born here

TRY shepherd's tea,
made from alpine
herbs, at a sheepfold
in the rolling hills
around Şapartoc

LUNCH on
Transylvanian
delicacies such as
beef tripe soup and
supă de găluşte
(chicken soup with
dumplings)

ROMANIA

VISIT Mesendorf's
fortified church, home
to Gothic towers,
Baroque paintings,
and a gorgeous
Wegenstein organ

ROMANIA

Fortified Villages
of Saxon
Transylvania

ADMIRE Viscri's
powder-blue
farmhouse owned
by Prince Charles,
now a local rural
training center

Viscri

(34)

Fortified Villages of Saxon Transylvania

LOCATION Romania **START/FINISH** Sighişoara/Viscri **DISTANCE** 30 km (19 miles)
TIME 1 day **DIFFICULTY** Moderate **INFORMATION** The Prince of Wales guesthouse
can be booked at https://zalan.transylvaniancastle.com

*You'll feel like you've pedaled back in time on this ride, as you roll through beech
forests, endless wildflower meadows, and pretty Saxon villages that could be lifted
straight out of the pages of a children's book.*

You're likely to see more horse-drawn carts than cars on
this wonderfully varied route between Sighişoara, the
jewel in Transylvania's crown, and the UNESCO-listed
village of Viscri. The ride starts on paved roads, but that
quickly gives way to gravel, and then dirt in the beech
and oak forests that follow the high contours of the
countryside. These woodlands are home to Europe's
largest population of brown bears—although you're much
more likely to catch a glimpse of a red deer flashing
through the trees, or hear the hoot of a pygmy owl.

Wildflower meadows of bright yellows and pinks usher
you into the village of Mesendorf, which makes a great
stop for a local lunch. As you climb back up into the hills,
hospitable shepherds might treat you to a slice of fresh
cheese and a cup of mountain tea. It's largely downhill
after this point, so sit back and enjoy the descent through
yet more idyllic meadows to Viscri, a gorgeously
traditional Saxon village with a fortified church—a relic of
the 16th century, when the realms of religion and war
were inextricably intertwined. As you cruise into the
cobbled "main street," keep an eye out for the local herd
of cattle returning from their day on the pastures, peeling
off into their owners' gates in an evening ritual that's been
going on for over 800 years.

PRINCE CHARLES IN SAXON TRANSYLVANIA

One of the most prominent landlords in the region is the unlikely figure of the UK's Prince Charles, who bought two houses here in 2006—one in Mălâncrav and one in Viscri. The prince himself still spends a few days a year in the latter; the rest of the time, it serves as a training center, giving local people free instruction in farming, heritage preservation, and traditional handicrafts.

Top The spiky skyline of Sighișoara **Above** A brown bear in the forests of the Carpathian Mountains

35

EV 6: From Budapest to the Black Sea

LOCATION Hungary, Croatia, Serbia, Bulgaria, and Romania
START/FINISH Budapest/Constanța **DISTANCE** 932 miles
(1,500 km) **TIME** 2 weeks **DIFFICULTY** Moderate
INFORMATION https://en.eurovelo.com/ev6; this stretch of
the EV 6 is not as well signposted as the western sections, so
carry maps and research your route carefully beforehand

*This grand tour of southeast Europe sees you
ride through five countries as you follow mighty
waterways from Budapest to the Black Sea.*

It's hard to imagine a grander cycling adventure than the
EuroVelo 6, which, in its entirety, runs all the way across Europe
from west to east. The route's final third, from the Hungarian
capital of Budapest to the shores of the Black Sea at Constanța
in Romania, is EuroVelo at its wildest and least traveled, dotted
with Neolithic monuments and splendid Baroque towns.

Make the most of Budapest's muscle-soothing thermal baths
and dine on Eger wine and Magyar cuisine in the city's fantastic
restaurants, fortifying body and soul before you head off south
into the Hungarian countryside. Following the bend of the
mighty Danube, you'll reach areas of stunning wilderness such
as Gemenc, where boars and stags roam in forests of oak, elm,
ash, and willow, and rare insects like Freyer's purple emperor
butterflies flit through the trees. Crossing into the northeastern
corner of Croatia, you'll have earned a drink at Baranja, where
underground wine cellars have been carved into the sandy
earth. There's more gorgeous landscape in the form of Kopački
Rit, where wooden walkways plot a path above one of Europe's
largest wetlands.

▶

The mighty Danube flowing through Iron Gates Natural Park in Romania

The human landscape here gives the natural one a run for its money. Osijek's old town is a riot of Baroque architecture, while further east, at Vukovar, the prehistoric site of Vučedol exhibits echoes of a culture rich in art, folklore, and shamanistic religion. Your constant companion on this leg of the journey is exquisite Croatian cuisine—you'll find there's no better fuel for whipping along on two wheels than platefuls of *pašticada* (Dalmatian beef stew), while packets of baklava serve not just as the perfect sugar-rich energy boost, but also a reminder of the region's Ottoman past.

Into Serbia, you'll ride in the shadow of the mighty fortress of Petrovaradin and explore modern art galleries in Belgrade—the perfect place to take stock for a day or two, indulge in some of Europe's most raucous nightlife, and delve into the complex collision of Ottoman and Yugoslavian history that characterizes so much of the journey.

Belgrade's cosmopolitanism is soon a distant memory as nature reclaims the trail. At the Iron Gates, the Danube plunges

THE NAMING OF LAKE SREBARNA

Numerous legends describe how Lake Srebarna got its name, which means "silvery." One is that it comes from the reflection of the moon on the lake's surface; another claims that a mythical boat, housing a horde of silver, is hidden on one of the lake's swampier shores.

A third, more historically grounded, theory suggests that it takes its name from Srebrist, an Ottoman khan who died fighting near the lake.

*Below The endless landscapes of southern Bulgaria **Right** Belgrade's Church of St. Sava, one of the largest Orthodox churches in the world*

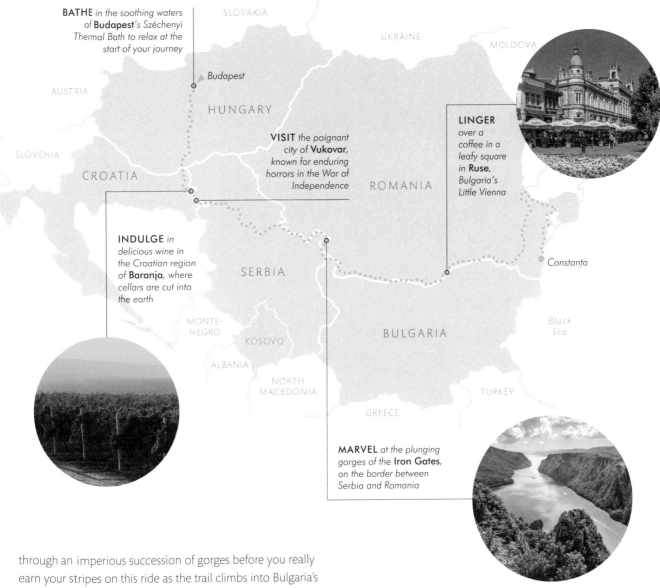

BATHE in the soothing waters of **Budapest**'s Széchenyi Thermal Bath to relax at the start of your journey

SLOVAKIA

UKRAINE

MOLDOVA

AUSTRIA

Budapest

HUNGARY

VISIT the poignant city of **Vukovar**, known for enduring horrors in the War of Independence

ROMANIA

LINGER over a coffee in a leafy square in **Ruse**, Bulgaria's Little Vienna

SLOVENIA

CROATIA

INDULGE in delicious wine in the Croatian region of **Baranja**, where cellars are cut into the earth

SERBIA

Constanţa

MONTE-NEGRO

KOSOVO

BULGARIA

Black Sea

ALBANIA

NORTH MACEDONIA

TURKEY

GREECE

MARVEL at the plunging gorges of the **Iron Gates**, on the border between Serbia and Romania

through an imperious succession of gorges before you really earn your stripes on this ride as the trail climbs into Bulgaria's hilly countryside. Bird-watchers will be in paradise here—the riverbanks are alive with raptors, shelducks, pelicans, and more—while the city of Ruse is well worth lingering for a while. Known as Bulgaria's Little Vienna, this is a place of dreamy spires and Rococo palaces.

Ruse's maximalism is rendered all the more striking by the serene landscapes that follow. Your journey ends on the Danube–Black Sea Canal, passing through wetlands smothered in water lilies and along the reedy shores of Lake Srebarna. You'll finally meet the Black Sea at Constanţa; Orthodox churches, grand mosques, and Greek statues tell the story of Romania's oldest city. It's a fitting finish to a cycle that began, all that time ago, in Hungary's contemporary capital.

another way

After Serbia's Iron Gates, you can choose to cross straight into Romania rather than traveling via Bulgaria—a route that takes you through the Banat Mountains and down into a gentle floodplain beginning at Drobeta Turnu-Severin.

BY RAIL

Let the train take the strain; there can be few finer ways of seeing Europe than from the comfort of a train car. Climb aboard a vintage steam train or a coastal tram. Ride first class or travel on a pass. Whether you're indulging in the nostalgic romance of the Orient Express or trundling through Italy on a sleeper train, you can rest assured you'll always be on the right track.

Previous page The Jacobite train chugging over Glenfinnan Viaduct in the Scottish Highlands

AT A GLANCE
BY RAIL

FINLAND

ESTONIA

LATVIA

LITHUANIA

BELARUS

UKRAINE

MOLDOVA

ROMANIA

SERBIA

KOSOVO

BULGARIA

N. MAC.

GEORGIA

ARMENIA   AZERBAIJAN

GREECE

TURKEY

CYPRUS

KEY TO MAP

Long route ··············

End point ●

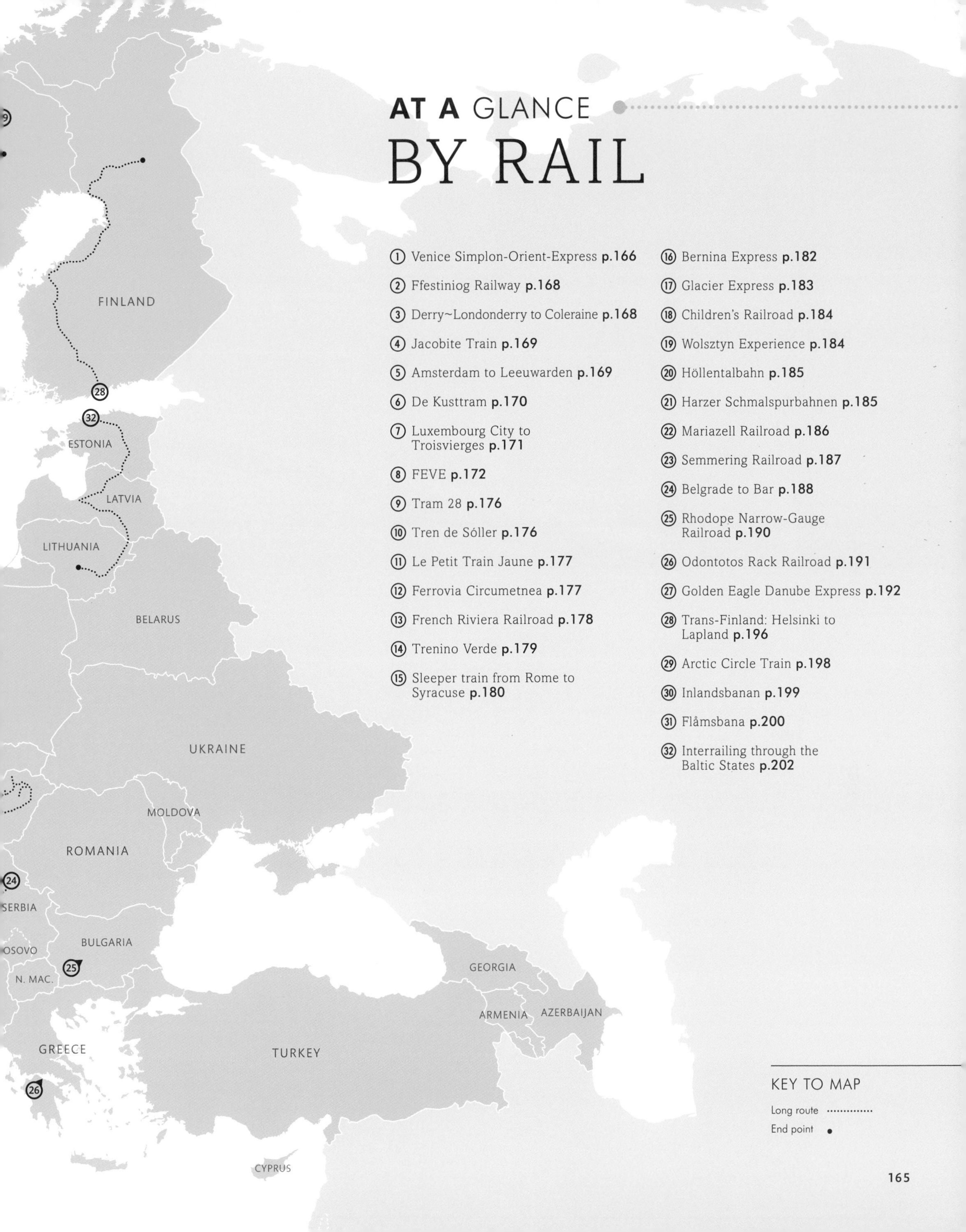

①

Venice Simplon-Orient-Express

The Venice-Simplon-Orient-Express, on its way through Switzerland

LOCATION France to Italy **START/FINISH** Paris/Venice **DISTANCE** 713 miles (1,148 km) **TIME** 18 hours **INFORMATION** www.belmond.com/trains/europe/venice-simplon-orient-express; train runs Mar–Nov

One of the world's most storied train journeys, the Venice Simplon-Orient-Express *conjures images of glamour, style, and* la dolce vita. *Climb aboard and immerse yourself in the golden age of travel.*

Brought vividly to life in novels such as Agatha Christie's *Murder on the Orient Express* and Ian Fleming's *From Russia with Love*, the iconic *Venice Simplon-Orient-Express* train journey from Paris to Venice exudes style and indulgence.

At the Gare de l'Est in Paris, cabin stewards in deep-blue uniforms greet guests, ushering them aboard the gleaming train cars. Step inside and you'll be transported to a bygone era of 1920s decadence. The interiors are the epitome of

luxury, reflecting stunning Art Deco designs, with gorgeous carved marquetry, hand-embroidered fabrics, and opulent silks.

Once the train has pushed off, its comforting, rhythmic sound will lull you into a reverie for the duration of a journey that takes you down through the length of France and then into Switzerland, where you'll be rewarded with archetypal Alpine scenery of quaint villages and snowcapped mountains. Arriving on Italian soil,

you'll glide across the grasslands of Lombardy and the Veneto, reaching Venice in the late afternoon—you can watch the sun set over the Grand Canal, coloring the city pink.

Along the way, expect impeccable service and an exquisite—and bountiful—series of culinary treats: loosen your belt for a four-course dinner, breakfast, a three-course lunch, and, finally, afternoon tea. All you need to do is sit back (in style) and admire the surroundings as you're whisked across Western Europe on one of the world's most iconic train journeys.

YOUR CARRIAGE AWAITS

The train's carriages are steeped in history: King Carol of Romania is said to have held romantic rendezvous in Sleeping Car 3425; the panels in Dining Car 4141 were created by glass designer René Lalique; while Sleeping Car 3309 is part of the original train that in 1929 was stranded for ten days in snow near Istanbul, inspiration for Agatha Christie's *Murder on the Orient Express.*

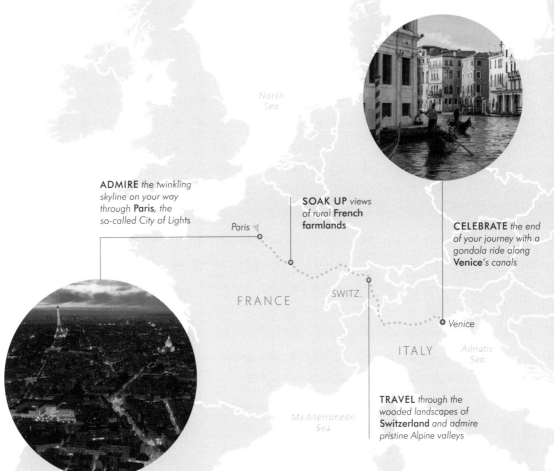

ADMIRE *the twinkling skyline on your way through* **Paris,** *the so-called City of Lights*

SOAK UP *views of rural* **French farmlands**

CELEBRATE *the end of your journey with a gondola ride along* **Venice**'s *canals*

North Sea

Paris

FRANCE

SWITZ.

ITALY

Venice

Adriatic Sea

Mediterranean Sea

TRAVEL *through the wooded landscapes of* **Switzerland** *and admire pristine Alpine valleys*

Mussenden Temple, perched on the cliffs above Benone Strand

② Ffestiniog Railway

LOCATION Wales **START/FINISH** Porthmadog/ Blaenau Ffestiniog **DISTANCE** 13½ miles (21.5 km) **TIME** 1½ hours **INFORMATION** www. festrail.co.uk

The Ffestiniog Railway's heritage steam train serves up scenic drama with a large helping of history as it chugs through Snowdonia's thrilling mountainscape. The world's oldest narrow-gauge railroad opened in 1836 to transport tens of thousands of tons of slate between the mining town of Blaenau Ffestiniog and the harbor down at Porthmadog. Steam trains and a passenger service were introduced in the 1860s, and some of these hardy locomotives still haul the gleaming handcrafted train cars today.

The train leaves peaceful Porthmadog with a whistle and crosses the estuary along the cob, a human-made seawall, before taking the steep climb up a lush, green, wooded valley. Tracing the graceful curve of the tracks (there's even a spiral at Dduallt), it passes lonely station houses and timeless hamlets as the view slowly changes to windswept moorland and rugged mountains. The still waters of Llyn Ystradau announce the beginning of the end of the track, as the train slows to a stop at Blaenau Ffestiniog.

HISTORY OF THE FFESTINIOG RAILWAY

When slate was first industrially quarried in Blaenau Ffestiniog, it was transported to the sea by road and river boat. The rail route was incorporated by an act of Parliament and relied on gravity—and the brave souls who operated the brakes.

③ Derry~Londonderry to Coleraine

LOCATION Northern Ireland **START/FINISH** Derry~Londonderry/Coleraine **DISTANCE** 33 miles (53 km) **TIME** 45 minutes **INFORMATION** www.translink.co.uk; hourly service year-round

Once described by Michael Palin as "one of the most beautiful rail journeys in the world," the rail line from Derry~Londonderry to Coleraine delivers first-class views of Northern Ireland's brooding coastline. It rumbles along mile after mile of shore, clinging to the mudflats around the sweeping southern fringes of Lough Foyle. Look for porpoises breaching the waters and peregrine falcons hovering on the thermals above.

It's at the Benone Strand dunes, however, where the true treasures are to be found. Here lie 7 miles (11 km) of golden sands and—teetering on a wind-buffeted cliff above—the iconic domed roof of the Italian-style Mussenden Temple. You'll catch a quick glimpse before the train slips into the darkness of two tunnels, blasted into the rock below. When you emerge on the other side into the neat streets of Castlerock and then onward to Coleraine, you'll wonder if it was all just a mere figment of your imagination.

4 Jacobite Train

LOCATION Scotland **START/FINISH** Fort William (return) **DISTANCE** 84 miles (135 km) **TIME** 4 hours **INFORMATION** https://westcoastrailways.co.uk; steam train operates twice daily May–Sept & once daily Apr & Oct

Wizards and muggles alike will be spellbound by the views from Scotland's most famous train, the *Jacobite*. Better known as the *Hogwarts Express* in the Harry Potter films, this steam train transported students to the fictional school of Hogwarts. While there's unfortunately no wizarding school at the end of the line, true magic does await, as you rumble loch-side from Fort William to coastal Mallaig, leaving dramatic Highland landscapes of emerald glens and moody mountains in your wake.

Seeing it on the big screen cannot prepare you for the Glenfinnan Viaduct, whose 21 concrete arches curling high above the Finnan River are even more magnificent in the flesh. To the delight of passengers—and the onlookers poised with cameras on the ground below—the train often pauses here, belching steam and granting bewitching views of glittering Loch Shiel and the shoreside Glenfinnan Monument. Whatever your take on magic, the great sorcery of this scenery is such that you'll be a firm believer by the time you reach Mallaig.

Steam spouting from the Jacobite as it passes over Glenfinnan Viaduct

5 Amsterdam to Leeuwarden

LOCATION The Netherlands **START/FINISH** Amsterdam/Leeuwarden **DISTANCE** 68 miles (109 km) **TIME** 2 hours **INFORMATION** www.ns.nl

In spring, the upper decks of the InterCity trains that shuttle across the Netherlands showcase the country in full bloom. The 12,350 acres (5,000 hectares) of tulip fields that grow east of Amsterdam, in the province of Flevoland, offer a kaleidoscope's twist of color, as you head out from the city limits through the Dutch-pancake-flat countryside and along the shoreline of the Markermeer. After the flowers and the flotillas of sailing ships, you might see wild horses as you journey through the Oostvaardersplassen Nature Reserve, or a textbook windmill as the train curves north into Friesland, the Netherlands' most characteristically independent province. The triumphs in this final stretch are the geometric fields that recall the designs of mind-bender M. C. Escher (who grew up in Leeuwarden), and the meditative fresco of creaky canal houses and farmlands where Friesian horses—also native to the area—gallop free.

another way

To see more of the Netherlands, ride the InterCity from Groeningen to Eindhoven, via Utrecht. In such a short time, you'll see every Dutch cliché in the guidebook (windmills, canals, polders, tulips), but also a vast swathe of the country that most travelers miss.

Left *De Kusttram cruising along the seafront*
Above *Strolling along the sands at De Haan*

⑥ De Kusttram

LOCATION Belgium **START/FINISH** De Panne/Knokke-Heist
DISTANCE 42 miles (67 km) **TIME** 2½ hours **INFORMATION**
https://dekusttram.be

Hop aboard the world's longest tramline to discover Belgium's short but mighty North Sea coast, a world of outdoor art, bustling ports, and sandy strands.

Belgium's seaboard isn't very long: it's just 42 miles (67 km) from De Panne, on the French border, to Knokke-Heist, on the Dutch. But it is varied, scenic, and supremely accessible—De Kusttram (Coast Tram) runs the entire length of this sandy shore, year-round, with services leaving every ten minutes or so.

There are 68 stops; just ring the bell when you want to get off. But where? Perhaps start in De Panne, where you can walk around the historic cottages of the Dumont Quarter and into the Westhoek nature reserve's unbroken dunes. Continue to the charming village of Oostduinkerke, where shrimp fishermen still work on horseback, before spending time in cosmopolitan Ostend, Belgium's biggest port—don't miss the Mu.ZEE's extensive collection of fine and modern art and a chance to gorge on the freshest Ostend oysters. Stop at De Haan, to stroll the comely belle-époque seafront. Then finish in Knokke-Heist, to combine browsing antique stores with spotting storks and spoonbills in the brilliantly biodiverse Zwin nature park.

COASTAL CULTURE

Every three years (since 2003), the Beaufort Triennial brings outdoor art to Belgium's beaches and promenades. Almost 40 works have become permanent fixtures, encompassed in the Beaufort Sculpture Park, which extends right along the country's coast. Each installation is easily accessible by Kusttram—hop off at Oostduinkerke Duinpark, for instance, to see *The Wanderer*, or at Mariakerke Bad for *Pillage of the Sea*.

Luxembourg City to Troisvierges

LOCATION Luxembourg **START/FINISH** Luxembourg City **DISTANCE** 80 miles (130 km) **TIME** 2½ hours return **INFORMATION** www.cfl.lu

The Grand Duchy of Luxembourg may fit into France over 200 times, but it packs in an awful lot. Take a (free) train from the capital to explore its forest-covered hills and rich history.

One of Europe's most picture-perfect capitals, Luxembourg City is a marvelous mishmash of narrow cobbled streets perched high above river gorges. It's also the perfect jumping-off point for a Grand Duchy adventure.

Take a train north, nabbing a left-hand window seat for glorious views of the fortress remains as you pull out. There's no need to fret about the ticket inspector as, remarkably, transportation here is free of charge. The urban landscape quickly fades as golden wheat fields begin to stretch out toward distant pine-wrapped hills. Views of lazily meandering rivers, steeply set vineyards, and precariously perched castle ruins are punctuated by darkness, as you weave in and out of tunnels. Fortunately, regular stops allow your eyes time to adjust to sights like the pastel-colored houses of Ettelbruck (also known for its General Patton Memorial Museum) and the 12th-century Clervaux Castle, a shining white beacon amid endless green forest.

Troisvierges is the final town before you hit Belgium—and its train fares. Discover its history as the first stop of the German advance west during World War I, before heading back to the capital.

Luxembourg City, the starting point for this cross-country trip

another way

There are many scenic rail journeys to be had from Luxembourg City—and all for free. Board a train to the striking Larochette Castle, the Roman town of Echternach, or the family-friendly Parc Merveilleux.

The gorgeous beach town of Ribadesella, in Asturias

⑧

FEVE

LOCATION Spain **START/FINISH** Bilbao/Ferrol **DISTANCE** 404 miles (650 km) **TIME** 3 days **INFORMATION** www.renfe.com/es/en/suburban/cercanias-feve

Unmarked on most maps, the train line that runs along Spain's north coast has an edge-of-the-world feel, compounded by the surrounding landscapes.

In a country of fantastic train journeys, the narrow-gauge FEVE line might just be Spain's best, cresting the northern coast and affording magnificent views over the Bay of Biscay and the plummeting gorges inland.

Your journey begins in Bilbao, a cultural hub surrounded by the magnificent green hills of the Basque countryside. It's worth lingering here to explore the modern treasures of the Guggenheim Museum and feast on some *pintxos* before making for the belle-époque magnificence of Bilbao-Concordia train station and boarding the modern, comfortable FEVE carriage.

The train rumbles slowly through the Basque and Cantabrian countryside, affording scenic panoramas that no road can reach. An early highlight comes outside the town of Treto, where a railroad bridge crosses the Ría de Treto—a river that snakes into a swampy estuary as it prepares for its meeting with the Cantabrian Sea. Grasslands and forests begin to be peppered with boxy red-brick houses as civilization emerges

◀ ▶

CANTABRIAN BROWN BEARS

As the train rattles through rugged regions like the Picos de Europa, you probably won't be too far away from a Cantabrian brown bear. Once roaming the whole Iberian Peninsula, the bear population has been significantly reduced but is on the rise, and tourism is actually helping. Although you almost certainly won't see one directly from the train, bear-watching is bringing significant amounts of money into crucial strongholds like Somiedo Natural Park.

▶

in the form of Santander, a lively spot to disembark. Delve into the contemporary art exhibitions of Centro Botín, a sleek waterfront complex beside the palm-fringed Pereda Garden, and head for the city's most handsome space, El Sardinero. Here, Art Nouveau buildings like the magnificent Gran Casino line a splendid stretch of sand, perfect for kicking back and sunbathing or enjoying a refreshing dip.

> Forested hills are haunted by the ruins of old wooden houses, wobbling on stilts

Back on the train, the line winds away from the coast and into the foothills of the Picos de Europa, a mighty mountain range that served as a first glimpse of Europe for seafarers from the Americas. Bears and wolves roam the hills here, but your experience will be of human habitation, at sleepy towns like Cabezón de la Sal, a jumping-off point for walks through the neck-craningly gargantuan sequoia forest that lines the hills nearby.

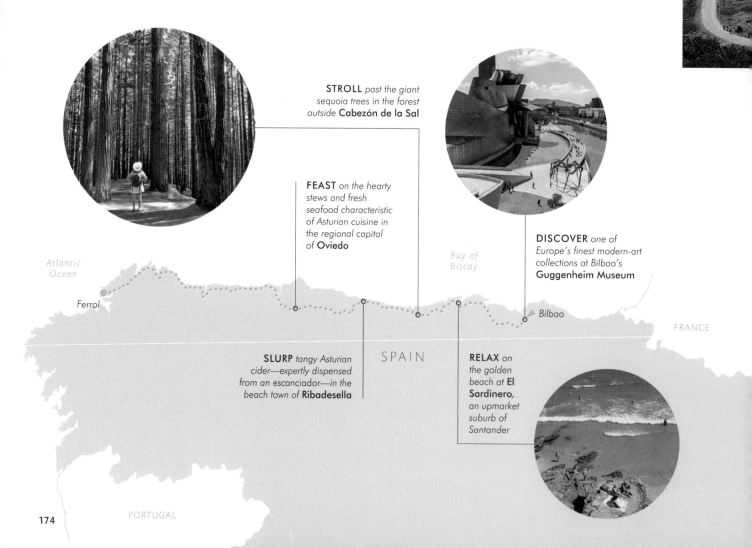

STROLL *past the giant sequoia trees in the forest outside* **Cabezón de la Sal**

FEAST *on the hearty stews and fresh seafood characteristic of Asturian cuisine in the regional capital of* **Oviedo**

DISCOVER *one of Europe's finest modern-art collections at Bilbao's* **Guggenheim Museum**

Atlantic Ocean

Bay of Biscay

Ferrol

Bilbao

FRANCE

SLURP *tangy Asturian cider—expertly dispensed from an escanciador—in the beach town of* **Ribadesella**

SPAIN

RELAX *on the golden beach at* **El Sardinero,** *an upmarket suburb of Santander*

PORTUGAL

Above left The foothills of the Picos de Europa *Above right* FEVE trains in Oviedo Station

An undeniable perk of train travel is that it negates the need for a designated driver. Take full advantage—responsibly, of course—at the seaside town of Ribadesella, where Asturian cider is high on the menu. Refreshing yet earthy, sweet yet tart, this is a lovely drop, traditionally poured from above head height to create a light foam. The gastronomic delights continue in Oviedo, capital of Asturias, whose glorious medieval streets shelter atmospheric restaurants serving the best of the region's cuisine: hearty bean stew with sausage and pork shoulder; bowlfuls of juicy clams; and platters of *cabrales*, a face-scrunchingly piquant blue cheese.

The FEVE saves some of its most gorgeous landscapes for the final leg. The forested hills outside San Román are haunted by the ruins of old wooden houses, wobbling on stilts—jump off here to explore La Peña cave, home to animal paintings dating back to the Ice Age. Back toward the coast, the horizon becomes a jumble of craggy cliffs, montane woodlands, and arcs of honeyed sand as the train passes nature reserves like Punta Fuciño de Porco before angling back inland for the final trundle—past crumbling castles and verdant Galician countryside to the harbor town of Ferrol.

another way

To travel northern Spain's railroads in supreme style, opt for a journey on *El Transcantábrico Gran Lujo*, a luxurious sleeper train that runs west from San Sebastián to Santiago de Compostela, stopping at Bilbao, Santander, and other stations on the FEVE route.

Tram 28 trundling through the streets of Lisbon

9 Tram 28

LOCATION Portugal **START/FINISH** Praça Martim Moniz/Campo Ourique, Lisbon **DISTANCE** 4½ miles (7 km) **TIME** 1 hour **INFORMATION** It's cheapest to buy tickets from a Metro station

It's a sight that says Lisbon as much as a Portuguese custard tart: the sunny-yellow Tram 28, trundling up and down the steep hills of the capital's historic neighborhoods. Lisbon's street-cars were born in 1873, originally introduced from America and pulled by horses; they've been electrified since 1901, but their characteristic rattle and squeak still evokes the age of animal power. The brass handrails and polished wood of the passenger cars recall a more glamorous era, their style unchanged since the 1930s.

There are six streetcar lines, but 28 is the most iconic, crawling through some of the city's most atmospheric areas. Jump on at Praça Martim Moniz to ensure you snag a seat, then sit back and enjoy a succession of must-see sights: the Portuguese parliament building, the robust Sé (cathedral) and the hill-clinging neighborhoods of Alfama and Graça.

10 Tren de Sóller

LOCATION Mallorca, Spain **START/FINISH** Palma/Sóller **DISTANCE** 17 miles (28 km) **TIME** 1 hour **INFORMATION** https://trendesoller.com

The polished-mahogany cars of the historic *Tren de Sóller* rattle up and down the narrow-gauge railroad between Mallorca's capital Palma and the handsome mountain town of Sóller. The 17-mile (28-km) journey takes in stunning views of plains and olive-tree-dotted countryside before the big climb—where it snakes through 13 tunnels and crosses several bridges and the dramatic Cinc Ponts viaduct. Just before Sóller, the train pulls in at a station viewpoint where you can hop off to take in jaw-dropping views across the Serra de Tramuntana—the vista gives you an inkling of the daunting task faced by engineer Pedro Garau when he tackled the challenge of building a rail line in this steep and unforgiving terrain. The pristine brass detail, wrought-iron decoration and bare wooden seats are exactly as they were in 1912, when the train first started operating on this remarkable route. Time doesn't seem to have troubled the backstreets of Sóller, either, which makes a fittingly historic finish to the journey.

another way

If you'd like to continue your journey a further 3 miles (5 km) to the pretty beachside Port de Sóller, you can jump on the tiny 1913 electric tram at Sóller's train station or below the main square—make sure you purchase a combined train-and-tram ticket.

11 Le Petit Train Jaune

LOCATION France **START/FINISH** Villefranche de Conflent/Latour de Carol **DISTANCE** 39 miles (63 km) **TIME** 2½ hours **INFORMATION** www.pyrenees-cerdagne.com/en/le-train-jaune-english

Iconic train journeys aren't all about speed. The canary-yellow wagons of *Le Petit Train Jaune* trundle up through the Pyrenees in their own good time, ascending some 3,000 ft (700 m) from Villefranche de Conflent to Latour de Carol (via the even loftier station of Bolquère) over the course of some two and a half hours, skirting the border with Spain in the process. The mountain views en route are as voluminous as you'd expect, particularly during summer, when there's the option of open-air seating.

The hot, craggy grandeur of the Pyrenean range has a character of its own, while the track's numerous bridges and tunnels are testament to an astonishing feat of engineering, with work on the line beginning back in 1903. Despite its measured pace and toy-train color scheme, the service is still part of the national SNCF network—just think of it as occupying the opposite end of the spectrum to France's ultramodern TGVs.

12 Ferrovia Circumetnea

LOCATION Sicily, Italy **START/FINISH** Catania/Riposto **DISTANCE** 68 miles (109 km) **TIME** 3 hours **INFORMATION** www.circumetnea.it

With its snowcapped peak and gentle slopes gracefully falling into the Mediterranean, beautiful Mount Etna is a sight to behold. To see it up close, board the Circumetnea Railroad, which—as the name suggests—circumnavigates the base of Europe's most active volcano. Built at the end of the 19th century, this narrow-gauge railroad line was designed to connect the villages at the base of Mount Etna. Today, the journey begins in Catania, a gritty working city that was a major port in antiquity. From here, the train heads through the outskirts, alongside residential houses flanked by lava rocks, and then past traditional Sicilian villages. The landscape alternates between starkly volcanic and abundantly fertile, lush with prickly pear orchards, citrus groves, and pistachio plantations. Mount Etna, soaring into the clouds, is your constant companion throughout.

Mount Etna towering above the villages of the Val di Catania

⑬

French Riviera Railroad

LOCATION France, Monaco, and Italy **START/FINISH** Marseille, France/Ventimiglia, Italy **DISTANCE** 161 miles (259 km) **TIME** 4 hours **INFORMATION** www.sncf.com/en; around eight trains a day ply this route

Grab a window seat and settle back for a ride along the timeless Côte d'Azur, with plenty of opportunities to break the journey in the region's effortlessly stylish resorts.

When it comes to glamour, few commuter routes can compare with the French Riviera railroad. The trains are functional rather than fancy, and many of the passengers are simply heading to or from work or school. Yet the line showcases the very best of the Côte d'Azur—chic resorts, golden sands, and the azure waters of the Mediterranean—for a fare that won't break the bank.

Dating back to 1872, the railroad runs from the chaotic and characterful streets of downtown Marseille to the refined Italian city of Ventimiglia via the Principality of Monaco. The best approach is to hop on and off, rather than travel the whole line in one fell swoop. This lets you follow in the footsteps of Hollywood stars on the famous Promenade de la Croisette in Cannes, sample a classic salade niçoise on the seafront in Nice, lose yourself in the mind-bending artworks of the Musée Picasso in charming Antibes, and test your luck at the legendary casinos of Monte Carlo.

Monaco's marina—and the waters that give the Côte d'Azur its name

another way

For a similarly scenic coastal journey, travel by train down the beautiful Italian Riviera from the historic Ligurian port of Genoa and on to the waterfront city of Civitavecchia, which gazes out over the Tyrrhenian Sea.

Trenino Verde

(14)

LOCATION Sardinia, Italy **START/FINISH** Palau/Tempio **DISTANCE** 37 miles (59 km) **TIME** 3½ hours **INFORMATION** www.treninoverde.com

Capo d'Orso rock formation, standing above the town of Palau

The "Little Green Train" is an unbeatable way to explore Sardinia, winding from the ocean to the mountains through cork oak and granite and past ancient megalithic tombs.

Rumbling from Sardinia's show-stopping coastline to its rugged interior, the Trenino Verde is island train travel at its very best. The line's most scenic stretch begins in the town of Palau, where pine forest crests a sandy bay and Capo d'Orso, a rock formation in the shape of a giant bear, silently guards the coast. The train chugs its way on a narrow-gauge track through the wilds of the Gallura region, past the relics of ancient civilizations: stone cairns mark the site of so-called giants' graves at Coddu Vecchiu, where Bronze Age peoples buried their dead.

Disembark at Lake Liscia to stretch your legs on the waterfront walking trails, or take a boat trip across the lake to see a group of magnificent olive trees, over 1,000 years old and gnarled by the ravages of time. Cork woods enclose the little town of Calangianus—there's even a museum here dedicated to the tree's spongy bark—while more megalithic mystery awaits at the tombs of Pascaredda. The train climbs higher on its final stretch, up the foothills of slabstoned Mount Limbara to the town of Tempio. Here, the granite that forms Gallura's craggy landscape coalesces into stately medieval squares, lined with bars ripe for enjoying a glass of local Moscato wine.

> The Trenino Verde is island train travel at its very best

⑮

Sleeper train from Rome to Syracuse

The harbor below Castello Ruffo, in the Calabrian town of Scilla

LOCATION Italy **START/FINISH** Rome/Syracuse **DISTANCE** 365 miles (588 km)
TIME 1 day **INFORMATION** www.trenitalia.com

The sleeper train from Rome to Sicily is ferried across the Strait of Messina. Soak up the scenery as the sun sets, then wake up in a city that blends Greek, Roman, Norman, and Baroque architectural styles.

You'd be forgiven for thinking you can't reach Sicily by rail from the Italian capital. After all, there's no underwater tunnel connecting the mainland to the largest island in the Mediterranean. The journey, however, is very much possible, with the train ferried across the Strait of Messina, a narrow stretch that separates the eastern tip of Sicily from the western tip of Calabria—one of the very few places in the world where a train is transported above water.

Cozy up in your little sleeper cabin and watch the world go by as you swoosh through Italy. As dusk descends on the Colosseum, the train leaves Rome and heads south, passing Mount Vesuvius in the gathering dark, wispy plumes of sulfur-rich steam circling up from its crater.

As the train's rhythmic rocking lulls you to sleep, Campania passes by outside, then a sliver of Basilicata. At Villa San Giovanni, in the sun-kissed region of Calabria, the carriages are unhooked and

KEEP an eye out for the looming silhouette of **Mount Vesuvius**, mainland Europe's most active volcano

Adriatic Sea

ITALY

Rome

FUEL up on hearty Roman fare before settling into your Sicily-bound carriage

Tyrrhenian Sea

Ionian Sea

CATCH dawn breaking over **Calabria**, home to pristine beaches and a dramatic stretch of coastline

WATCH the train being unhooked and rolled onto a ship to cross the **Strait of Messina**

Syracuse

CELEBRATE the end of your journey with a performance at **Syracuse's** Greek theater

another way

The 37-mile (60-km) Trabocchi Line travels along the Trabocchi Coast, offering bellissimo views of central and southern Italy. Take your bike and make the return journey on the Via Verde, which traces the railroad and affords more spectacular panoramas.

separated, and then rolled onto a ship fitted with railroad tracks. The journey across the narrow strait is short—about 20 minutes—and, before you know it, you'll be pulling into the train station of Syracuse, a city home to spectacular Roman and Greek ruins. Grab some lunch (Sicily's cuisine makes the most of island-grown ingredients including citrus fruits, almonds, and ricotta) and head for the city's amphitheater—the perfect way to bookend your trip.

The Greek theater at Syracuse, Sicily

(16)

Bernina Express

LOCATION Italy to Switzerland **START/FINISH** Tirano/St. Moritz
DISTANCE 37 miles (60 km) **TIME** 4 hours **INFORMATION**
www.rhb.ch/en/panoramic-trains/bernina-express

This panoramic train ride offers a made-for-the-movies landscape of snow-white glaciers, soaring peaks, and elegant mountain villages.

Connecting Tirano in northern Italy to the glamorous Swiss ski resort of St. Moritz, the *Bernina Express* travels along the highest rail track in the Alps. The bright red Rhaetian Railway train makes the trip without cog wheels, carving its way through 55 tunnels, over 196 bridges, and up gradients of up to 70 percent.

The scenery changes dramatically as the journey gets under way. As you leave behind the warmer Mediterranean climes of Tirano on the ascent toward the Swiss border, swaying palm trees make way for picture-perfect Alpine landscapes, with glaciers carpeting the mountainside and jagged peaks soaring into a deep blue sky. The train zips past the magnificent Palü Glacier, home to Alp Grüm, renowned for being the only Swiss hotel and restaurant accessible exclusively by train (or on foot). It soars above Ospizio Bernina, at 7,392 ft (2,253 m), with the waters of Lake Bianco and Lej Nair glistening in the distance, and winds past glorious glaciers before reaching St. Moritz, Switzerland's most fashionable mountain resort. The train was designed specially with this Alpine panorama in mind—the roof is made entirely of glass, so you'll be able to soak up fabulous views every chug of the way.

another way

The Gotthard Express connecting Lugano/Bellinzona and Lucerne is a spectacularly scenic five-and-a-half-hour journey that also includes a section aboard a steamboat. Panoramic carriages ensure you make the most of the stunning scenery.

Autumnal trees greeting the Bernina Express as it crosses a viaduct

(17) Glacier Express

LOCATION Switzerland **START/FINISH** St. Moritz/Zermatt **DISTANCE** 180 miles (290 km) **TIME** 8 hours **INFORMATION** www.glacierexpress.ch

Switzerland's mountain scenery is world-famous, and this historic narrow-gauge train shows exactly why, winding from the glam resort of St. Moritz to Zermatt, in the shadow of the Matterhorn.

Capturing snowy landscapes from a carriage on the Glacier Express

It was 1930 when the *Glacier Express* first rolled along the rails between St. Moritz and Zermatt, and the service remains now what it was then: a scintillatingly scenic tourist train.

Its flashy red livery and panoramic windows have come to represent a kind of benchmark for European rail adventures, serving up snow-capped Alpine landscapes that swoop and soar and leave you scrabbling for superlatives. Similarly pleasing is the fact that it bills itself as the world's slowest express train, with an average speed of just 24 mph (38 kph). This is not the kind of country you want to rush through, after all.

Both the start and end points of the journey are classy destinations in their own right—it's hard to beat Zermatt's backdrop of the mighty Matterhorn—and you can expect plenty of onboard comforts, but the real luxury of a journey like this is the chance to wallow in the sheer scale of the mountain scenery. The train wasn't named by accident: the valleys, ridges, and slopes might be dotted with cowherds' huts and log-pile cottages but they were scoured into shape by shelves of ice. To be transported through it all is a joy.

Old steam locomotives at a depot in Wolsztyn

18 Children's Railroad

LOCATION Hungary **START/FINISH** Hűvösvölgy, Budapest (return) **DISTANCE** 7½ miles (11.5 km) **TIME** 2–3 hours return **INFORMATION** https://gyermekvasut.hu

One of Budapest's little-known marvels, the Children's Railroad is remarkably, as the name suggests, run by kids. Trips on Train Line 7 begin at Gyermekvasútas Otthon, a school that doubles as an extracurricular training ground for this novel railroad—the point of it all is to instill a sense of discipline and comradeship in young teens. A half-day tootle along the tracks winds through the gently forested slopes of the Buda Hills and, while chug-chugging along the rails at 12 mph (20 kph), you'll glide through parts of suburban Budapest few visitors see. There are Danube views without distraction, lookout towers, and forest playgrounds to explore. The high point (literally) of the return journey is wooded János-hegy, the loftiest point of the city at 1,732 ft (528 m) and home to the ornamental Elizabeth Lookout, named after Hungary's Queen Elizabeth, who visited in 1882.

CHILDREN'S RAILROADS

Children's railroads originated in the former USSR, when the first opened in 1932 in Moscow. Over the next six decades, more than 50 others were built across Eastern Europe by the youth section of the Communist Party. Many still remain today, with some, like Park Railroad Maltanka in Poland, using vintage miniature steam engines.

19 Wolsztyn Experience

LOCATION Poland **START/FINISH** Wolsztyn/Leszno **DISTANCE** 30 miles (48 km) **TIME** 1½ hours **INFORMATION** www.thewolsztynexperience.org; the Wolsztyn Experience Society's 7-night footplating holidays include four round-trips from Wolsztyn to Leszno

Anyone who loves everything about vintage locomotives—from the squeal of the whistle to the hiss of the steam—will be in seventh heaven in Wolsztyn, western Poland. Here, steam trains provide regular, timetabled services on the national rail network, chugging along to Leszno and Poznań. Even better, if you've always dreamed of being a steam-train driver, you can ride in the engine itself by booking a footplate course with the Wolsztyn Experience Society. Run by British steam-train enthusiasts, this organization is dedicated to the preservation of Poland's historic railroad, operating since 1886.

The countryside in these parts isn't the prettiest—the route, which is largely straight and flat, passes through mile after mile of rather featureless farmland—but for nostalgia buffs, that's beside the point. It's all about the trains; so much so that as well as footplate-riding, the society also arranges special engine-shed visits and run-pasts for keen photographers.

20 Höllentalbahn

LOCATION Germany **START/FINISH** Freiburg/
Villingen **DISTANCE** 46 miles (75 km) **TIME** 1½
hours **INFORMATION** www.hochschwarzwald.de

When Germans crave freedom or yearn for the
solitude of nature, they go to the Black Forest—
and a train ride through this southwestern
swathe of woodlands and half-timbered towns
will give you the perfect insight into exactly why.
The Höllentalbahn heads through the area's
greatest hits, but don't let its English name—
literally, Hell Valley Railroad—put you off. The
nickname stuck because it's considered the
steepest railroad in the country, rising more
than 1,970 ft (600 m) from Freiburg to
Hinterzarten and at a gradient of 5.5 percent.

This being Germany, the engineering is
eye-popping, as are the bridges and the
viaducts, and the valley highs and peekaboo
glimpses in between when speeding out of
tunnels. It is impossible to spend time on the
train and not be tempted to get off at Titisee,
one of Germany's most beautiful lakes and a
place where your eyes will work overtime
taking in all the natural splendor.

another way

*The 3-Seenbahn, or Three Lakes
Railroad, is only 12 miles (19 km)
long, but it branches off from the
Höllentalbahn and packs in plenty—
namely, detouring from the Titisee to
rattle past Windgfällweiher and the
Schluchsee, two more of the Black
Forest's most beautiful pleasure lakes.*

21 Harzer Schmalspurbahnen

LOCATION Germany **START/FINISH**
Wernigerode/Brocken **DISTANCE** 15 miles
(24 km) **TIME** 1 hour 45 minutes **INFORMATION**
www.hsb-wr.de

With 48 stations, a grand collection of working
steam locomotives and around 87 miles (140 km)
of track carrying over a million passengers each
year, the Harz mountains are a hit with number-
crunching transportation buffs. But a journey on
the Harzer Schmalspurbahnen is definitely not
just for trainspotters and *Thomas the Tank Engine*
fans. This charming vintage railroad is in fact a
working transportation system that's been in
continuous service since 1887.

For visitors, the most popular route is the
Brockenbahn, which winds up the forested
slopes of Brocken mountain, northern Germany's
highest peak, from the town of Wernigerode to
the summit. From time to time, special trips are
available, with extras such as an onboard brunch,
lunch or whiskey tasting included in the fare. For
spectacularly romantic views, visit in winter,
when the conifers are laden with snow.

*The Harzer Schmalspurbahnen
steaming through the snow in winter*

Mariazell Railroad

LOCATION Austria **START/FINISH** St. Pölten/Mariazell **DISTANCE** 56½ miles
(91.5 km) **TIME** 2 hours **INFORMATION** www.mariazellerbahn.at

*Traveling by train through the white-etched Alps is always a joy, no more
so than when discovering spectacular scenery on a narrow-gauge
pilgrimage in the Styrian foothills.*

In the late 19th century, travelers came by the thousands to visit Mariazell, a pilgrimage center in Austria's Styria region, to view an image of the Virgin Mary carved in wood. That gave cause to build this narrow-gauge railroad to transport pilgrims across the difficult Alpine terrain, and today trains still carry the curious through the Pielach valley to Mariazell Basilica, where the venerated Catholic object is now enshrined.

The scenic trip is worth it regardless of your spiritual beliefs. En route, the rail line passes waterfalls, mountain farms, and towns. There's Weinburg, home to a pioneering climbing center; Frankenfels, known for cave tours; and Gösing, ideal for stretching legs in the Ötschergräben gorges.

Until the inception of modern trains, Mariazell was accessible only by steam-pulled carriage, but today there are several options, depending on the time of year you're traveling. For VIP luxury, opt for the first-class panorama carriage (summer weekends only). On a budget? Buy a ticket for the Himmelstreppe, the journey at its most frill-free. To see it as the original pilgrims once did, it's all aboard the 100-year-old vintage locomotive.

*Above A curving viaduct on the
Mariazell Railroad line Right Mariazell
Basilica, the end point for pilgrims*

Semmering Railroad

LOCATION Austria **START/FINISH** Gloggnitz/Mürzzuschlag **DISTANCE** 25 miles
(41 km) **TIME** 1½ hours **INFORMATION** www.semmering.com

*An engineering feat with sublime mountain views, the Semmering
Railroad offers a little piece of history alongside some of Austria's
finest scenery. Bag yourself a window seat and prepare to be wowed.*

One of just a handful of railroads inscribed on the UNESCO World Heritage List, the
Semmering Railroad, or Semmeringbahn, earns its place as a piece of stupendous
engineering. Built between 1848 and 1854, it was one of the greatest of its time, with
14 tunnels, 16 viaducts, and 110 bridges along its route. Today, trains still chug along its
25 miles (41 km) of historic tracks from Gloggnitz to Mürzzuschlag, taking in some of
Austria's spectacular mountain scenery over the course of the 90-minute journey.

The railroad winds its way up through the verdant Semmering Pass and the
Schwarza and Auerbach valleys before its most dramatic section a few miles from its
final destination. Here, the train tiptoes along the Kalte Rinne Viaduct before trundling
through the nearly 1-mile (1.5-km) Semmering Tunnel, which opens out onto the
precipitous slopes of the Alpine Roschnitz valley. Expect to gaze out at rocky cliffs,
bucolic farmsteads, and towering pine forests—and don't forget to look back at those
striking viaducts as you round the corner and chug away.

*A train dwarfed by
peaks as it crosses
Krausel Klause Viaduct*

SUMMER ARCHITECTURE

Watch for
Semmering's charming
"summer architecture,"
handsome homes and
hotels—all carved
wooden balconies,
towering turrets, and
pointed gables—that
popped up all over
town in the mid-19th
century with the
arrival of the railroad.

CROATIA

ROMANIA

Belgrade

SERBIA

ENJOY *the thrum of* **Belgrade,** *Serbia's lively and historic capital city, before hopping aboard*

BOSNIA AND HERCEGOVINA

GAZE *at the* **Montenegrin mountains** *as the train heads south toward the coast*

TAKE *a wander around the mix-and-match buildings of* **Podgorica,** *the unassuming capital of Montenegro*

MONTE-
NEGRO

BULGARIA

KOSOVO

NORTH
MACEDONIA

ALBANIA

Bar

*Adriatic
Sea*

CELEBRATE
journey's end on the beach in **Bar,** *with views of the Adriatic*

(24)

Belgrade to Bar

LOCATION Serbia to Montenegro **START/FINISH** Belgrade/Bar **DISTANCE** 296 miles (473 km) **TIME** 1 day **INFORMATION** www.zeleznicesrbije.com and www.zcg-prevoz.me

Who needs luxury? This day-long journey from the Serbian capital to the Montenegrin coast might not be an upmarket affair, but the widescreen Balkan scenery is as fine as it gets.

When Europe's greatest rail experiences get spoken about, attention tends to fall on the timeless inter-city routes and iconic mountain journeys of Western Europe. Far fewer plaudits go the way of this workaday north-to-south passenger service through the Balkans—yet among those in the know, Belgrade to Bar is as hallowed a prospect as the *Orient Express*.

This has nothing to do with luxury—the ten-hour journey is one of the cheapest day-rides you'll find in Europe—and everything to do with the lands shifting past the windows. The views are a treat for almost the full duration of the trip, with wide cornfields and massing hills, but they reach their scenic apogee among the mountain ranges of Montenegro, as the train chugs high above glinting rivers before gradually descending to the shores of the Adriatic.

But this is also a track with a story to tell. Originally begun back in 1950, the line wasn't fully opened until 1976, when Yugoslavian ruler Tito regularly traveled along it in his opulent *Blue Train*. Then, as now, the long journey from Belgrade down to Bar passed through 254 tunnels and crossed 435 bridges, statistics that say plenty about the region's toppling topography, and the extraordinary engineering feat that underpins the whole route.

another way

Via Dinarica calls itself "A Mega Hiking Trail across the Western Balkans" and provides the opportunity to experience the region on foot. Covering eight countries in total—including both Serbia and Montenegro—the initiative also promotes responsible tourism.

The views are a treat
for almost the full
duration of the trip

Right *Mala Rijeka Viaduct,*
once the highest railroad
bridge in the world
Below *Tara River Canyon*

Rhodope Narrow-Gauge Railroad

LOCATION Bulgaria **START/FINISH** Septemvri/Dobrinishte **DISTANCE**
78 miles (125 km) **TIME** 4 hours **INFORMATION** www.bdz.bg

*The "Alpine Railroad of the Balkans" delivers a timeless angle on
Bulgaria's most spectacular mountainscapes—and a lesson in
how to slow down on the only narrow-gauge line in the country.*

The battered trains and branch lines of Bulgaria's railroad network possess a
mystique that few others in Europe can. Together they offer rail travel in its
purest form on journeys that force their passengers to slow down to a speed
that has almost been forgotten in the past half-century. Opened in 1945, the
Septemvri to Dobrinishte line does just that, taking you on a very deliberate
dawdle through the Rhodopes, the Rila, and the Pirin mountain ranges, up
steep gradients and around corkscrews that celebrate the golden age of rail
travel. Quite unlike other narrow-gauge rides that have been polished up
elsewhere, there are still plenty of creaks and cranks to savor—cue an original
steam locomotive and two retro carriages. And the scenery is extraordinary.
After the tunnels, the arch viaducts, and then Avramovo, the highest station in
the Balkans, the train pulls into Bansko, a Bulgarian ski resort brimming with
hotels and the gateway to the slopes of Todorka peak.

*Sunrise hitting the
Rila mountains
behind the village
of Avramovo*

another way

*To explore further east from the
Bulgarian capital Sofia, board the
Istanbul–Sofia Express, a 355-mile
(571-km) journey that runs daily
between the two cities, offering
an adventurous glimpse into the
sleeper rides of yesteryear.*

㉖ Odontotos Rack Railroad

LOCATION Greece **START/FINISH** Diakopto/Kalavryta **DISTANCE** 14 miles (22 km)
TIME 1 hour **INFORMATION** www.odontotos.com

A scenic ride through plane trees and wildflowers to the poignant mountain town of Kalavryta, this historic railroad has been ferrying passengers up the Vouraikos Gorge in western Greece since 1896.

Chugging its way from the Gulf of Corinth into the mountainous region of Achaea, this wonderfully scenic railroad journey hugs the walls of the Vouraikos Gorge, carved out over the ages by the snaking river of the same name. The train passes over narrow bridges and beneath towering rock formations, and past sheer valley walls alive with wildflowers: here the yellow flash of aurinia petals, there the deep purple of campanula. Up above, honey buzzards and kestrels hover in pursuit of prey; peer down at the river and you may even spot otters frolicking on its banks.

Humans have left their mark here, too. Jumping off the train at the mountain village of Zachlorou offers the chance to explore the Mega Spilaio monastery, in a huge cave that has housed Christian hermits for millennia. Kalavryta, meanwhile—the route's end point—is a gorgeous mountain town whose Byzantine churches and leafy streets are tinged with tragedy: hundreds of men and boys were massacred here during World War II. Visit the moving memorial to the fallen, and then head for happier times in town: a bowl of steaming wild boar stew in a taverna and the sound of bouzouki music carried on the breeze.

The track running between steep-sided cliffs in the Vouraikos Gorge

HERACLES AND BOURA

Given the awe-inspiring landscapes, it's no surprise to learn that Vouraikos has a place in ancient Greek mythology. Legend has it that Hercules was in love with a woman named Boura, who lived by the sea close to what is now the gorge's mouth. Hercules, impatient to reach her, tore through the landscape with his bare hands, creating the great scar in the earth that is now the Vouraikos Gorge.

Golden Eagle
Danube Express

LOCATION Hungary **START/FINISH** Budapest (loop) **DISTANCE** Various
TIME 7–8 days **INFORMATION** www.goldeneagleluxurytrains.com

*All packed for adventure? Then board this once-in-a-lifetime
train on a journey from Budapest into the dusty plains and
vineyards of Hungary's cowboy-inhabited hinterlands.*

Of all the luxury trains you can ride around the world in today—Europe's
Orient Express; South Africa's *Blue Train*; India's *Maharajas' Express*; Australia's
The Ghan—the *Golden Eagle Danube Express* is the one that offers more
than five-star service and premium suites. By following the rail less traveled,
it explores a part of central and southern Europe still unknown to many
travelers. Depending on which route you choose, it leaves its terminus station
in Budapest to crisscross Romania, Bulgaria, North Macedonia, Serbia, Bosnia

Left *Budapest, the start and end point of this luxurious circuit through Hungary*
Above *Bathers in Széchenyi Thermal Bath*

and Herzegovina, Montenegro, and more. Seen from your couchette or the decadent dining car, spectacular and scantly populated mountains, lakes, and forests slide by the window almost as a demo reel, offering a rudimental education on why slow travel by train is so much more than your final destination.

With so many routes to pick from—and once-in-a-lifetime prices to match—it can be tricky to know where to begin. The classic itinerary for train lovers, however, is the all-Hungarian affair, which gently reveals places, sights, and colors not featured in many guidebooks. Board your train in Budapest, a city that finely balances modern Buda with historic Pest, making sure you go for a sybaritic dip at the gloriously decadent Széchenyi Thermal Bath before the guard's whistle blows at Nyugati Station. From here, the train wends toward Balaton Uplands National Park, a vast patchwork of wide mountaintops and basins, emerging to arrive in social-media-friendly Keszthely. Overlooking Lake Balaton, the shoreline city is crammed with grand palaces and townhouses, including Festetics Palace, home to more historic counts than you'd find at a mathematics symposium.

As well as wedding-cake Baroque palaces, you're on the lookout for medieval towers, and the historic old town of Sopron fits the bill with its 13th-century Fire Tower; after dizzying yourself with the ▶

another way

Like most luxury train operators, the Golden Eagle Danube Express offers more than one life-affirming route. In fact, the hotel-on-wheels has a succession of pinch-yourself trips to experience, with other memorable excursions tootling from Budapest to Prague via Krakow or to Venice via Belgrade, Mostar, Sarajevo, and Ljubljana.

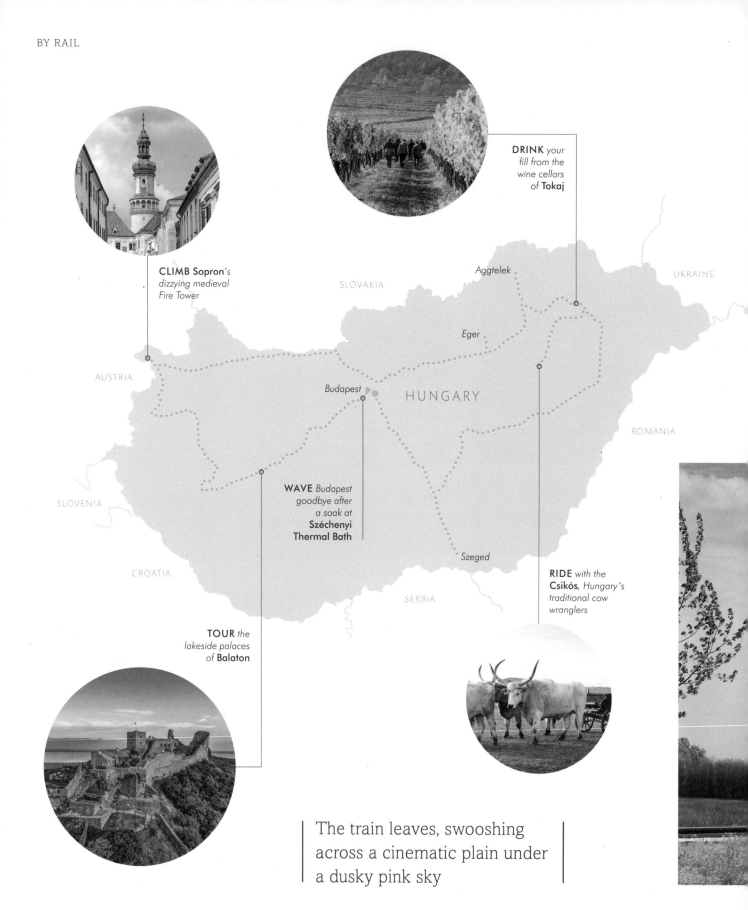

DRINK *your fill from the wine cellars of* **Tokaj**

CLIMB Sopron's *dizzying medieval Fire Tower*

SLOVAKIA

Aggtelek

UKRAINE

Eger

AUSTRIA

Budapest

HUNGARY

WAVE *Budapest goodbye after a soak at* **Széchenyi Thermal Bath**

SLOVENIA

ROMANIA

CROATIA

Szeged

SERBIA

RIDE *with the* **Csikós**, *Hungary's traditional cow wranglers*

TOUR *the lakeside palaces of* **Balaton**

The train leaves, swooshing across a cinematic plain under a dusky pink sky climb up the 200-step corkscrew staircase, you'll need to lie down in your luxury en-suite compartment as the train rambles on.

A less obvious highlight is Hortobágy National Park, where the Csikós, the cow wranglers of the East Hungary plains, continue to lead lives that lie somewhere between the image of a lonely livestock rancher and the fantasy of a Wild West cowboy. Before the train leaves, swooshing across a cinematic plain under a dusky pink sky, you might get lucky and see the national park's other imagination-sparking resident: long-legged cranes, which migrate through the area by the thousands.

Later in the journey, as the train begins its homeward leg back to Hungary's exceptionally tailored capital, there's time for one last stop: the crowd-pleasing wine cellars of Tokaj, where oenophiles reckon the world's most exquisite sweet wines are made. Reason enough to stock up on souvenirs to take home, or toast as you make that final push back to Budapest. This is what memories on the rails are made of.

THE CSIKÓS

The Csikós are cow wranglers, who dress in flowing cornflower-blue gowns and waistcoats and wear crane feather–brimmed hats that recall the days of legendary highwayman Dick Turpin. The men learn to ride as young as one year old, and, like their forbears, continue their almost medieval profession out on the *puszta*, the dusty plains of Hortobágy National Park.

Heading out into the Hungarian plains

Trans-Finland: Helsinki to Lapland

LOCATION Finland **START/FINISH** Helsinki/Kemijärvi **DISTANCE** 600 miles (966 km) **TIME** 4 or 5 days **INFORMATION** www.visitfinland.com

This long trundle north takes in Finland's finest towns, its proudest traditions, and a landscape of forests and lakes that's the hallmark of any memorable Finnish train journey.

A river crossing in the wilds of Finnish Lapland

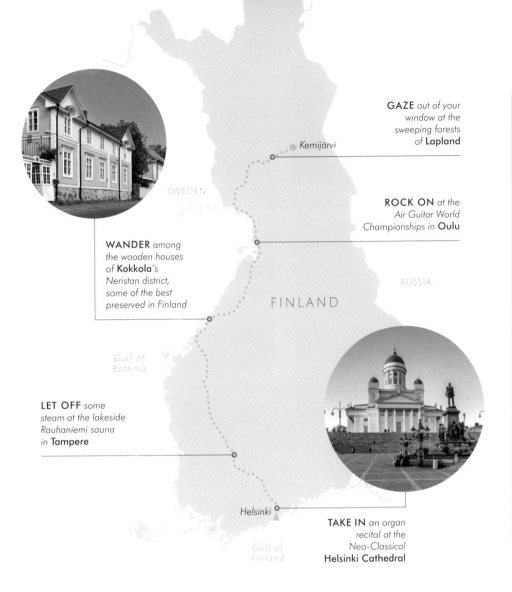

GAZE *out of your window at the sweeping forests* of **Lapland**

Kemijärvi

SWEDEN

ROCK ON *at the Air Guitar World Championships in* **Oulu**

RUSSIA

WANDER *among the wooden houses* of **Kokkola**'s *Neristan district, some of the best preserved in Finland*

FINLAND

Gulf of Bothnia

LET OFF *some steam at the lakeside Rauhaniemi sauna in* **Tampere**

Helsinki

TAKE IN *an organ recital at the Neo-Classical* **Helsinki Cathedral**

Gulf of Finland

THE SCREAMING MEN OF OULU

Mieskuoro Huutajat is a choir that doesn't sing a note. Instead they "bellow and scream and cry," according to composer Petri Serviö, who founded the group in 1987. Dressed in black suits but sounding like they'd be more at home in a soccer stadium, the "shouting choir," also known as The Screaming Men of Oulu, is made up of around 30 performers. Their loud renditions of the Finnish national anthem and other patriotic songs has been likened to the Māori haka.

Spread along the scenic shores of the Gulf of Finland and mixing a cutting-edge design district with the graceful old architecture of its landmark cathedrals, Helsinki can be a hard place to leave. But there's a whole country ahead of you on this bottom-to-top rail trip through Finland, so leave you must.

A-to-B-ers might opt for the night train to Kemijärvi, but this is a journey you won't want to sleep through. Instead, take the western branch line and hop off along the way. Tampere, Finland's second-largest urban center and a vibrant college town, is up first. This is the sauna capital of the world, so take your pick from one of the 50-plus toasty rooms that are peppered along the surrounding lakefronts. Then it's on to the Gulf of Bothnia: first stop Kokkola, with its charming neighborhood of yellow and white wooden houses; then Oulu, the cultural capital of northern Finland. This is the home of the "shouting choir," and there's normally some kind of concert or festival going on—if you're here in August (and you happen to have a talent for playing an invisible instrument), drop by Rotuaari Square for the Air Guitar World Championships, held in Oulu since 1996. You can even take part yourself.

As memorable as all that might be, the lasting impressions of this ride are likely to be the thick taiga that swamps the trackside as you make your way through Lapland. This lush forest is a sanctuary for elk, reindeer, wolverines, and brown bears—so keep your eyes peeled on the last leg into Kemijärvi.

Left *Abisko National Park in winter*
Above *Houses in the Lofoten Islands*

(29)

Arctic Circle Train

LOCATION Sweden to Norway **START/FINISH** Kiruna/Narvik **DISTANCE** 82 miles (132 km)
TIME 2 hours **INFORMATION** www.scandinavianrail.com

The Northern Lights and the Midnight Sun might top many travel hit lists, but there's as much joy to be had in the quiet adventures and empty spaces of northern Scandinavia.

Riding the rails of one of the world's northernmost lines is unlike any other train journey. At this latitude, the horizon curves like a crescent moon and the landscape feels empty apart from the stunted dwarf pines and herds of reindeer. But that's not what makes this corner of Lapland so extraordinary. Come in winter and you'll be treated to a multicolored disco above your head when the Northern Lights stream in so fast they could be witchcraft. Come in summer and you'll experience midnight light and a place where time never feels in short supply.

To find life this far north in the Arctic Circle, you'll want to hop off at some of the train's stops,

spending a night or two in places like Björkliden, Låktatjåkka, and Vassijaure. In particular, Abisko National Park is recast as a snow globe in winter and ripe for exploring by cross-country skiing or snowmobiling. At other times, warmer temperatures bring flowering alpine meadows and wild camping adventures to Torneträsk, Scandinavia's largest Arctic lake.

As the train leaves the mountain plateau for the Norwegian coast, brown gradually gives way to green and blue—Narvik rewards with orca-watching excursions, while delightful Lofoten, where the coast's true beauty emerges, offers adventures in abundance.

Inlandsbanan

LOCATION Sweden **START/FINISH** Mora/Gällivare **DISTANCE** 663 miles (1,067 km) **TIME** 2 days **INFORMATION** https://res.inlandsbanan.se; daily departure mid-Jun–Aug; travel before mid-Jul to experience the Midnight Sun

A train crossing the Storstupet Canyon

Take a slow ride through Sweden's forests on the Inlandsbanan, *a leisurely train service that travels up from Dalarna County to the stark wildernesses of Lapland.*

Most passengers aboard the *Inlandsbanan* are here for one thing: crossing the Arctic Circle as the train trundles north from central Sweden to Lapland. Better known in their frozen, wintry states, these forest-dominated landscapes are so thoroughly deserted of human life that every lonely hamlet or scenic river-crossing becomes an event that'll have you glued to your window.

The pace of the journey is leisurely and punctuated by the frequent squeal of brakes as elk emerge from the pine and spruce to wander across the tracks. Food is a highlight, too—the guides onboard help you navigate the local delicacies sold at tiny Lapland towns along the way, with smoked salmon, foraged cloudberries, and even reindeer on the menu.

While the route requires you to overnight at lakeside Östersund before continuing along the final stretch of railroad to Gällivare, many passengers hop on and off at will, embarking on hiking routes that disappear into fairy-tale forests or stopping to learn about the nomadic Sami culture at a local heritage museum. However many days you spend aboard, you'll find no better excuse for slow travel at its most magnificent.

another way

Extend your journey by opting for a 10-day package tour of the railroad, which runs from the original but less-frequently traveled start of the route, Kristinehamn, with additional stopovers in Arvidsjaur and Vilhelmina.

DISCOVER *the* **Flåm Railway Museum**

OGLE Aurlandsfjord *from the Flåm shoreline*

Flåm

CHUG *past storybook hamlets on the way up into* **Aurland's** *mountains*

NORWAY

GET *wet in the spray of* **Kjosfossen waterfall**

Myrdal

BREATHE *in the mountain air at* **Myrdal**

Flåmsbana

LOCATION Norway **START/FINISH** Flåm/Myrdal **DISTANCE** 12½ miles (20 km) **TIME** 2 hours **INFORMATION** www.norwaysbest.com/flamsbana

With thousands of fjords, glacial valleys, and mountains to discover, Norway defies expectations. An opportunity to see these thrilling shifts in landscape awaits on the Aurlandsfjord.

Judging by the fjord-scapes, waterfalls, and odd-looking rock formations—look hard and you might find one that's the spitting image of a wolf or a polar bear, or even someone in your family—the visual feast along the Flåmsbana sightseeing route leaves little retina room for much else. In only 12½ miles (20 km), the vintage train delivers the greatest hits of Norway in microcosm, marrying the ever-variegated scenery of the Flåm Valley and its sapphire-blue river with a spectacular feat of engineering. Completed in 1940, there are no fewer than 20 tunnels, 18 of which were built by pick and shovel over two decades, and it is one of the steepest standard gauge lines in the world.

All journeys begin at the end of the Aurlandsfjord, a tributary of the far-mightier Sognefjord, before winding—literally—up to the high mountains at Myrdal station. At one point, the train royally shows off, performing an acrobatic 180-degree turn while inside a tunnel. It's the most beautiful slow journey imaginable, made even slower by a stop at Kjosfossen waterfall, where passengers can soak it all in from their seat, or hop off for a platform selfie, with added glacial spray.

Logistics-wise, Norway can be difficult to travel around quickly, thanks to its leviathan-size fjords and rampant wilderness. The Flåmsbana, however, makes light work of this challenge: end station Myrdal is a stop on the Bergen Line, meaning a ride on the Flåm Railroad easily fits into a cross-country itinerary between the Western Fjords and Oslo.

NORWAY

Flåmsbana

another way

The Flåm Railroad might be Norway's best known, but it's far from the only one. For a journey longer—and wilder—buy a ticket for the Rauma Line, a 71-mile (114-km) jaunt from Bjorli to Åndalsnes.

The Flåmsbana,
winding its way up the
Flåm Valley to Myrdal

(32)

Interrailing through the Baltic States

LOCATION Estonia, Latvia, and Lithuania **START/FINISH** Tallinn/Kaunas
DISTANCE 517 miles (832 km) **TIME** 2 weeks **INFORMATION** www.interrail.eu;
buy Interrail's "10 days within 2 months" pass to visit every one of the destinations
mentioned in this route

*Pack your rail pass for a train ride through this little-visited
Baltic enclave of charming towns, bog-spattered wilderness,
and soaring fortresses.*

"Fairy-tale" is an analogy much used to describe Baltic trio Estonia, Latvia, and Lithuania. And true, their museum-worthy old towns, cornucopia of castles, and thick forests may well have you believing you've stepped into a world penned by Hans Christian Andersen. Yet the most fairy-tale-like thing, perhaps, is the thrill of the unknown that envelops these three tiny nations. With their long stints under Soviet rule and being tucked away in a corner of the continent, the Baltic countries—on a through-route to Finland and Russia— have never been the obvious option for a train trip.

> The thrill of the unknown envelops these three tiny nations

But Estonia and Latvia joined Lithuania on the Interrail program in 2020, which means there has never been a better time to roam the region by rail. For now, all use Russian gauge tracks, too, unlike the majority of Europe, making them inviting places to explore altogether in one long locomotive ride.

And a wealth of attractions awaits. Not in the way of bombastic sights, rather in the plenitude of gentle spells cast by enchanting towns of East-meets-West architecture, in the shards of a stark yet intriguing Soviet legacy, and in the urbane culture that has ▶

Left The rooftops of Rīga's Old Town
Below Lyduvėnai Bridge, one of the longest in Lithuania

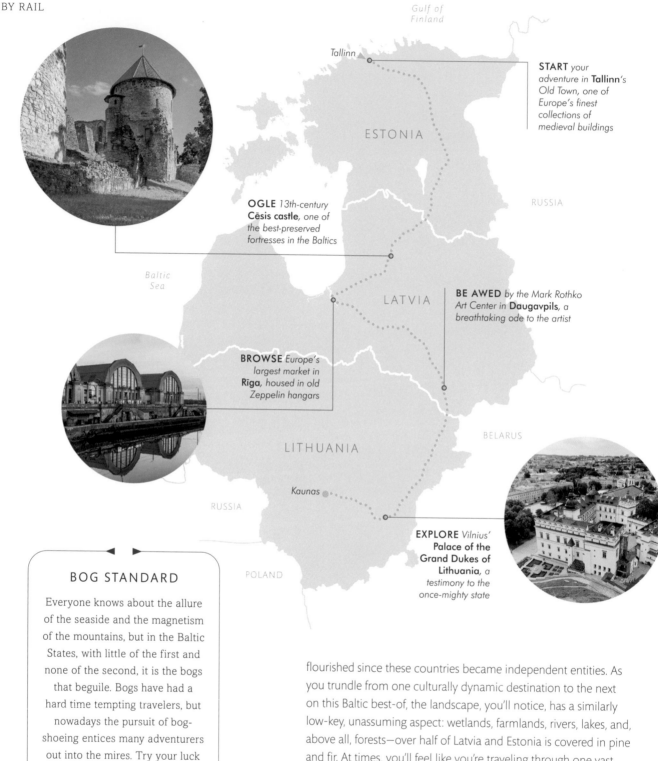

Gulf of Finland

Tallinn

START *your adventure in* **Tallinn's** *Old Town, one of Europe's finest collections of medieval buildings*

ESTONIA

RUSSIA

OGLE *13th-century* **Cēsis castle,** *one of the best-preserved fortresses in the Baltics*

Baltic Sea

LATVIA

BE AWED *by the Mark Rothko Art Center in* **Daugavpils,** *a breathtaking ode to the artist*

BROWSE *Europe's largest market in* **Rīga,** *housed in old Zeppelin hangars*

LITHUANIA

BELARUS

RUSSIA

Kaunas

POLAND

EXPLORE *Vilnius'* **Palace of the Grand Dukes of Lithuania,** *a testimony to the once-mighty state*

BOG STANDARD

Everyone knows about the allure of the seaside and the magnetism of the mountains, but in the Baltic States, with little of the first and none of the second, it is the bogs that beguile. Bogs have had a hard time tempting travelers, but nowadays the pursuit of bog-shoeing entices many adventurers out into the mires. Try your luck in particularly bog-rich Estonia: Kõnnu Suursoo bog in Põhja-Kõrvemaa Nature Reserve covers a huge swathe of swampy terrain.

flourished since these countries became independent entities. As you trundle from one culturally dynamic destination to the next on this Baltic best-of, the landscape, you'll notice, has a similarly low-key, unassuming aspect: wetlands, farmlands, rivers, lakes, and, above all, forests—over half of Latvia and Estonia is covered in pine and fir. At times, you'll feel like you're traveling through one vast nature reserve. But then, just as the sensation sinks in, out of the distance emerges a town studded with castles, cathedrals, and charming old burghers' houses.

The capitals of Tallinn (Estonia), Rīga (Latvia), and Vilnius (Lithuania) are the journey's only stop-offs that Baltic first-timers are likely to have heard of. Expect a montage of turrets, domes, and magnificent medieval buildings in each, packed with pretty museums and wrapped with cobblestone streets. But the take-your-breath-away moments might just come in between. Tartu tantalizes with its elegant 18th-century center enlivened by Estonia's most esteemed university—and the student population that comes with it. Latvia's rails take you to Cēsis, brandishing one of the Baltic's best-preserved castles, and Daugavpils, birthplace of abstract artist Mark Rothko with a sensational art center dedicated to him within the city's fortress. The end of the ride is Kaunas, a place with excellent museums, an exquisite Baroque monastery, and the kind of artistic trappings that come with being a European City of Culture.

Watch this track-space, though: the highly anticipated Rail Baltica project, which aims to connect major destinations in all three nations by train from Warsaw and Helsinki, is set to catapult train travel here further into the spotlight. Book your Baltic berth before cars get crowded.

> ## Expect a montage of turrets, domes and magnificent medieval buildings

another way
Take the same route and slow it right down, adding stops in Latvia such as Sigulda (for Turaida Castle) or Jūrmala (for fantastic beaches). Or extend journey's end from Kanaus to Klaipėda to finish with some Lithuanian beach time.

Left Passenger trains in Vilnius Station
Below Town Hall Square, the focal point of Tallinn's Old Town

BY WATER

Fishing villages and forest-fringed lakes. Pelicans and polar bears. From the Arctic to the Aegean, the scale and variety of Europe's waters are astounding. Take an expedition ship around Svalbard or a river tour down the Rhine; raft the Tara Canyon in Montenegro or ferry-hop through the Greek Islands. Whether you cruise, sail, paddle, or float, time on the water is always time well spent.

Norwegian
Islands

㉙
SVALBARD

ICELAND

SWEDEN

NORWAY

㉚

㉝

DENMARK

②

①

⑰

③

UNITED
KINGDOM

⑨

⑯

IRELAND

NETHERLANDS

⑤

POLAND

⑥

GERMANY

④

⑦

⑧

BELGIUM

CZECH
REPUBLIC

LUX.

SLOVAKIA

⑱

FRANCE

⑮

AUSTRIA

HUNGARY

⑭

SWITZ.

⑳

SLOVENIA

CROATIA

⑫

⑲

BOSNIA-
HERZ.

㉓

⑬

㉑

MONTE-
NEGRO

⑪

ITALY

㉒

⑩

ALBANIA

PORTUGAL

SPAIN

Previous page The colorful town of
Varenna, on the shores of Lake Como in Italy

AT A GLANCE
BY WATER

KEY TO MAP

Long route ············

End point ●

Far-reaching views of Loch Ness from Dores Beach

Great Glen Canoe Trail

LOCATION Scotland **START/FINISH** Corpach/Inverness **DISTANCE** 60 miles (97 km) **TIME** 5 days **INFORMATION** greatglencanoetrail.info; some open-water experience necessary; guided trips and luggage transfers available

Canoe or kayak along Scotland's Caledonian Canal, from the Atlantic to the North Sea, taking in ancient clan castles, deep lochs, and some of Scotland's finest food along the way.

Slicing through the Great Glen—Scotland's own rift valley, surrounded by gnarly hills and mountains that shimmer with snow for much of the year— the Caledonian Canal is an engineering wonder. Its 60 miles (97 km) connect a series of sea and inland lochs, creating a passage from the Atlantic to the North Sea. The Caledonian has been used as a working waterway since 1822 but today serves as a spectacular route for visitors to venture deep into these dramatic landscapes.

Setting off from Corpach on the shores of Loch Linnhe, you'll paddle in whatever vessel you choose along the canal's calm waters, quickly leaving behind civilization as you get deeper into the wild Highlands. Out here, if it's not other boaters or hikers on the towpath, you might have otters, red squirrels, or even ospreys and golden eagles for company as you float along.

Loch Lochy is your first taste of open water. From here, looking south on a clear day, you'll get glorious views of the towering Nevis Range in the distance, often snowcapped and always majestic. Loch Oich is home to the ruins of Invergarry Castle, which can be reached from a small pontoon on

FINISH *in* **Inverness** *with a dram of whisky and a few local oysters*

Inverness

PADDLE *past the ruins of* **Urquhart Castle,** *a much fought-over medieval fortress*

EXPLORE *the shores of* **Loch Ness,** *always on the lookout for the eponymous monster*

SCOTLAND

WATCH *boats tackle* **Neptune's Staircase,** *an engineering feat of eight locks*

Corpach

SEE *the regal* **Nevis Range** *in the distance, all snow-topped and spectacular*

THE NESSIE HUNTER

Everybody knows the legend of the Loch Ness monster. Nessie, as the elusive creature has been monikered, has still never been officially sighted, but that hasn't stopped one man dedicating his life to looking for her: Steve Feltham has been on the hunt for the Loch Ness monster since 1991. Living on lochside Dores Beach in a static van, you'll either see him making clay models of Nessie or out on the water, seeking her scaly back breaching the surface.

> You might have otters, ospreys, and golden eagles for company as you float along

the western side. And at Fort Augustus you'll find your way onto the fabled (and choppy) waters of Loch Ness, more than 22 miles (36 km) long and 754 ft (230 m) deep in parts—deep enough to hide a monster. There's more water in Loch Ness than in all of the rivers and reservoirs in England and Wales combined, and you'll be paddling on it for what feels like an eternity before squeezing back into the narrow canal for the run into Inverness.

② Sea-kayaking in the Outer Hebrides

Kayakers on a white-sand beach, the Sound of Barra

LOCATION Scotland **START/FINISH** Castlebay, Isle of Barra (return) **DISTANCE** 8–15 miles (13–24 km) per day; route varies depending on weather and experience **TIME** 1 week (return) **INFORMATION** www.clearwaterpaddling.com; trips Apr–Sept; book in advance

These far-flung watery islands and islets are perfect to explore by kayak: you'll spot seals, otters, and eagles as you paddle alongside bleached shell beaches and machair grassland.

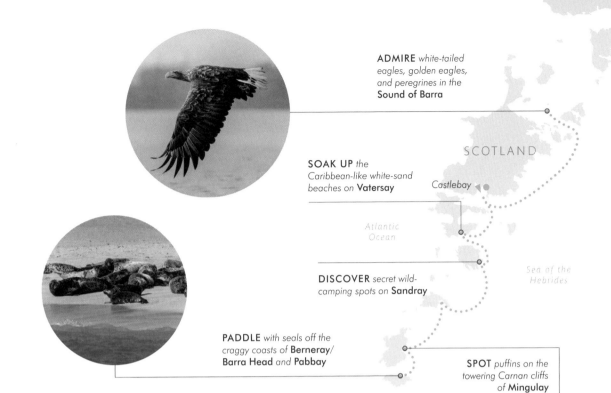

ADMIRE white-tailed eagles, golden eagles, and peregrines in the **Sound of Barra**

SOAK UP the Caribbean-like white-sand beaches on **Vatersay**

SCOTLAND

Castlebay

Atlantic Ocean

Sea of the Hebrides

DISCOVER secret wild-camping spots on **Sandray**

PADDLE with seals off the craggy coasts of **Berneray/ Barra Head** and **Pabbay**

SPOT puffins on the towering Carnan cliffs of **Mingulay**

The archipelago that is the Outer Hebrides (also known as Na h-Eileanan Siar, or the Western Isles) is a unique and off-the-beaten-track destination reached only by plane, or by ferry from Skye or Oban. There are around 220 islands in the chain, with the largest inhabited outcrops including— from north to south—Lewis and Harris, North Uist, Benbecula, South Uist, and Barra. Submerged prehistoric forests, standing stones, burial sites, and chambered cairns all add to the powerful sense of history on these islands, where the predominant rock type is Lewisian Gneiss, the oldest rock in Europe, formed up to 3 billion years ago. Today, communities have strong Gaelic traditions and there's a distinct independence from the Scottish mainland.

Offshore the magic continues. Shallow turquoise lagoons connect to the sea where sheer cliffs, sea caves, rocky archways, and huge stacks demarcate the craggy coastline. Kayaking in this grand and wild scenery will make you feel small and awe-inspired. Beginners can stick close to land and enjoy gliding through serene and sheltered waters, but for the ultimate sea-kayaking experience you can paddle south to the end of the Outer Hebrides, wild camping along the way. Stop at Vatersay (the southernmost and westernmost inhabited island) before making a push to the remote islands of Sandray, Pabbay, Mingulay, and Berneray/Barra Head to spot nesting puffins, razorbills, and guillemots. Finally, head north along the rocky shoreline of Barra and up into the broad blue stretch of the sheltered Sound of Barra, where—with a bit of luck—you might glimpse dolphins and basking sharks.

another way

Clearwater Paddling offers tall-ship kayaking tours to Orkney and the hard-to-reach islands of the remote St. Kilda archipelago, using the ship as a comfortable base for the week and exploring the islands' cliffs and wildlife-rich coastlines by kayak each day.

A traditional narrow boat moored by the bridge in Graiguenamanagh

③

Barrow River

LOCATION Ireland **START/FINISH** Tullamore (return) **DISTANCE** 150 miles (240 km) **TIME** 1 week **INFORMATION** www.riverbarrow.net

Drift along the Barrow River to a bucolic backdrop of reedy riverbanks, crumbling castles, and waterfront pubs.

If you're going to get nowhere fast, there can surely be fewer places better than the Barrow River in County Kildare. Yellow iris, cuckooflower, and the heavily scented meadowsweet line the riverbanks; herons let your barge get tantalizingly close before launching off across the water. Each lock you pass through comes complete with a traditional white-washed house and resident lockkeeper, ready for a chat and—this being Ireland—to offer some pointers on where to raise a glass of Guinness that evening.

For nearly 200 years, steel-boarded narrow boats have plied the Grand Canal network, first trans-porting peat to Dublin and beyond and latterly ferrying tourists through the bucolic countryside. Hop aboard a working slice of 1950s river life and spend a languid week cruising along the Grand Canal and down the Barrow River, one of the most beautiful navigable stretches in Europe.

You'll average a leisurely 4 mph (6 kph) or so, following a daily routine of moorings off, engine on, slow chug to the next ruined castle or cozy local. Double locks present the occasional obstacle, but it's easy to slip back to tranquility again—just flick the engine into neutral and you'll be surrounded by silence, with nothing but the soothing slosh of water against the bow as your narrow boat glides calmly through the reeds.

Lundy Island

LOCATION England **START/FINISH** Lundy Island Harbour (return)
DISTANCE 9 miles (14 km) **TIME** 2 days **INFORMATION**
Accommodation must be pre-booked via www.landmarktrust.org.uk

A weekend paddleboard around Lundy Island promises squawking seabirds, searingly beautiful scenery, and some truly intriguing caves ripe for exploring.

Almost 12 miles (20 km) off the coast of Devon, stranded in the Bristol Channel, Lundy Island has seen human activity for around 3,000 years. There's evidence of Bronze and Iron Age settlements, and Vikings are responsible for its name, meaning Puffin Island. Today, the best human activity involves getting out on the water with a paddleboard to explore its craggy, cave-pocked coastline. While you might not meet many puffins along the way (their population has dwindled thanks to nonnative rats), you're sure to spot penguin-like guillemots, striking razorbills, and Manx shearwaters that patrol the skies and nest in the cliffs.

The perspective is spellbinding from the water. The island's western side is all smooth granite with natural slipways and layered sea stacks, while its eastern shores are peppered with wildflowers in spring and summer. You could probably do this paddle in a day, but the real pleasure is taking your time to explore its sea caves or hopping off your board for a brief snorkel to see the stony corals that lie beneath. Lundy was the UK's first ever marine conservation area—look for gray seals as you float, and if you're lucky you might even spot a dolphin, pilot whale, or harbor porpoise.

***Top** Lundy Island, on the horizon **Above** Guillemots clinging to a craggy rock face*

another way

If watery adventures aren't for you, explore Lundy Island by foot on its coastal paths. A 4-mile (6-km) route takes you around the northern half of the island, affording endless ocean views.

The tranquil Wye River meandering through wooded hills and rolling farmland

5

Wye River

LOCATION England and Wales **START/FINISH** Ross-on-Wye/
Chepstow **DISTANCE** Up to 100 miles (160 km) **TIME** 2–4 days
INFORMATION www.visitdeanwye.co.uk, www.wyevalleyaonb.org.uk

*Take to the winding Wye River for some fine British
scenery, a few enthralling rapids, and to see what all
the fuss was about in Wordsworth's famous poem.*

Few rivers in the world command such enchanting scenery as the
Wye. This twisting waterway, which has its source in the Welsh
Cambrian mountains and empties out into the Severn Estuary
around Chepstow, passes through quaint villages, handsome
market towns, and remote farmsteads, offering a mesmerizing view
of rural Britain. Whether you choose to canoe its most navigable
length—around 100 miles (160 km)—or simply choose a section to
explore over a day or two, the Wye promises great reward.

Most trips begin from Ross-on-Wye, a charming market town
that was made famous among travelers in the late 1700s by William
Gilpin's *Observations on the River Wye* book. It was this writing that
established the "Wye Tour," an alternative to the European Grand
Tour for those who couldn't afford such adventures abroad. From
here, you'll paddle southward through Kerne Bridge and Lydbrook,
and past Symonds Yat Rock, where you can climb out of your
canoe and hike up to the viewpoint for one of the region's most
iconic vistas of the sloping valley.

It's spectacular birding country here, so look for goshawks and
sparrowhawks, hovering kestrels, and soaring buzzards in the skies
and trees that surround the river; with a bit of patience and good
luck, you might even spot a peregrine falcon. Though always be
careful to keep an eye on the waters, too—there are a few rapids

THE DEVIL'S PULPIT

There are myriad
myths and legends
across the Wye Valley,
but the Devil's Pulpit is
perhaps its most
famous. This rocky
viewpoint looms over
the ruins of Tintern
Abbey and is well
worth the steep climb
up the hills. It's said
that the Devil himself
created this rugged
outcrop, to try to turn
the Cistercian monks
that prayed there away
from their religious
leanings. Henry VIII
succeeded where
Satan failed when he
had the monastery
destroyed in 1536.

along this stretch of the Wye, which require a little focus and a lot of mettle to tackle in your canoe. It's bumpy and bouncy, but the ride is short-lived: it's largely a tranquil waterway from here onward, so once you've mastered the rapids, you can return your gaze to the surrounding scenery.

And it's plain sailing onto delightful Monmouth. This unassuming market town has lovely independent shops and some regal Georgian buildings, but most intriguing is its big music history: the likes of Queen, Oasis, and Simple Minds all recorded songs here at Rockfield Studios. It also became the UK's first official "Bee Town" in 2020, thanks to its work preserving habitats for essential pollinators like honeybees; stop off to pick up some local honey or swig a glug of mead.

> Once you've mastered the rapids, you can return your gaze to the surrounding scenery

Right *Ross-on-Wye, Herefordshire* **Below** *Bigsweir Bridge, connecting England and Wales*

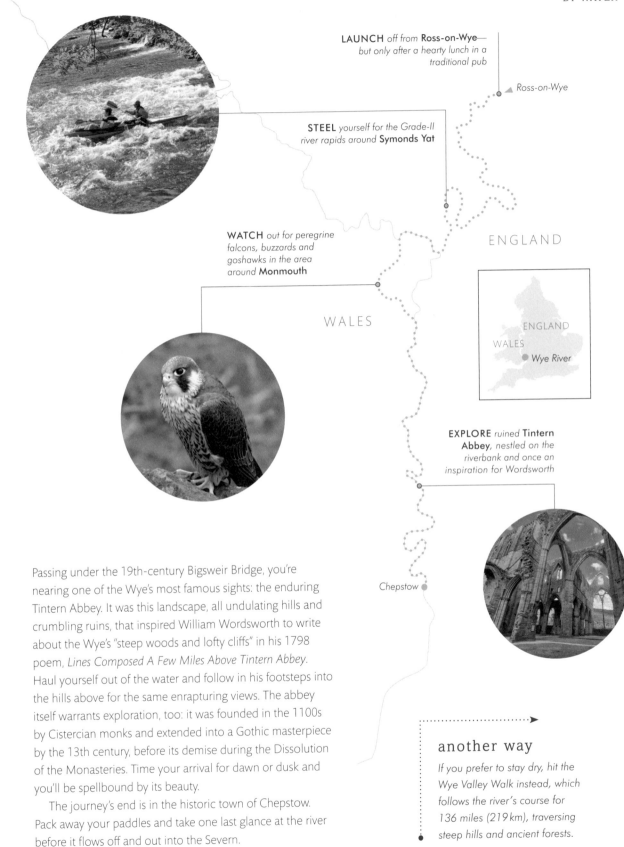

LAUNCH *off from* **Ross-on-Wye**—
but only after a hearty lunch in a traditional pub

Ross-on-Wye

STEEL *yourself for the Grade-II river rapids around* **Symonds Yat**

ENGLAND

WATCH *out for peregrine falcons, buzzards and goshawks in the area around* **Monmouth**

WALES

ENGLAND
WALES
Wye River

EXPLORE *ruined* **Tintern Abbey**, *nestled on the riverbank and once an inspiration for Wordsworth*

Chepstow

Passing under the 19th-century Bigsweir Bridge, you're nearing one of the Wye's most famous sights: the enduring Tintern Abbey. It was this landscape, all undulating hills and crumbling ruins, that inspired William Wordsworth to write about the Wye's "steep woods and lofty cliffs" in his 1798 poem, *Lines Composed A Few Miles Above Tintern Abbey*. Haul yourself out of the water and follow in his footsteps into the hills above for the same enrapturing views. The abbey itself warrants exploration, too: it was founded in the 1100s by Cistercian monks and extended into a Gothic masterpiece by the 13th century, before its demise during the Dissolution of the Monasteries. Time your arrival for dawn or dusk and you'll be spellbound by its beauty.

The journey's end is in the historic town of Chepstow. Pack away your paddles and take one last glance at the river before it flows off and out into the Severn.

another way

If you prefer to stay dry, hit the Wye Valley Walk instead, which follows the river's course for 136 miles (219 km), traversing steep hills and ancient forests.

6 Mon & Brec Canal

LOCATION Wales **START/FINISH** Goytre Wharf–Brecon **DISTANCE** 27 miles (42 km) **TIME** 4 days **INFORMATION** https://canalrivertrust. org.uk

Cutting through the spectacular Brecon Beacons National Park, the Monmouthshire & Brecon (or Mon & Brec) Canal, built in the late 19th century, is a blissful way to see some of Wales' finest scenery—and exploring it by narrow boat is the best way forward. Start from the tranquil Goytre Wharf, a former industrial hub with a collection of well-preserved historic limekilns, and head north on your journey to Brecon. As you chug along the still waters of this leafy canal, you'll leave behind the bustle of the wharf and enter into a peaceful, bucolic landscape. The rotund hills of the Brecon Beacons rise up around you as you pass through Llangattock and Talybont-on-Usk. It's not all relaxation: you've five locks to contend with as you get closer to Brecon, each one hand-operated. Happily, though, this hard work is well rewarded with a Welsh rarebit in one of the town's many charming pubs.

Barges on the Monmouthshire & Brecon Canal

7 The Thames

LOCATION England **START/FINISH** Cricklade/ Teddington **DISTANCE** 140 miles (224 km) **TIME** 4 to 6 days **INFORMATION** www.visitthames.co. uk/things-to-do/boating/stand-up-paddle-boarding

Now here's a stand-up paddleboarding trip to remember. England's "royal river" unfurls for almost 218 miles (350 km) from a soggy field in the Cotswolds to the expanse of the North Sea. The Thames is best known as the waterway that flows imperiously through central London, although for the bulk of its length it threads among gentle meadows and bucolic countryside. It departs its source as little more than a trickle but soon widens out to become a fully fledged river, passable by small watercraft.

And that's where you come in. The navigable, non-tidal part of the Thames technically begins at Cricklade Bridge in Wiltshire and finishes at Teddington in southwest London, an epic stretch that can be paddleboarded in four to six days. You'll pass through (or around, as you should really portage) more than 40 locks, and spend much of your time immersed in a world of ducks, narrow boats, and open fields. Camping's an option, as are hotels and B&Bs; ending the evenings at traditional riverside pubs along the way is obligatory.

another way

The Thames Path National Trail is a 183-mile (294-km) hiking path that follows the river from its source to the Thames Barrier—or, indeed, vice versa. Allow up to two weeks for what is an unforgettable walk.

The historical houses of Korenlei and Graslei facing each other across the Leie

⑧ Leie River

LOCATION Belgium **START/FINISH**
Sint-Martens-Latem/Gravensteen, Ghent
DISTANCE 8 miles (13 km) **TIME** 3 hours

Starting in Sint-Martens-Latem, southwest of
Ghent, a paddleboard on the section of the Leie
River that runs through northwest Belgium is a
paddle of two parts. It begins amid a rural stretch
of weeping willows and water lilies, where
manicured lawns run up to stately mansions,
houseboats are moored at regular intervals, and
yacht clubs tempt with riverside terraces. Cross
the Ringvaart canal, though, and you're heading
into the heart of medieval Ghent. The river
narrows and you start passing one majestic
building after another: the Old Fish Market;
St. Michael's Church; Korenlei and Graslei, eyeing
each other across the river, the facades of their
picture-perfect guildhalls reflected in the water.
Fork left and you come to the stout walls of
12th-century Gravensteen, the Castle of the
Counts, an impressive enough sight from
street level but truly remarkable from down
on the water.

⑨ 11 City Tour

LOCATION Netherlands **START/FINISH**
Leeuwarden (loop) **DISTANCE** 136 miles
(220 km) **TIME** 5 days **INFORMATION**
www.sup11citytour.com

Big skies and a vast watery landscape are your
constant companions on the 11 City Tour, a
stand-up paddleboarding challenge that follows
a circuit through Friesland from the provincial
capital of Leeuwarden. Dreamed up by Anne-
Marie Valeria Reichman, a Friesland native, the
route connects the 11 historic cities of the
Netherlands' most northerly province.

You'll pass through Sneek, with its emblematic
waterpoort (a 17th-century defensive gate), the
attractive pilgrimage town of Bolsward, and
Hindeloopen, once a bustling shipping center
but now a placid maze of narrow alleyways and
wooden bridges. You'll overnight—in a comfy
traditional Friesland sailing boat—in Dokkum,
Franeker, Workum, and Sloten. And you'll paddle
down canals lined with gable-roofed houses,
through forests and peat bogs, and along the
wind-buffeted shoreline of IJsselmeer. The course
record is under 24 hours. You'll have five glorious
days to take it all in.

THE ELFSTEDENTOCHT

The 11 City Tour is a
modern-day take on the original
Elfstedentocht, an ice-skating
event first held in 1909. Around
15,000 amateur skaters take part,
including (in 1986) one Willem-
Alexander, the future king of the
Netherlands. The race can only
take place when the ice is at least
6 inches (15 cm) thick—which
last happened in 1997.

Left *Vila Nova de Gaia* **Above** *Terraced vineyards in the Douro Valley*

⑩ Douro Valley

LOCATION Portugal **START/FINISH** Vila Nova de Gaia/Porto
DISTANCE 62 miles (100 km) **TIME** 1 day **INFORMATION** Boat
tours can be booked at www.livingtours.com

*Laze your way through Portugal's Valley of Gold on
a river cruise, stopping off at wine lodges to sample
the port for which this region is justly famous.*

Winding down the Rio Douro on a traditional riverboat, a glass of port
in hand, drinking in the view of rolling vineyards and historic wine
lodges—there are worse ways to spend the day.

From the pleasingly ramshackle riverfront of Vila Nova de Gaia,
a city across the Rio Douro from Porto, your riverboat passes under
the looming girders of Porto's Dom Luís I Bridge and heads east,
into the lush green wine country of the Douro Valley. This is the
heartland of port wine—a fact not lost on the British, who set up
innumerable wine lodges here. Look out for elegantly crumbling
quintas adorned with names like Cockburn, Taylor, and Yeatman
breaking up the vineyards.

In the port town of Pinhão, disembark to visit one such estate: the
Symington property of Quinta do Bomfim. Taste the white, tawny, and
ruby wines that have been lovingly made here since 1896, and learn
about the process with a factory tour. Back on board, wind lazily back
toward Porto, as the sunset casts aglow the vineyards of the valley
walls. It's clear why they call it the Rio Douro—the River of Gold.

PORT WINE

What distinguishes
port from ordinary
wine is the process of
fortification. A
brandy-like spirit is
added to the wine
during the
fermentation process,
which enhances both
alcohol and sugar and
lends port its
characteristic thick
sweetness. Often
enjoyed as a dessert
wine, port was long
prescribed for
apparent medicinal
benefits in times
past—these days, it's
best considered a tonic
for the soul, rather
than the body.

⑪ Nervión River

LOCATION Spain **START/FINISH** Town Hall Bridge (return) **DISTANCE** 15 miles (24 km) **TIME** 2 hours **INFORMATION** www.bilbaoturismo.net

Frank Gehry's stunning Guggenheim Museum in Bilbao

The bold Basque city has reinvented itself over the past three decades, pivoting from grimy port to cultural icon. Make a journey along its vital waterway to witness this masterly metamorphosis up close.

Bilbao has become a byword for urban regeneration. Following the opening of Frank Gehry's ground-breaking Guggenheim Museum in 1997, the previously down-at-heel port has been transformed into an art-and-architecture hub. And one of the best ways to see all this change is by boat.

Founded in the 14th century, Bilbao sits just inland from the Bay of Biscay, with the Nervión River flowing through its center, out to sea. Catch a boat along this lifeblood waterway and you'll not only glide past the spruced-up buildings of the Old Town and the rippled silver waves of the Guggenheim but also Santiago Calatrava's curvaceous Zubizuri bridge, the vast Euskalduna Concert Hall, and old industrial areas that have been turned into stylish new residential and cultural districts, like the previously abandoned Zorrotzaurre peninsula. You'll also pass impressive wharfs and docks that provide a reminder of the city's productive past.

Finally, at the river's mouth, lies the extraordinary Puente Colgante, or Hanging Bridge. Built in 1893 to link both banks without impeding those all-important ships, it's the world's oldest transporter bridge, and continues to convey people and vehicles across, via a gondola suspended on cables from vertiginous towers. It's a working relic of Bilbao's past in a city fixed firmly on the future.

another way

At the other end of Spain, take a cruise through Seville's history on the Guadalquivir River, passing the Torre del Oro, the 19th-century houses of the Triana district and Isla de la Cartuja.

(12)

The Dordogne

The beautiful village of La Roque Gageac, on the northern bank of the Dordogne

LOCATION France **START/FINISH** Argentat/Mauzac **DISTANCE** 106 miles (170 km)
TIME 9–12 days **INFORMATION** https://canoedordogne.com/en

Steer your canoe down the Dordogne River, through one of France's most romanticized regions—where you'd be wise to relish the scenery rather than rush past it.

Glorious food. Age-old châteaux. Wooded hills and soaring limestone cliffs. The reasons to head to the Dordogne are endless, but this come-hither corner of France is more than just somewhere to unwind. The bucolic 106-mile (170-km) section of the river between Argentat and Mauzac could have been purpose-built for a canoeing adventure, providing historical drama, deep views, and the chance to paddle through some kinder, gentler realm where inboxes and rolling news have little bearing.

The journey starts off as a deliciously quiet affair, but you'll have more company on the famously sumptuous stretch between Souillac and Beynac-et-Cazenac, a section marked by clifftop castles and honey-hued medieval towns. Things get more serene again as you continue downstream, although the all-enfolding loveliness of the Dordogne countryside never lets up.

Whether you're powering from A to B or taking things slowly, you'll find a range of accommodation options, from riverside campsites to luxurious B&Bs. Make sure you join those dots with plenty of lazy lunch stops and fine-dining dinners—this is one of France's top foodie destinations, after all.

13 Canal du Midi

LOCATION France **START/FINISH** Toulouse/Étang de Thau
DISTANCE 150 miles (240 km) **TIME** 10 days **INFORMATION**
www.french-waterways.com/waterways/south/canal-midi

*A boat gliding
lazily along the
Canal du Midi*

*Board a canalboat and cruise along France's most famous
waterway to enjoy the plane tree-dappled countryside of
the languid south.*

As legacies go, the creation of the Canal du Midi takes a beating.
Between 1667 and 1694, engineer Pierre-Paul Riquet built a 150-mile
(240-km) artificial waterway between France's south coast and the city
of Toulouse, in the process creating a through-route from the Atlantic
to the Mediterranean. His achievement was recognized in 1996 (not
before time) by UNESCO, who inscribed the canal onto the World
Heritage List and called it "not only a technical feat, but also a work of
art." Its highest point, the Seuil de Naurouze, is some 623 ft (190 m)
above sea level, but no less remarkable is the way in which the canal
has become a living, breathing part of its surroundings.

Which all means the waterway is also a hugely popular pleasure-
ground for hire boats. Dozens of locks lie between Toulouse and the
sea, as does a region of quintessential French scenery, complete
with sunflower fields, traditional orchards, and age-old villages.
Chugging along the waterway as the canal curves through the
countryside (cheese and wine for lunch? *pourquoi pas?*) is an
unfettered delight, even at busy times during the *grandes vacances*
of high summer.

another way

*If you'd rather be in the
saddle than at the tiller, it's
possible to cycle alongside
the canal on largely flat
paths, with optional detours
to the likes of Carcassonne,
Narbonne, and Béziers.*

(14)

The Rhine

LOCATION Switzerland, Germany, France, and the Netherlands **START/FINISH** Basel/Amsterdam **DISTANCE** 468 miles (750 km) **TIME** 8 days

Drift through the heart of Europe on this classic cruise along one of the continent's longest and prettiest rivers, beginning in Switzerland and finishing off in spirited Amsterdam.

Not all rivers are created equal. Beginning its life high in the Swiss Alps, the Rhine flows across the European map for 760 miles (1,230 km), forming not just a major landmark but—in many cases—an official border between nations. By the time it flows through the medieval heart of Switzerland's Basel, it's not only well on its way toward the North Sea but wide enough to accommodate substantial passenger vessels, making it one of the continent's top-tier options for a multi-day river cruise.

> There's a golden-era charm to the idea of gliding through the countryside

There's a golden-era charm to the idea of gliding through the countryside on what is, essentially, a floating hotel, watching wineries and castles slide past as the hours drift by with the current. If ocean cruising can tend toward gimmicky facilities (skydiving simulator, anyone?), river cruising still has tradition at its core, with an emphasis on comfort, relaxation, and, of course, the scenery itself. It generally takes eight days or so to travel from Switzerland to the coast, which is more than long enough to be lulled by the Rhine's sedative powers.

Shore excursions add to the overall experience. North from Basel, the first major settlement of note is Strasbourg, a fascinating ▶

Left *The Lorelei, in Germany's Upper Middle Rhine Valley*
Below *Strasbourg's historic quarter*

Left *Amsterdam, a fitting finale for this river tour* **Above** *Niederwaldtempel, overlooking the Rhine at Rüdesheim am Rhein*

THE LEGEND OF THE LORELEI

The Lorelei, in Germany's Upper Middle Rhine Valley, looks much like any large riverside promontory—it's steep, tree-covered, and made of slate—but it has a tale to tell. Legend associates it with a beautiful maiden who launched herself into the river after being betrayed by a lover. The well-known story, which these days forms part of any Rhine commentary worth its salt, goes on to tell us that she then became a ghostly siren, luring fishermen to their deaths.

French border city with a half-timbered Old Town and a towering cathedral. Several hours of cruising later, the Baroque charm of Germany's Heidelberg—a muse for so many authors and composers—is a further highlight, followed soon after by the Rheingau wine region, famed for its Riesling. Which brings us onto one of the truisms about a Rhine cruise: the slopes and forests that flank the river look even prettier when you've got a chilled glass of white in your hand.

Continuing north, you're now traveling through quintessential Rhine gorge landscapes, the hilly banks lined with fortresses, village steeples, and medieval towns. This section of the river valley has been inscribed onto UNESCO's World Heritage List for the way in which it combines natural beauty with centuries of human influence, inspiring countless artists and bringing a soft-focus, storybook feel to the river scenery—terraced vineyards, age-old ruins, and all.

After you've passed through Bonn, formerly the capital of West Germany, the old-meets-new buzz of Cologne is the next big attraction along the river. It has the largest Gothic cathedral in northern Europe, a twin-spired colossus that finds a natural home in this architecturally rich, culturally layered city.

The same description can just as easily be applied to your final disembarkation point. Amsterdam isn't technically on the Rhine, but the presence of the Amsterdam-Rhine canal allows the colorful Dutch capital to form a fitting finale to a trip along the river. You'll now have some 468 miles (750 km) of river cruising under your belt, not to mention a week's worth of good food and drink, but this is emphatically not a city to be missed. Take time to wander the canals and to visit the Rijksmuseum and Van Gogh Museum—a suitably arty way to wrap up a trip that places beauty and aesthetics front and center.

another way

The Danube is another of Europe's wide and wonderful rivers, and a cruise along its length allows you to visit big-hitting cities such as Budapest, Vienna, and Bratislava. Come in December to enjoy the Christmas markets.

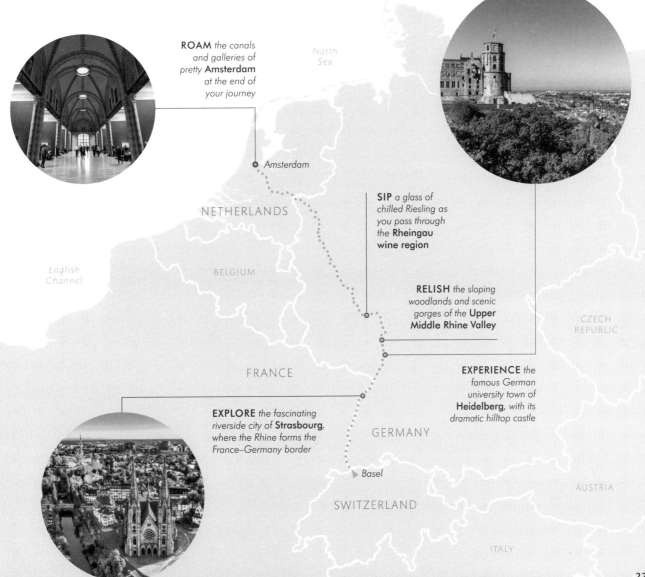

ROAM *the canals and galleries of pretty* **Amsterdam** *at the end of your journey*

North Sea

Amsterdam

NETHERLANDS

English Channel

BELGIUM

FRANCE

SIP *a glass of chilled Riesling as you pass through the* **Rheingau wine region**

RELISH *the sloping woodlands and scenic gorges of the* **Upper Middle Rhine Valley**

CZECH REPUBLIC

EXPERIENCE *the famous German university town of* **Heidelberg,** *with its dramatic hilltop castle*

GERMANY

EXPLORE *the fascinating riverside city of* **Strasbourg,** *where the Rhine forms the France–Germany border*

Basel

AUSTRIA

SWITZERLAND

ITALY

15

Bodensee

LOCATION Germany, Austria, and Switzerland **START/FINISH**
Various **DISTANCE** Varies **TIME** 7–10 days **INFORMATION**
www.bodensee.eu/en

*The Bodensee is an intriguing alternative to Europe's
traditional beachy breaks, where you can paddle out
from historic island towns to castles and vineyards.*

Finding an away-from-the-crowds destination for a watery break in
Europe—with islands, beaches, and tropical gardens with a sense of only
just being discovered—is harder than ever these days. And yet, paddling
the Bodensee (or Lake Constance, to give it its English name), it can feel
like the answer has been here all along.

Despite its size (it's the second largest in Europe), the lake is
surprisingly overlooked, offering canoeing and kayaking that few other
lakes can match. Start with a canoe tour on the Swiss side from Stein am
Rhein to the Schaffhausen waterfalls, or explore the German Riviera by
kayaking from Lindau island to the lakefront vineyards of Meersburg.
Tourism has hardly altered the shoreline here and, as well as a fringe
of crowd-free beaches, one last push could bring you to Mainau, an
island with a castle and botanic gardens. Alternatively, base yourself in
Konstanz, where the streets are filled with Gothic churches and former
monasteries puffing out their chests. From here, nature reserves and
islands tucked away in the lake's riverine headwaters await.

another way

*Kayaking or canoeing too
much work? Bodensee-
Schifffahrt operates ferries
from all landing points on the
German lakeside from March
to October. The Bodensee
Card PLUS offers free use of
passenger ferries, as well as
discounts at more than 160
activities around the lake,
including—naturally—
canoeing and kayaking.*

*The dramatic
entrance to the
Bodensee at
Lindau*

Left *Boathouses lining Mirowsee*
Above *A kayaker paddling along Schwaanhavel River*

(16)

Mecklenburg Lake District

LOCATION Germany **START/FINISH** Kanustation Mirow/Wesenberg **DISTANCE** 22 miles (35 km) **TIME** 2 days **DIFFICULTY** Moderate to challenging **INFORMATION** www.mecklenburgische-seenplatte.de; best Apr–Oct

Kayak in quiet exhilaration through a soothingly beautiful landscape of woods and water on a paddle-camping trip in Germany's Mecklenburg Lake District.

It's oh so quiet. Tucked away between Berlin and the Baltic is one of Germany's most enchanting secrets: the Mecklenburg Lake District, a fretwork of more than 1,000 lakes, most of which you've probably never heard of. But its remoteness is its greatest pull. Kayak away from the shore and suddenly you are alone, at one with the woods and the water. It's the perfect place for an off-the-radar adventure. There are few people, and even fewer interruptions—just the ever-changing light reflecting in the expanses of glassy water, an open horizon, and a starry, starry night sky at the end of a day's paddling.

Kanustation Mirow at the southern tip of Mirowsee rents out kayaks and canoes and can recommend memorable paddling routes. One such spin over lock and quay takes you to Wesenberg via a necklace of beautiful lakes and backwaters, with an overnight camp at Gobenowsee. As you paddle, time slows and nature feels breathtakingly close, whether in the silence of dawn or the pastel pinks of sunset. Bring along swimming gear for refreshing dips at unmapped beaches, and binoculars for fleeting glimpses of kingfishers, cranes, white-tailed eagles, and ospreys. From Wesenberg, taxis and canoe shuttles can get you back to base camp.

Striking Český Krumlov, a UNESCO World Heritage site

⑰ Møns Klint

LOCATION Denmark **START/FINISH** Klintholm Havn (return) **DISTANCE** 12½ miles (20 km) **TIME** 7–8 hours **INFORMATION** www.moensklint.dk; book guided trips with Camp Møns Klint (www.campmoensklint.dk); prior kayaking experience required

Denmark's outdoors is generally gentle, but around Møns Klint's high, mighty chalk cliffs, the landscape becomes a much more rugged proposition. This coastline is the key reason the island of Møn was designated Denmark's first UNESCO Biosphere Reserve, and while the wood-fringed white rock face that plummets into a pastel-blue Baltic Sea is lovely viewed from land, you need to take to the water if you want to truly appreciate it. And because all fine things merit a suitable buildup, this kayak from Klintholm Havn is the perfect way to make that picture-book paddle. The out-and-back route swoops from white-gold strands and farmland to cliffs towering up to 419 ft (128 m); beaches pepper the route, even along the cliff base, so kayakers have plenty of stunning spots to stop at. Clamber up the wooden stairs at Stranden Møns Klint to the state-of-the-art Geocenter, which waltzes you through 70 million years of Danish geological history, before the return paddle.

another way

For a shorter paddle, you can use Busene Have, south of the hamlet of Busene, as an alternative put-in point. It's less than 2½ miles (4 km) of paddling from here to Møns Klint and you'll still get to see the most magnificent scenery.

⑱ Vltava River

LOCATION Czech Republic **START/FINISH** Vyšší Brod/Český Krumlov **DISTANCE** 23 miles (38 km) **TIME** 2 days **INFORMATION** www.malecek.cz, www.loderafty.cz; trips include all equipment, transportation, and a night's camping halfway along the route

The Vltava is the Czech Republic's longest river, flowing 270 miles (435 km) across the country before emptying into the Elbe just north of Prague. It makes for a beautiful journey—passing through tranquil woodland and tiny villages—but a long one, so settle on the short stretch between Vyšší Brod and Český Krumlov for an excellent two-day taster. This bucolic cruise through South Bohemia has become something of a rite of passage for locals, and the water bubbles with boats in summer, when floating bars dole out bottles of beer to thirsty paddlers—you'll need to keep your wits about you if you want to ride the river's weirs without taking a dunking. Drifting languidly past the region's gentle scenery is the main appeal, although the route is bookended by a couple of towering landmarks: Vyšší Brod's Cistercian monastery and the lofty castle that waits by the finishing line in Český Krumlov, a dramatic ending to any journey.

(19)

Lake Como

LOCATION Italy **START/FINISH** Como/Varenna
DISTANCE 12 miles (20 km) **DURATION** 2 hours
INFORMATION www.navigazionelaghi.it

There's no better way to soak up all the glamour of Lake Como than from the water. Hop onto a traditional steamer at the jetty in Como and take in the scenery as you travel north toward Varenna. Age-old fishing villages speckle the shore, while grand villas stand majestically by the shoreline. Look out for gorgeous Villa del Balbianello, which sits on a wooded promontory jutting out into the lake, and don't miss beautiful Villa Carlotta, a 17th-century mansion with spectacular landscaped gardens tumbling down to the shore. You'll pass Bellagio, the "Pearl of the Lake," a charming lakefront town dotted with stylish boutiques and shaded by oleander and lime trees. Your journey ends in Varenna, one of the lake's most romantic towns, home to a web of steep, pedestrianized cobbled streets offering gorgeous glimpses of the lake.

◀ ▶

WE'VE BEEN EXPECTING YOU, MR. BOND

The Italian Lakes' stunning landscapes have long captivated filmmakers, not least the directors of James Bond. As your boat glides past Villa del Balbianello, you'll recognize the area from *Casino Royale*; the exhilarating chase scene at the beginning of *Quantum of Solace* was filmed at nearby Lake Garda.

(20)

Soča River

LOCATION Slovenia **START/FINISH** Bovec **DISTANCE** Varies **TIME** 1–3 hours
INFORMATION www.socarafting.si

The impossibly emerald waters of the Soča River are an astonishing sight. This fast-flowing waterway winds its way through Slovenia's Soča Valley, one of the country's top sustainable tourism destinations. The wilderness here is indeed pristine: tall, lanky pines clad the hillsides and rocky granite boulders pepper the riverbed. It's those white-gray rocks that make floating down the Soča so thrilling—and the fact that you'll be doing it on a hydrospeed, a sort of water sled that you clasp between your hands. Hydrospeeds bring you much closer to the action than a raft can, and as the water gushes over the rocks, so do you, clinging on for dear life. Calmer sections of the river offer a chance to take in the surrounding scenery: look toward the arresting Julian Alps as you meander along its lazy flow.

Kayaking and hydrospeeding down the Soča

Yachting around Croatia's Islands

The sun rising over Mljet island

LOCATION Croatia **START/FINISH** Split/Dubrovnik **DISTANCE** 235 miles (365 km)
TIME 3–5 days **INFORMATION** Cruise availability, facilities, and itineraries vary

Along the lengthy coastline between Split and Dubrovnik lies a scattering of around 1,000 islands, some inhabited by slow-living locals and others left wild and empty, ripe for exploration.

Croatia's Adriatic coast is yachtie heaven: warm, calm seas; hundreds of islands to cruise around; and plenty of craggy coves in which to drop anchor for an afternoon of ultimate escapism. Start your journey from Split, a cultural hub on the Dalmatian coast, and set sail for Hvar, a tiny island with a big personality. Explore ancient fortresses and lavender fields by day, then finish with cocktails overlooking the ocean by night.

Vis comes next, a sleepy isle home to the spectacular, almost entirely sheltered Stiniva Beach, with its azure waters lapping gently on the shingles. From here, beeline for Korčula, where a merry tangle of medieval streets makes up an enchanting old town, and verdant vineyards and olive groves groan with produce inland. Korčula has some rare sandy beaches, so make time for a spot of sunbathing before coasting over to understated

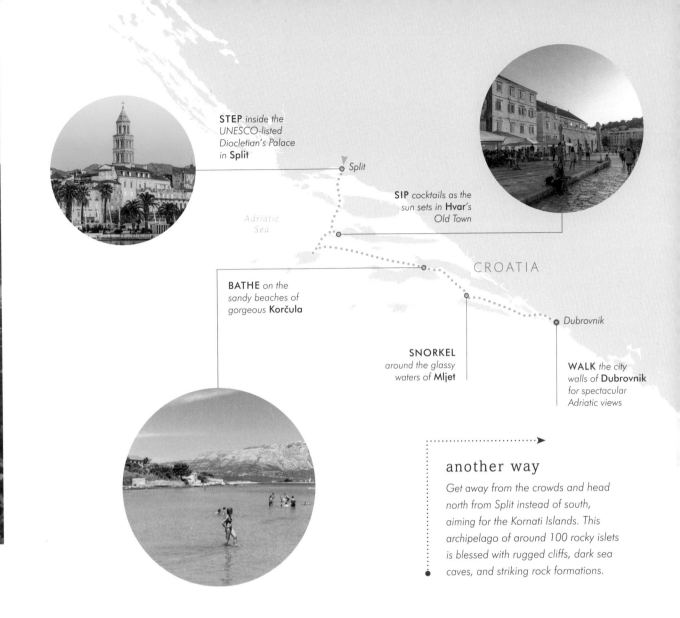

STEP *inside the UNESCO-listed Diocletian's Palace in* **Split**

Split

Adriatic Sea

SIP *cocktails as the sun sets in* **Hvar's** *Old Town*

CROATIA

BATHE *on the sandy beaches of gorgeous* **Korčula**

SNORKEL *around the glassy waters of* **Mljet**

Dubrovnik

WALK *the city walls of* **Dubrovnik** *for spectacular Adriatic views*

another way

Get away from the crowds and head north from Split instead of south, aiming for the Kornati Islands. This archipelago of around 100 rocky islets is blessed with rugged cliffs, dark sea caves, and striking rock formations.

Mljet. This long, thin, forested isle stretches 1,640 ft (500 m) from east to west and has a pair of shimmering lagoons and some of the most intriguing underwater life in its crystal-clear seas. Spend a day swimming or snorkeling, or simply walking among its Roman ruins and over its handsome, hilly interior. If you can tear yourself away, Dubrovnik is calling, a city famous for its ancient walls, vast palaces, and cobbled streets. Here your trip ends with spectacular views out over the Adriatic—best enjoyed with a glass of Croatian white at one of the city's classy seafood joints.

Dubrovnik's city walls standing tall over the Adriatic

Kotor's Old
Town and the
Bay of Kotor

(22) Bay of Kotor

LOCATION Montenegro **START/FINISH** Kotor
Old Town (return) **DISTANCE** 4 miles (6 km)
TIME 3 hours **INFORMATION** https://kotor.travel

*Paddle in awe through Montenegro's
fabulous fjord-like inlet and beneath
beautiful karst mountain slopes.*

It's hard not to feel small while sitting on a kayak in
the middle of the Bay of Kotor. This craggy inlet on
Montenegro's sparkling Adriatic coast is surrounded
by some utterly striking mountain peaks, reaching
as high as 5,577 ft (1,700 m) above sea level. From
down here, you'll be reminded of your place in
the pecking order as you paddle around between
medieval old towns and quaint fishing villages,
drifting along on the calm waters.

Kayaking is easy here: the bay's sheltered position
means you don't need to struggle against strong
currents or bouncing waves; instead you'll find a
serenity little afforded to those on land. Most trips
begin from Kotor's busy Old Town, a tiny tangle of
narrow streets lined with stone houses characterized
by green shutters and terra-cotta rooftops. From here,
you can paddle past the city's outskirts, enjoying
views of its Venetian walls and the old fort that
presides over the town, and then onto quieter coves
where locals sun themselves on rocky, shell-strewn
beaches. You might stop to see a historic church
perched on a cliff high above the water, or to don a
mask and snorkel and dive into the refreshing sea—
if you can tear your eyes away from majestic Mount
Lovćen, towering in the distance, that is.

Whitewater rafters navigating around rocks in the Tara River

(23) Tara Canyon

LOCATION Montenegro **START/FINISH** Šljivansko/Radovan Luka
DISTANCE 15 miles (25 km) **TIME** 6 hours **INFORMATION** www.
visit-montenegro.com; trips run May–Sept

Flowing through the deepest canyon in Europe, the turquoise waters of the Tara River are excellent for rafting, whether you're a pro or an absolute beginner.

Yes, you'll get wet. You may even fall out of your inflatable boat. But there's nothing more thrilling than tackling the rapids as a team, paddling furiously with the roar of the river and the yells of your guide ringing in your ears.

The Tara Canyon, the 50-mile (80-km) natural gash at the heart of the beautiful, UNESCO-protected Tara River Basin Biosphere Reserve, is a superb place to test your mettle. With famously clean water, bubbling cascades, and Class III–V rapids, it lends itself to anything from short excursions to three-day adventures, traveling the navigable section in its entirety with side-trips by vehicle along the way. The classic six-hour paddle from Šljivansko to Radovan Luka visits beautiful waterfalls and swimming spots, breaking halfway for a local-style BBQ lunch. Varying in altitude between around 1,475 to 8,200 ft (430 to 2,500 m), the canyon and its surroundings have a spectacularly rich biodiversity, with some species of flora dating back to the Ice Age. As well as stately trees and numerous species of fish, this is a prime habitat for eagles, wolves, and bears—so you never know whose tracks you might spot on the riverbanks.

another way

The upper reaches of Bosnia's Neretva River, carving through a deep valley and passing under waterfalls, are just as varied for white-water rafting. Some stretches are perfect for pottering; others are heaven for adrenaline junkies.

Ferry-hopping around the Greek Islands

LOCATION Greece **START/FINISH** Athens/Santorini **DISTANCE** 167 miles
(368 km) **TIME** 10 days **INFORMATION** www.gtp.gr/routesform.asp

*The Cyclades island of
Santorini, justifiably
famous for its sunsets*

*Jump between some of Greece's most iconic islands on this
relaxed boat tour through the Cyclades, home to ancient ruins,
magnificent food, and some of the Mediterranean's finest beaches.*

PARTY until dawn on the white sands of Paradise Beach, the nightlife hot spot on **Mykonos**

Athens ▼

GREECE

Aegean Sea

TURKEY

VISIT the Vallindras distillery on **Naxos** and sample the tart local liqueur, kitron

FEAST on the **Cyclades'** culinary specialties, like kopanisti cheese and kakavia, an ancient fish soup

CLAMBER up the walking trails of **Paros'** nature reserve, rich in coastal views and pockmarked with caves

Santorini

WATCH Santorini's famous sunset from the atmospheric Prophet Elias monastery, one of the island's finest viewpoints

A carefree tour of the glorious Greek Islands, guided by the whims of the ferry schedule and the whiff of *gyros* emanating from waterfront tavernas, is travel at its most blissful. The possibilities are endless here, but a superb starting point is the "Route of Diamonds," taking in a string of glittering gems in the Aegean Sea.

Leaving Athens in your wake, you'll make ground on the storied shores of Mykonos. This is an island legendary in every aspect: Zeus and Heracles are said to have done epic battle with fearsome giants here. Today, it's the party gods who look down on the Hellenic answer to Ibiza, but be sure to take a break from sipping Mythos beer on Paradise Beach to visit the gorgeous whitewashed Panagia Paraportiani church. Paros is an altogether more relaxed affair, where Byzantine churches loom above fishing harbors, jet-skis carve a wake in the Aegean blue, and rural wineries reward inland exploration. This is a place to linger over lip-smacking traditional delicacies, like octopus with fava and roasted lamb.

History buffs, meanwhile, will be itching to get to Naxos, where grand Venetian mansions line the narrow streets and an unfinished temple to Apollo frames a cloudless sky. The most glorious sight is saved for last, however: the shores of Santorini, an island chain rearing spectacularly from the flooded caldera of an ancient volcano, where world-beating sunsets draw the curtain on days spent roaming ancient ruins and relaxing on red-sand beaches.

another way

For all their positives, ferries serving the Greek Islands are notoriously unreliable, with ever-changing timetables. If greater control is what you're after, charter a yacht from Syros with Cyclades Sailing and set sail under your own steam.

㉕ Matka Canyon

LOCATION North Macedonia **START/FINISH** Matka Dam (return) **DISTANCE** 6 miles (10 km) **TIME** 2 hours **INFORMATION** www.matkacanyon.com; kayaks are available to rent on Matka Lake

Changing with the light from glowing emerald to deepest indigo, the glossy waters of Lake Matka in the Matka Canyon are perfect for paddling: in fact, apart from the licensed boats that cruise along the lake, kayaks are the only watercraft allowed here. The canyon, a beautiful, biodiversity-rich limestone gorge around 11 miles (17 km) southwest of the North Macedonian capital of Skopje, is particularly serene on sunny days, but even if the weather's gray, there's visual poetry in the texture of the rock and the broken reflections of trees.

Keep watch for interesting plants, birds, and butterflies as you go: the canyon is home to several species that aren't found anywhere else in Europe. Its walls are dotted with flooded caverns, and in Vrelo Cave, a particularly deep complex at the southwest end of the lake, walkways allow visitors to admire the stalagmites, stalactites, nooks, and crannies colonized by bats.

Kayaking in the Matka Canyon

㉖ The Black Sea

LOCATION Bulgaria **START/FINISH** Varna (return) **DISTANCE** 150 miles (240 km) **TIME** 6 days **INFORMATION** https://bulgaria travel.org; Varna has a variety of yachting operators that offer bareboat charters and crewed yacht rentals

The waters of this vast inland sea have always been untroubled by the kind of traffic that scoots around the Aegean and the Adriatic. Even now, the Bulgarian Black Sea coast is a far quieter destination than the Greek Islands or Croatia. But don't let that put you off: the local yachting scene is rapidly picking up, with fancy new marinas appearing along the shore.

Varna, a port town with long-standing sailing traditions, makes a good starting point for a leisurely southbound sail. You could overnight in the sunny beach resort of Sveti Vlas, the charming historic enclave of Sozopol and the sleepy coastal village of Tsarevo before heading north again. Within and beyond the lovely Burgas Bay, you'll pass Bulgaria's five rather mysterious Black Sea islands, all named after saints. Only one monastery still remains, on St. Anastasia Island, dedicated to "The Healer." Which is rather fitting for this soothing sail.

HOW THE BLACK SEA GOT ITS NAME

There's almost no life in the deepest waters of the Black Sea. More than 7,200 ft (2,200 m) deep, it contains high concentrations of hydrogen sulfide, making it the most oxygen-depleted basin on Earth. All the area's peoples had a name for it, but it was the ancient Bulgar name, meaning both Great and Black, that stuck.

Pelicans taking flight in the Danube Delta

28 Nemunas River Delta

LOCATION Lithuania **START/FINISH** Mingè/ Vente **DISTANCE** 9 miles (15 km) **TIME** 6 hours **INFORMATION** www.nemunodelta.lt

The Nemunas River flows across Lithuania, splitting into a dense network of waterways as it nears the coast before emptying into the shallow waters of the Curonian Lagoon. Kayaking trips into this reedy delta of fishing villages and ancient light-houses depart from Mingè, a pretty anchorage that's known as the "Venice of Lithuania." It's quite a stretch, but as with Mingè's northern Italian namesake, the river here serves as the village's main street—there are no bridges connecting the houses on the east bank with those on the west.

In spring, the delta floods, and you'll be paddling past islands that are hills at any other time of the year; in the fall, up to 3 million birds pass over the Venté Cape each day on their migration south. Beyond Venté, across the open lagoon, you'll be able to make out the migrating dunes of the Curonian Spit, a natural sand barrier—and a UNESCO World Heritage site—that keeps the Baltic Sea at bay.

27 Danube Delta

LOCATION Romania **START/FINISH** Tulcea (return) **DISTANCE** 93 miles (150 km) **TIME** 1 day **INFORMATION** www.romaniatourism. com; wildlife-spotting chances are increased on longer trips of 3–5 days

The mighty Danube River meets the Black Sea in Europe's second-biggest, best-preserved river delta, a web of reed-rimmed watery channels, lakes, and marshland that forms a haven for the continent's most varied and abundant gathering of birdlife. No wonder our feathered friends have found Elysium here. Few European regions this big have such a low human population density, and several utterly different ecosystems coexist, making this a magnet for the 330-odd avian species residing here full-time, plus myriad migratory birds, too.

Typical day trips by boat traverse dreamy channels as far as Letea to see Europe's northern-most subtropical forest, an entrancing place where spreads of trees intermingle with sandy desert from the area's stint as a seabed in the geological past. Exploring each of these innu-merable waterways would take several lifetimes. The birdlife changes by the week, and the entire wetland is in constant flux: no two boat trips in the delta, therefore, can ever be the same.

Riverfront houses lining the "main street" in Mingè village

Svalbard

LOCATION Norway **START/FINISH** Longyearbyen (return) **DISTANCE** 473 miles
(762 km) **TIME** 1 week **INFORMATION** https://en.visitsvalbard.com; best
May–Sept; landings are dependent on weather and sea-ice conditions

*Embark on a small-group expedition cruise to Svalbard for close-ups of
polar bears, walruses, and seals; icebergs; and dazzling glaciers as the
Midnight Sun burns in summer skies.*

Nothing prepares you for Svalbard. The final stop
before the North Pole, a mere 500 miles (805 km)
of pack ice away, this High Arctic archipelago is a
place of savage beauty. In summer, the ice melts
just enough to allow expedition ships to cruise its
crystal waters. Boats weave in and out of glacier-
lined fjords in search of the wildlife you've waited
a lifetime to see: seals, walruses, humpback whales,
and—everyone's favorite—polar bears. Choose
a small-group, eco-friendly, expert-led cruise for
prime wildlife-spotting potential.

Spitsbergen is the most accessible island, and
this trip takes you right up to its northwestern

fringes. As you strike out into open sea, the epic
scale, otherworldly light, and remoteness of the
island hits deeply. The week-long voyage kicks off
in Longyearbyen, one of the world's northernmost
towns, then curves northwest via Forlandet
National Park, once a whaling station and now a
reserve for black guillemots, barnacle geese, seals,
sea lions, and walruses. From here boats cruise
north to glacier-rimmed Kongsfjorden, landing
at the former coal-mining town of Ny Ålesund.

Pushing further toward the Pole, you'll touch
upon North West Spitsbergen National Park, where
dark mountains rear like shark fins above mirror-

Left Smeerenburgbreen glacier, on the island of Amsterdamøya *Below* A longed-for glimpse of Svalbard's resident polar bears

another way

To get even closer to the wildlife, join a week-long guided kayaking and camping expedition, taking you deep into the heart of Spitsbergen's fjords; Longyearbyen is the starting point for kayaking adventures on Isfjorden (www.wildlife.no).

BRING binoculars for the bird cliffs of **Fuglesongen** in the island's northwest, home to Svalbard's largest colony of little auks

GASP in wonder at the glacial majesty of **Monacobreen** as you weave among the icebergs of Liefdefjorden

LAND on the island of **Amsterdamøya** to explore the 17th-century whaling town of Smeerenburg

CLAMBER up **Irgensfjellet** on Blomstrandøya for soul-stirring views over glaciers and razor-edge mountains

LOOK out for beluga whales splashing in iceberg-dotted waters on a Zodiac cruise to **Lilliehöökbreen glacier**

Longyearbyen

SVALBARD

like waters and great glaciers. Weather permitting, you'll sail as far as 80 degrees north, entering the realm of polar bears who ride the floes and icebergs to hunt for seals. Looping back west, you'll get to cruise the shallow straits of Blomstrand and glimpse the glittering expanse of Monacobreen glacier as you head through the Liefdefjorden. Then it's time for the return voyage back to Longyearbyen—and back to civilization.

Greenland Sea

Barents Sea

A ship making its way between the pop-up mountains of Geirangerfjord

(30) # Western Fjords

LOCATION Norway **START/FINISH** Bergen/Ålesund **DISTANCE** 473 miles (762 km) **TIME** 5 days **INFORMATION** www.visitnorway.com; best spring to fall

Chugging across Norway's western fjords is like seeing the world afresh in all its nature-gone-wild glory. And in this glacier-carved landscape, ferry is the ideal way to go.

The level of beauty in the western fjords is outrageous: misty waterfalls spill down cliffs that whoosh up to great snow-tipped crags; Viking churches and rainbow-bright timber villages hug serene and lonely shores; and sea eagles glide above waters in shades of blue and green that are off the color chart. When the sun shoots out of the clouds, everything gleams.

Bagging a top-deck seat on a ferry is the best way to dip in and out of the fjords that so intricately filigree the country's west. Begin in Hanseatic Bergen, clasped between seven mountains, allowing time to tour the historic Bryggen wharf district. From here, boat it across sapphire-blue, mountain-rimmed Sognefjord, Norway's longest fjord at 127 miles (204 km). Factor in a side-trip across the radiant Lustrafjord by dinky ferry to Urnes Stave Church; dwarfed by its colossal backdrop, the 12th-century church is Norway's oldest place of worship and a UNESCO World Heritage site.

The journey north stitches together lyrical scenery: peak-fringed Fjærlandsfjorden and Innvikfjorden and glacial-green Oppstrynsvatnet lake. Hop back on the ferry to navigate Geirangerfjord, perhaps fairest of them all with its pop-up mountains and plunging waterfalls such as The Seven Sisters and The Bridal Veil. You'll end in the Art Nouveau coastal town of Ålesund, which sits on a fishhook-shaped peninsula and is famous for its seafood and whale sightings. Not a bad way to call it a day.

another way

If the fjords seem vast from a ferry, just imagine how they must feel in a kayak or canoe. Paddling away from the crowds on ink-blue waters in the hush of morning is pure magic. Many of the major fjords offer kayak rental and multi-day guided tours.

The Arctic by Icebreaker

LOCATION Finland **START/FINISH** Kemi (return) **DISTANCE** Varies **TIME** 4 hours
INFORMATION www.experience365.fi; runs Dec–Apr; shuttle buses carry passengers
from Kemi and Rovaniemi to the harbor

*Set off on a wintry adventure in the frozen Gulf of Bothnia on board
the* Sampo, *the only icebreaker to offer mini-cruises, for the chance
to experience Lapland from a unique perspective.*

Setting out before dawn to spend a short winter day on a frozen sea may seem like an eccentric idea. But just wait until you hear the next bit: you'll be invited to slide in. Passengers on the *Sampo*, safely encased in Arctic rescue dry suits, get the chance to float in a patch of icy water the ship has helpfully cleared. Once back on board, you can warm up with a hot drink.

Built in Helsinki in 1960, the *Sampo* is a truly impressive vessel. It was designed to withstand extreme weather conditions, and its ice-class hull can break through solid ice up to 78 inches (2 m) thick.

The *Sampo* kept the shipping lanes in the Gulf of Bothnia clear of ice for nearly 30 years up to 1987, when the town of Kemi recommissioned it as a tourist attraction. It still breaks up the ice, but it also takes passengers on short, educational trips. During your cruise, you can take a look at the engine room and chat to the crew about all things technical. And take that icy dip, if you dare.

THE SAMPO

Kemi's trusty icebreaker is named after a mythical object that features in the Finnish epic poems that helped inspire J. R. R. Tolkien to write *The Lord of the Rings*. Forged by a master blacksmith, the Sampo was imbued with magical properties, and brought misfortune to all those who attempted to steal it.

The Sampo *plowing through pack ice in the Gulf of Bothnia*

32
Finnish Lakeland

LOCATION Finland **START/FINISH** Oravi (return) **DISTANCE** Varies **TIME** Varies
INFORMATION www.visitsaimaa.fi

*Midsummer, when daylight never truly fades, is the time to immerse yourself
in this two-tone world of deep blue water and dark green spruce forest,
gliding in between the thousands of islands on Finland's largest lake.*

How to choose where to venture for water-based fun in Finnish Lakeland, where lakes cover a quarter of the region and are so numerous no one has ever been able to accurately count them? The greatest lake of all, Saimaa, is an oar-inspiring start point. Europe's fourth-largest natural freshwater lake, with around 1,700 sq miles (4,400 sq km) of surface area, 13,710 islands, and the longest coastline of any lake on the planet, Saimaa flexes its inlet-riven tentacles far and wide. At points, sinuous headlands and occasional road crossings seem to subdivide the lake, yet on it stretches, through different basins and under different

*Kolovesi
National Park,
bordering Lake
Saimaa*

names, from Lappeenranta in the south to Joensuu in the north, a distance of 145 miles (234 km).

Yet for all Saimaa's statistics, the one thing you'll notice as you put in and paddle off from the woodsy village of Oravi, poised between Linnansaari and Kolovesi national parks, is the quiet. The masses do not come here, or if they do, they are so dispersed it's as if the cobalt waters and conifer-flanked cliffs, channels, islands, and isthmuses exist just for you—and the rich birdlife that call these waters home. Sliding across still, silent Saimaa, you'll soon see why so many Finns equate Lakeland with paradise.

THE SAIMAA RINGED SEAL

One of the world's last surviving freshwater seals, the Saimaa ringed seal is so endangered that numbers hover around just 400 pairs; you might be lucky enough to see one while kayaking the lake. Bankside snow cover is important for the seals, as they build lairs in it to give birth, and warmer winters contributed to declining numbers. Fortunately, the construction of seal snow banks has helped reverse this decline.

Stockholm Archipelago

LOCATION Sweden **START/FINISH** Stockholm (return) **DISTANCE** Varies
TIME Varies **INFORMATION** www.visitstockholm.com

A tiny fishing harbor on one of the skerries near Stockholm

How many cities offer a serene sailing break among verdant islands and dynamic neighborhoods? Stockholm's archipelago is an idyllic place to while away some time on the water.

The effortlessly cool Swedish capital has sustainability on the mind, with promises to become carbon neutral by 2040 and a number of fossil-free transportation options already available. You can have your own low-impact vacation here by using a little wind to power your sails as you take to the water. Beyond the city center, you'll find yourself cruising among beach-fringed atolls, uninhabited skerries, and forested islands dotted with copper-colored summer houses.

The sailing is easy, with light winds to carry you forth and few tides to disrupt your flow—the only hurdle is deciding where to set sail for next. You could opt for the islands of Vaxholm and Svartsö, brightened up by their painted wooden houses, or moor up at Grinda, the city's wild-swimming capital in fair weather. So difficult is your choice, you'll want to extend your trip to see it all. And the locals will tell you to just do it: in Sweden, the freedom to venture into nature—*allemansrätten*—is a human right.

another way

If you're feeling active, hop in a sea kayak to explore Stockholm's archipelago. You'll get closer to the beautiful beaches and craggy coves, and have the freedom to hop out and onto land wherever you like.

INDEX

ACKNOWLEDGMENTS

DK Eyewitness would like to thank the following authors for their contribution to this book:

Rob Ainsley hasn't cycled all his life. Not yet anyway. He has five and a half bikes, all with rack and mudguards, and is collecting international End to Ends—some (eg Cuba) taking longer than others (eg the Faroes). He writes for cycling magazines about his native Yorkshire, Britain, the world, and everywhere else, and blogs on e2e.bike.

Sarah Baxter is a travel journalist, author, hiker, and runner. She is a Contributing Editor of *Wanderlust* magazine and writes for many other publications, including *The Guardian*, *The Telegraph*, and *The Times*. She is the author of *A History of the World in 500 Walks* and several titles in the Inspired Traveller's Guide series, and has contributed to more than a dozen guidebooks.

Kerry Christiani is an award-winning travel writer and photographer based in the wild Cambrian Mountains in Mid Wales. Never happier than when hoofing up a mountain or diving into the sea or snow, she has traveled all seven continents, contributing to dozens of travel guides, books, and articles for publishers including *National Geographic Traveler*, *The Times*, and *The Independent*. Her website is kerryawalker.com and she can be found on Twitter @kerryawalker.

Kiki Deere was brought up bilingually in London and northern Italy and has seen her work published in major travel publications including *The Telegraph*, *Conde Nast Traveler*, and Culture Trip. You'll find her tucking into culinary specialties to discover local flavors or exploring the great outdoors, whether skiing in the Alps or soaking up Lake Como's sights from the water. Follow her on Twitter @kikideere.

Keith Drew is a freelance travel writer and editor who writes about unusual places with an interesting story to tell for *The Telegraph* and BBC Travel among others. He is the cofounder of family-travel website Lijoma.com, a curated selection of inspirational itineraries to destinations like Iceland, Jordan, Sri Lanka, and Japan.

Steph Dyson is a bilingual freelance travel writer who's worked on more than a dozen guidebooks and written about sustainable adventure travel for publications across the globe, including CNN, *The South China Morning Post*, and *The Independent*. Addicted to getting truly off-the-beaten-path, she splits her time between the UK and Latin America and runs the award-nominated website Worldly Adventurer.

Emma Gregg is an award-winning travel journalist who has visited all seven continents. She specializes in responsible tourism, writing extensively about sustainable travel, including low-carbon, flight-free trips. Based in the UK, she loves forests, islands, and coral reefs, and is never happier than when embarking on a new adventure.

Lottie Gross is a travel writer and editor who has penned stories about everything from the heaving city streets of Mumbai to the quietest corners of Albania's beautiful coastline. She's a guidebook author in destinations such as India and the UK, and writes for British national newspapers as well as international magazines such as *AFAR* and *World Travel Magazine*.

Anita Isalska is a freelance writer and editor based in San Francisco. Anita writes about travel, technology, and outdoor adventures, especially hiking, cycling, and winter sports. Anita specializes in France, Eastern Europe, and her adopted home, California. Read her stuff on anitaisalska.com or find her on Twitter @anitaisalska.

Ben Lerwill is an award-winning freelance travel writer based in the English countryside. His specialist subjects include walking, wildlife, and train travel, and his work appears everywhere from *National Geographic Traveler* to *BBC Countryfile Magazine*. He is also a children's author, focusing mainly on nonfiction books.

Mike MacEacheran is an award-winning freelance travel journalist who writes for *The Times*, *The Telegraph*, *FT*, *The Guardian*, *National Geographic*, *The Washington Post*, *The Wall Street Journal*, *Conde Nast Traveler*, *Monocle*, *The Observer*, *Mail on Sunday*, Rough Guides, *The Independent*, and BBC Travel. He's reported from 115 countries and lives in Edinburgh.

Shafik Meghji is an award-winning travel writer, journalist, and author of *Crossed off the Map: Travels in Bolivia*. Specializing in Latin America and South Asia, he has coauthored more the 40 guidebooks for DK Eyewitness and Rough Guides, and writes for BBC Travel and Wanderlust, among others. He can be found at shafikmeghji.com and on Twitter and Instagram @ShafikMeghji.

Rachel Mills has coauthored guidebooks to New Zealand, India, Canada, Ireland, and Great Britain for both Rough Guides and DK Eyewitness, and is an expert in sustainable, responsible tourism. Follow her @rachmillstravel.

Joseph Reaney is a British travel journalist and editor who divides his time between the UK and Central Europe. As well as contributing to travel publications like DK Eyewitness, Lonely Planet, Rough Guides, and Fodor's, he is the owner and editor-in-chief of travel content writing agency World Words.

Dan Stables is a travel writer and journalist based in Manchester. He writes for a variety of print and online publications, and has authored or contributed to more than 30 travel books on destinations across Europe, Asia, and the Americas. Find his work at danielstables.co.uk, or on Twitter @DanStables.

Luke Waterson is a Wales-based adventure and culinary travel writer with a penchant for the UK outdoors, Scandinavia, and Eastern Europe, about which he writes for the BBC, *The Telegraph*, Adventure.com, *The Sunday Times*, and many others. Follow his recommendations about the best things to see and do in Wales at undiscovered-wales.co.uk.

Peter Watson is a travel writer and founder of outdoor travel blog Atlas & Boots. A keen trekker and climber, he can usually be found on the trails of the Greater Ranges of Asia. He's visited over 80 countries and is currently focused on climbing the seven summits—the highest mountain on every continent.

The publisher would like to thank the following for their kind permission to reproduce their photographs:

(Key: a-above; b-below/bottom; c-center; f-far; l-left; r-right; t-top)

123RF.com: 4kclips 90-91t, anetlanda 244tl, Wies?aw Jarek 64, Viktoriya Chursina 57crb, Martin Dworschak 186br, jenifoto 97b, Konstantin Kalishko 38t, Vadym Lavra 100bl, Aliaksandr Mazurkevich 197c, nata_rass 180tl, perekotypole 157t, rh2010 193tr, snr 204tl, iclar tac 183t

Alamy Stock Photo: agefotostock / T. Papageorgiou 107tl, agefotostock / Tolo Balaguer 142, All Canada Photos / Roberta Olenick 243cr, Anis-Photography 35cr, ARCTIC IMAGES / Ragnar Th Sigurdsson 65ca, Martin Bache 15tr, Albert Beukhof 213t, Stuart Black 129cl, blickwinkel 103tr, blickwinkel 109, Eva Bocek 43t, Piere Bonbon 125br, Richard Bradley 73cr, Michael Brooks 174crb, Krzysztof Browko 148-149, Adam Burton 215t, Chris Button 14br, Cathouse Studio 203br, David Cheshire 218bl, Dave Chia 33cr, Mohammed Anwarul Kabir Choudhury 129cb, Colouria Media / Kai-Uwe Och 199b, David Creedon 83br, Cro Magnon 174cl, Cro Magnon 233, Ian Dagnall 133cl, Ian Dagnall 210t, Ian Dagnall 211tr, Simon Dannhauer 41tl, Davidzfr 137bl, DB Pictures 181clb, DE ROCKER 143tr, Nikolay Dimitrov 160bl, Stephen Dorey - Gloucestershire 219tl, Athanasios Doumas 73cla, dpa picture alliance 185br, Robert Evans 005tl, 116-117, Everst 004br, 066-067, Jürgen Feuerer 95cl, funkyfood London - Paul Williams 114, Maria Galan 174br, Milan Gonda 239cl, Hemis / GIUGLIO Gil 46cr, Hemis / JACQUES Pierre 46tl, Kate Hockenhull 175tr, Image Professionals GmbH 239tl, Image Professionals GmbH / Linder, Bastian 62tr, Image Professionals GmbH / Meinhardt, Olaf 245br, imageBROKER 39b, imageBROKER / Alessandra Sarti 147tl, imageBROKER / Dirk Bleyer 65cr, imageBROKER / Egmont Strigl 57tl, imageBROKER / Stefan Kiefer 153cl, imageBROKER / Thomas Aichinger 186bl, Ivanita 56-57, Ivoha 25cla, Ivoha 28-29, jbdodane 188crb, KENAN KAYA 111br, Chris Keep 15crb, kevers 99br, Joana Kruse 92tr, LatitudeStock / David Forman 213crb, Hervé Lenain 95tr, Hervé Lenain 96tl, Hervé Lenain 139tl, Lumi Images 161cl, makasana photo 25tl, Nino Marcutti 234t, Stefano Politi Markovina 235tl, mauritius images GmbH 40, mauritius images GmbH 92bl, mauritius images GmbH 103clb, mauritius images GmbH / Catharina Lux 231tr, mauritius images GmbH / Hans Blossey 231tl, mauritius images GmbH / Volker Preusser 150tr, Gareth McCormack 23b, Joe McUbed 31b, David Milsen 158-159, Navin Mistry 21b, Jim Monk 15tl, Multipedia 161tr, Alexandr Muntean 237tr, Nature Picture Library / Brent Stephenson 213cla, Cum Okolo 135cr, Irina Papoyan 194br, Charlie Phillips 79b, Graham Prentice 156cr, Prisma by Dukas Presseagentur GmbH 228tr, M Ramírez 204crb, Sergi Reboredo 31cl, Radomir Rezny 146, robertharding / Miles Ertman 33t, Roger Cracknell 01 / classic 106b, RooM the Agency / coberschneider 153bl, ROUSSEL IMAGES 96tr, rudi1976 92tl, Markus Schoeffler 35tl, Neil Setchfield 121c, DAVID J SLATER 219cl, Lourens Smak 37tl, Soma 188tl, South of Kaçkar Mountains 112crb, James Sturcke 30tr, Andy Sutton 212b, Adrian Szatewicz 75br, Jochen Tack 229cr, The National Trust Photolibrary / Joe Cornish 215cr, Aleksandar Tomic 160br, Tomka 194bl, Urbanmyth 229cl, Velomorvah 140bl, Steve Vidler 123bl, volkerpreusser 151br, Alan Watson 154, Westend61 GmbH / Manuel Sulzer 49tr, Mieczyslaw Wieliczko 134b, Noppasin Wongchum 228tl

AWL Images: Walter Bibikow 49clb, Christian Kober 104

Belmond Ltd.: David Noton 166

Depositphotos Inc: anakul 63, AndrewMayovskyy 240bl, gsafarek 235tr, kydy 136t, rixipix 242-243tl, smoxx 107crb

Dreamstime.com: Acceleratorhams 120-121, Adam88x 184tr, Karl Ander Adami 60tr, Agami Photo Agency 138tl, Leonid Andronov 229bl, Christopher Babcock 235cl, Bbbrrn 113b, Magnus Binnerstam 62cra, Justin Black 18b, Eva Bocek 93br, Boris Breytman 83cr, Jason Busa 127b, Charlton Buttigieg 81b, Andrea Calzona 220bl, Diadis 226-227bl, Matthew Dixon 216, Dreamer4787 235br, Ekotini 57cl, Everst 75clb, Paola Garcia Broeders 219crb, Florin Ghidu 60bl, Apostolos Giontzis 106t, David Head 124, Helen Hotson 78-79t, Francesco Riccardo Iacomino | 76br, Jon Ingall 49b, Janusorlov 196b, Jaysi 225, Jcfmorata 238-239bl, Lukas Jonaitis 202-203bl, Dawid Kalisinski 22t, Ingus Kruklitis 132tr, Lerka555 197cl, Miroslav Liska 75tl, Anna Lurye 133bl, Peter Mallinger 189tr, Tomas Marek 005bl, 162-163, Mikel Martinez De Osaba 141t, Milllda 241br, MNStudio 58, Christian Mueringer 128, Mihai Neacsu 54, Neurobite 65tl, Nogreenabovetwothousand 187t, Sean Pavone 176tl, Petermladenov 190t, Pitsch22 19l, Michele Ponzio 181br, Porojnicu 47br, Basak Prince 50, Pytyczech 41tr, Dario Racane 144br, Rnijholt 169bl, Emma Ros 144tl, Scaliger 230bl, Richard Semik 214, Josef Skacel 002-003, Michal Stipek 93bl, Stock Tr 112br, Darius Strazdas 205bl, Tigger76 204cl, Roman Tiraspolsky 200clb, Nikolay Tsuguliev 198tl, Stefano Valeri 19tr, Vogelsp 182b, Tanja Wilbertz 26t, Ian Woolcock 17b, Ian Woolcock 122tl, Xantana 113c, 194tl, Evgeny Kharitonov 59tr

Getty Images: Marco Bottigelli 74, 82tl, 100tr, Ashley Cooper 243clb, Education Images 12-13, imageBROKER / Reinhard Pantke 126tl, Maya Karkalicheva 115tr, Mahaux Photography 75tr, Mahaux Photography 77, Ilan Shacham 155, Walter Rodriguez / 500px 246bl, Westend61 221tl

Getty Images / iStock: A-Basler 86, agustavop 94, AleksandarGeorgiev 155tl, AlenaPaulus 153crb, alessandro0770 150tl, AnatolyTiplyashin 115clb, Frank Anschuetz 27b, Aliaksandr Antanovich 51tr, anyaberkut 70-71bl, atosan 152, BackyardProduction 222tr, bluejayphoto 88tr, bodrumsurf 112tl, CalinStan 108, CalinStan 156cla, carstenbrandt 129br, Christiantdk 85t, Cloud-Mine-Amsterdam 223b, Dabitxu7 32, Will Dale 80tl, Andrey Danilovich 53, deanburn 20tl, DieterMeyrl 71br, dragonnano 200bl, Eva Corbella Fotografia 175tl, FooTToo 88cr, FooTToo 135tl, golfer2015 121t, GoodLifeStudio 161br, Gert Hilbink 137t, honza28683 151bl, HRAUN 72tl, IAM-photography 73br, jacquesvandinteren 95cr, Janoka82 42, Julia700702 178b, justhavealook 170tr, Kufner-Foto 145tr, Paola Leone 34b, LorenzoT81 52tl, lucentius 20tr, LUNAMARINA 31cr, mantaphoto 181br, mason01 179tr, mmeee 101, MNStudio 83tl, Muhur 110-111, naphtalina 30tl, oksanaphoto 198tr, olrat 227br, Eloi Omella 51tl, PocholoCalapre 171b, RolfSt 14bl, RossHelen 205br, RudyBalasko 89, ruivalesousa 224, rusm 232, Nazar Rybak 72tr, rzoze19 55, saiko3p 87, samael334 130-131, sankai 189b, SeanPavonePhoto 222tl, SeppFriedhuber 243tl, ShaunTurner 168tr, Adam Smigielski 137cr, Smitt 76tl, Calin Stan 241tl, StockPhotoAstur 172, Streluk 006-007, David Taljat 91tr, taranchic 92br, TomekD76 88tl, tony740607 48, tunart 236, Flavio Vallenari 19bl, Flavio Vallenari 211tl, vitfedotov 24b, zapatisthack 52b

Golden Eagle Luxury Trains: Andrea Peto 195b

Shutterstock.com: Nikiforov Alexander 200tl, Arjan Almekinders 36, Leonid Andronov 177br, Myroslava Bozhko 147clb, Antun Cerovecki 115tl, Diego Cervo 30cla, Creative Travel Projects 44-45, Szilard Csaki 194tc, Mostovyi Sergii Igorevich 84bl, imagIN.gr photography 191bl, iwciagr 61br, kasakphoto 004bl, 008-009, Elke Kohler 16t, Ale Koziura 132tl, LFRabanedo 98, lukaszimilena 005tr, 206-207, Gospodarek Mikolaj 102-103, Andy Morehouse 211cb, Gunter Nuyts 147crb, PHOTOGRAPHER GUI 95bl, Piotrwoz 79t, SankyPix 170tl, Vova Shevchuk 157br, slawjanek_fotografia 34t, Kochneva Tetyana 59, travellight 218tr, Umomos 247t, VladislavPichugin 46-47b, Radko Voleman 150crb, Luka Vovk 105

Unsplash: Bence Balla-Schottner 192-193, Lisa Barbosa Ribeiro 167bl, Damiano Baschiera 167cr, Roxxie Blackham 139br

Visitnorway.com: Øyvind Heen - fjords.com 201

Vrijheidsmuseum: Flip Franssen 37crb

Cover images:

Front: Alamy Stock Photo: Westend61 GmbH / Dieter Heinemann

Back: 123RF.com: Vadym Lavra cr; Getty Images: Ilan Shacham cb; Getty Images / iStock: Andrey Danilovich cl; Shutterstock.com: Diego Cervo ca

All other images © Dorling Kindersley

Project Editors Keith Drew, Elspeth Beidas
Senior US Editor Megan Douglass
Senior Designers Ben Hinks, Stuti Tiwari
Project Designer Bess Daly
Proofreader Kathryn Glendenning
Indexer Hilary Bird
Picture Researcher Marta Bescos
Senior Cartographic Editor Casper Morris
Jacket Designer Jordan Lambley
Jacket Picture Research Jordan Lambley
Senior Production Editor Jason Little
DTP Designer Rohit Rojal
Senior Production Controller Samantha Cross
Managing Editor Hollie Teague
Managing Art Editor Sarah Snelling
Art Director Maxine Pedliham
Publishing Director Georgina Dee

First American Edition, 2023
Published in the United States by DK Publishing
1745 Broadway, 20th Floor, New York, NY 10019

Copyright © 2023 Dorling Kindersley Limited
DK, a Division of Penguin Random House LLC
23 24 25 26 27 10 9 8 7 6 5 4 3 2 1
001–334347–Mar/2023

A catalog record for this book
is available from the Library of Congress.
ISBN: 978-0-7440-7780-3

DK books are available at special discounts when purchased in bulk for sales promotions, premiums, fund-raising, or educational use. For details, contact:
DK Publishing Special Markets,
1745 Broadway, 20th Floor, New York, NY 10019
SpecialSales@dk.com

Printed and bound in Malaysia

For the curious
www.dk.com

MIX
Paper | Supporting responsible forestry
FSC™ C018179

This book was made with Forest Stewardship Council ™ certified paper—one small step in DK's commitment to a sustainable future. **For more information go to www.dk.com/our-green-pledge**

The rapid rate at which the world is changing is constantly keeping the DK Eyewitness team on our toes. While we've worked hard to ensure that *Unforgettable Journeys Europe* is accurate and up-to-date, we know that roads close, routes are altered, places shut, and new ones pop up in their stead. If you notice we've got something wrong or left something out, we want to hear about it. Please get in touch at travelguides@dk.co.uk